Next-Generation Treatment Methods and Destinations in Dental Health Tourism

Ömer Faruk Şarkbay
https://orcid.org/0000-0001-9360-7634
İstanbul Gelişim University, Turkey

Aslı Kaya
https://orcid.org/0009-0009-3648-6608
İstanbul Gelişim University, Turkey

IGI Global
Scientific Publishing
Publishing Tomorrow's Research Today

Vice President of Editorial	Melissa Wagner
Director of Acquisitions	Mikaela Felty
Director of Book Development	Jocelynn Hessler
Production Manager	Mike Brehm
Cover Design	Jose Rosado

Published in the United States of America by
IGI Global Scientific Publishing
701 East Chocolate Avenue
Hershey, PA, 17033, USA
Tel: 717-533-8845 | Fax: 717-533-7115
Website: https://www.igi-global.com E-mail: cust@igi-global.com

Library of Congress Cataloging-in-Publication Data

LCCN: 2025031526 (CIP Data Pending)
ISBN13: 9798337341149
Isbn13Softcover: 9798337341156
EISBN13: 9798337341163
British Cataloguing in Publication Data
A Cataloguing in Publication record for this book is available from the British Library.

To our beloved families who have stood firmly behind us at every step, embraced us with love, and held our hand through every challenge. Your unwavering support, guidance, and affection have shaped who We are today and have been our greatest source of strength and motivation.

Editorial Advisory Board

Nurten Elkin, *İstanbul Gelişim University, İstanbul, Turkey*
İzzet Erdem, *Burdur Mehmet Akif Ersoy Üniversitesi, Burdur, Turkey*
Ramazan Erdem, *Süleyman Demirel University, Isparta, Turkey*
Hüseyin Eriş, *Harran University, Şanlıurfa, Turkey*
Afsun Ezel Esatoğlu, *Ankara University, Ankara, Turkey*
Berrin Filizöz, *Sivas Cumhuriyet University, Sivas, Turkey*
Durmuş Gökkaya, *Yozgat Bozok University, Yozgat, Turkey*
Mahruk Güneyli, *İstanbul Gelişim University, İstanbul, Turkey*
Ayşe Ispirli Turan, *Samsun Ondokuz Mayıs University, Samsun, Turkey*
Dilruba Izgüden, *Süleyman Demirel University, Isparta, Turkey*
Nadire Kantarcioğlu, *International Association for Scientific Research and Strategy Development UBSDER, Ankara, Turkey*
Ergün Kara, *Osmaniye Korkut Ata University, Osmaniye, Turkey*
Himmet Karadal, *Bolu Abant İzzet Baysal University, Bolu, Turkey*
Saadet Karakuş, *University of Health Sciences, Turkey*
Turgay Karalinç, *İstanbul Gelişim University, İstanbul, Turkey*
Emin Kaya, *Isparta University of Applied Sciences, Turkey*
Ramazan Rüçhan Kaya, *Uşak University, Uşak, Turkey*
Yasemi Nurbanu Kaya, *International Association for Scientific and Strategy Academic Research UBAAD, Bursa, Turkey*
Taşkın Kiliç, *Ordu University, Ordu, Turkey*
Semiha Kiliçaslan, *Malatya Turgut Özal University, Turkey*
Merve Kişi, *Süleyman Demirel University, Isparta, Turkey*
Neşe Kiskaç, *İstanbul Arel University, İstanbul, Turkey*
Dilek Kocabaş, *Akdeniz University, Antalya, Turkey*
Kaan Koçali, *İstanbul Gelişim University, İstanbul, Turkey*
Ebru Özlem Korkutata, *Çanakkale Onsekiz Mart University, Çanakkale, Turkey*
Aslı Metin, *Isparta University of Applied Sciences, Isparta, Turkey*
Aygen Oksay, *Süleyman Demirel University, Isparta, Turkey*
Semanur Oktay Alkan, *İstanbul Gelişim University, İstanbul, Turkey*
Aslı Ercan Önbiçak, *Independent Researcher, İzmir, Turkey*
Hikmet Emir Önbiçak, *Independent Researcher, İzmir, Turkey*
Arif Önder, *İstanbul Gelişim University, İstanbul, Turkey*
Fatma Türkan Özirmak, *İstanbul Gelişim University, İstanbul, Turkey*
Sümeyye Özmen, *Sakarya Uygulamalı Bilimler Üniversitesi, Sakarya, Turkey*
Fahri Özsungur, *Mersin University, Mersin, Turkey*
Aslıhan Kübra Sakarya, *İstanbul Gelişim University, İstanbul, Turkey*
Betül Sari, *Mersin University, Mersin, Turkey*
Ömer Faruk Şarkbay, *İstanbul Gelişim University, İstanbul, Turkey*
Burak Sayar, *Bitlis Eren University, Bitlis, Turkey*

Mortaza Chaychi Semsari, *Independent Researcher, Iran*
Mehmet Şengül, *Çağ University, Mersin, Turkey*
Osman Şenol, *Karadeniz Technical University, Trabzon, Turkey*
Akın Tekcan, *Amasya University, Amasya, Turkey*
Zeliha Tekin, *Muş Alparslan University, Muş, Turkey*
Dilaver Tengilimoğlu, *Atılım University, İstanbul, Turkey*
Bülent Tokat, *Kütahya Dumlupınar University, Kütahya, Turkey*
Aynur Toraman, *Süleyman Demirel University, Isparta, Turkey*
Yasin Tosun, *Economic Policy, Universität Siegen, Germany*
Emrah Tüncer, *İstanbul Gelişim University, İstanbul, Turkey*
Memiş Can Yardimci, *Afyon Kocatepe University, Afyon,Turkey*
Begüm Yaşçin, *İstanbul Beykent University, İstanbul, Turkey*
Arzu Yiğit, *Süleyman Demirel University, Isparta, Turkey*
Vahit Yiğit, *Süleyman Demirel University, Isparta, Turkey*
Necla Yilmaz, *Süleyman Demirel University, Isparta, Turkey*
İsmet Galip Yolcuoğlu, *İstanbul Gelişim University*, *İstanbul, Turkey*
Yonca Güneş Yücel Atalay, *İstanbul Gelişim University, İstanbul, Turkey*
Recep Yücel, *Kırıkkale University, Kırıkkale, Turkey*
Şebnem Yücel, *Konya Selçuk University, Konya, Turkey*
Hina Zahoor, *İstanbul Gelişim University, İstanbul, Turkey*

Table of Contents

Detailed Table of Contents

infrastructure, and foreign exchange, it also raises ethical and socio-cultural challenges, including inequality, resource allocation, and cultural homogenization. The chapter concludes that sustainable growth in dental tourism requires coordinated policies, ethical governance, and digital innovation to ensure equitable and patient-centered global healthcare mobility.

The increase in demand for cross-border dental treatment reflects not only individual patient preferences but also the transformation of global healthcare delivery models. To understand the multi-layered nature of this transformation, this book chapter aims to examine the dimensions of dental tourism—service delivery, organizational operations, and patient experience—using a holistic approach. In this context, the aim of this chapter is to examine the dynamics of dental tourism within a comprehensive framework by utilizing bibliometric analysis, document analysis, and SWOT analysis methods, based on existing research in the literature. To achieve the objective of the research, 70 studies retrieved from WoS were first examined using bibliometric analysis. Of these studies, the 10 most cited studies were subjected to document analysis. In the final stage of the research, a SWOT analysis was performed based on the studies examined. The findings of the research may provide insights for strategic planning in the dental tourism market.

This analytical review explores the role of sustainability and smart technologies in shaping dental health tourism destinations. By examining quantitative data from multiple countries, the study highlights how the adoption of eco-friendly practices, digital health tools, and tele-dentistry significantly improves patient satisfaction, operational efficiency, and destination competitiveness. Findings reveal strong positive correlations between sustainability measures and smart technology integration with higher tourist inflows and revisit intentions. The review emphasizes that combining innovation with environmental responsibility is essential for the long-term growth and success of dental health tourism, offering valuable insights for policymakers and industry stakeholders.

Dental tourism is on the increase as people go to other countries in search of affordable quality dental care. Such countries as India, Hungary and Mexico have more developed procedure such as implant and veneers at affordable prices. Online visibility and digital exchanges influence the notion of trust that plays a significant role in patient decision-making. This essay discusses the fact that dental clinics take online review of their business and digital promotion as well as the use of patient testimonials in order to establish credibility. Patients can obtain information through online reviews and digital marketing because of the little available in-person consultation. The confidence is determined by the reviews on such platforms as Google, Yelp, and Trustpilot, and the clinic visibility is impacted by SEO, content marketing, and social media. To succeed, there should be good marketing and ethical conduct.

Dental tourism, a segment of medical tourism, has witnessed substantial growth over the past two decades, emerging as a viable alternative for patients seeking affordable, high-quality dental care beyond their national borders. This phenomenon has been largely driven by rising healthcare costs in developed countries, long waiting periods for dental treatments,Dental tourism, a segment of medical tourism, has witnessed substantial growth over the past two decades, emerging as a viable alternative for patients seeking affordable, high-quality dental care beyond their national borders. This phenomenon has been largely driven by rising healthcare costs in developed countries, long waiting periods for dental treatments, lack of insurance coverage for certain procedures, and the globalization of healthcare services. As patients become more informed and mobile, dental tourism has become a mainstream option, with countries across Asia, Latin America, and Eastern Europe emerging as popular destinations.

The integration of Artificial Intelligence (AI), particularly deep learning, into dental radiology is revolutionizing the way oral diseases are diagnosed and managed. This chapter explores how convolutional neural networks (CNNs) and related deep learning techniques are being applied to interpret dental imaging modalities such as panoramic X-rays, periapical radiographs, and cone-beam computed tomography (CBCT). By leveraging large datasets, AI models can detect caries, periodontal disease, periapical lesions, and other abnormalities with accuracy comparable to or exceeding that of experienced clinicians. The chapter reviews current tools, architectures, and real-world applications, and discusses the benefits and challenges of adopting AI in clinical practice, including ethical concerns, data privacy, and model transparency. Through case studies and comparative evaluations, we demonstrate the transformative potential of AI-powered radiology in making dental diagnostics faster, more consistent, and accessible across varying healthcare settings.

The global rise of dental health tourism has created demand for more efficient, personalized, and technology-driven care models. This chapter explores how Artificial Intelligence (AI) is transforming dental health tourism by enabling smarter diagnostics, remote consultations, and optimized treatment planning even before patients travel. Through AI-powered imaging analysis, chatbots, virtual assistants, and predictive cost estimation tools, clinics can offer a seamless pre-travel experience tailored to individual patient needs. Additionally, machine learning models support clinicians in creating faster, more accurate treatment plans while maintaining high standards of care across borders. The chapter also addresses how AI enhances post-treatment monitoring through telehealth and digital platforms, ensuring continuity of care. Ethical, legal, and data privacy concerns in cross-border AI applications are also discussed.

Foreword

The relationship between healthcare and international mobility has never been more dynamic than it is today. As patients around the world become increasingly willing to cross national borders in pursuit of quality dental treatment, and as clinical technologies advance at a remarkable pace. These parallel developments make rigorous scholarly inquiry more pressing than ever. It is therefore with great pleasure that I write this foreword for Next-Generation Treatment Methods and Destinations in Dental Health Tourism, edited by Dr. Ömer Faruk Şarkbay and Dr. Aslı Kaya.

This volume arrives at a particularly opportune moment, as dental health tourism has evolved from a niche phenomenon into a significant component of the global healthcare economy. Millions of patients each year now travel abroad for procedures ranging from routine restorations to complex implantology and full-mouth rehabilitations. The motivations behind this movement are multifaceted—encompassing cost considerations, access barriers in their home countries, the pursuit of specialized expertise, and the desire to combine treatment with travel. Understanding these motivations, and the systems that serve them, requires precisely the kind of interdisciplinary inquiry that this book provides.

What distinguishes this edited collection from existing literature is its deliberate integration of two rapidly converging domains: the geographical and strategic dimensions of dental tourism destinations, and the technological revolution reshaping clinical dentistry. The chapters assembled here move fluidly between macro-level analyses of global dental tourism trends and micro-level examinations of artificial intelligence applications in dental diagnostics. They explore deep learning models for caries detection and oral cancer screening, as well as AI-driven approaches to personalized treatment planning. This breadth of scope, anchored in methodological rigor, makes the volume a valuable resource for scholars, practitioners, and policymakers alike.

The editors have succeeded in assembling a diverse group of contributors whose collective expertise spans health management, dental sciences, marketing, law, data science, and public health. Each chapter offers a distinct perspective while contributing to a coherent narrative about the present state and future direction of dental health tourism. From the legal and ethical complexities of cross-border care to the operational optimization of outpatient clinics through predictive modeling, the topics covered reflect the true complexity of this field.

I am confident that this book will serve as an essential reference for anyone seeking to understand how next-generation treatment methods and emerging destination strategies are jointly shaping the future of dental health tourism. It is a testament to the editors' vision and the contributors' dedication that such a comprehensive and timely work has been brought to fruition.

I commend this volume to its readers and trust that it will inspire further research, informed policy development, and improved clinical practice in the years to come.

Dilaver Tengilimoğlu
Faculty of Business Administration, Atılım University, Ankara, Turkey

Preface

Dental health tourism stands at a pivotal crossroads where next-generation treatment technologies meet the expanding geography of cross-border patient mobility. The rapid evolution of digital dentistry—encompassing artificial intelligence-assisted diagnostics, deep learning-based imaging, smart clinical workflows, and personalized treatment protocols—has fundamentally altered the quality and scope of care available to international patients. Simultaneously, new and established destinations continue to refine their healthcare infrastructure, regulatory environments, and marketing approaches to attract a growing global patient base. Grasping these interconnected developments demands a multidisciplinary and forward-looking scholarly perspective, which this volume endeavors to offer.

Next-Generation Treatment Methods and Destinations in Dental Health Tourism was conceived to fill a critical gap in the academic literature by bringing together original research on the technological, geographical, and strategic dimensions of contemporary dental health tourism. As editors, we envisioned this volume as a cohesive scholarly platform—one that examines not only where patients travel for dental care and why, but also how emerging technologies such as deep learning, AI-driven personalization, and predictive analytics are transforming the patient journey from initial consultation to post-treatment follow-up.

POSITIONING IN THE WORLD TODAY

The global dental care ecosystem is undergoing a period of accelerated change. On the demand side, patients increasingly seek affordable, high-quality treatments beyond their home countries, motivated by cost differentials, reduced waiting periods, and the appeal of combining medical procedures with travel experiences. On the supply side, destinations worldwide are investing in state-of-the-art clinical infrastructure, pursuing international accreditation, and adopting next-generation technologies to differentiate themselves in an increasingly competitive market.

Nations such as Turkey, Hungary, Mexico, Thailand, and India have emerged as prominent hubs, each leveraging distinct competitive advantages in pricing, expertise, and geographic accessibility.

Concurrently, technological breakthroughs are reshaping the clinical landscape of dentistry at an unprecedented pace. Convolutional neural networks and deep learning architectures are being deployed for automated caries detection, oral cancer classification, and radiographic analysis with remarkable accuracy. AI-driven virtual consultations and smart diagnostic tools are enabling clinics to offer seamless pre-travel assessments and personalized treatment plans to prospective dental tourists. This book addresses these converging trends with academic rigor, drawing on perspectives from health management, dental sciences, marketing, law, data science, and public health to present a holistic picture of where dental health tourism stands today and where it is headed.

INTENDED AUDIENCE

This volume is intended for a broad readership, including:

Academics and researchers in health management, public health, tourism studies, dentistry, and data science who wish to examine the dynamics of dental tourism through interdisciplinary lenses.

Healthcare administrators, dental clinic operators, and health tourism professionals seeking evidence-based strategies for marketing, patient management, and sustainable service delivery.

Graduate and postgraduate students enrolled in health tourism, health informatics, or dental public health programs who require both foundational knowledge and exposure to cutting-edge research.

Policymakers and regulatory authorities involved in shaping cross-border healthcare frameworks, patient safety standards, and the ethical governance of AI-driven dental technologies.

Through a combination of theoretical analyses, empirical investigations, and applied frameworks, this book serves the dual purpose of advancing scholarly understanding and informing real-world practice in the dental tourism sector.

CHAPTER-BY-CHAPTER OVERVIEW

Chapter 1. The Rise of Dental Tourism: A Comprehensive Overview of the Global Landscape

This chapter analyzes the drivers of cross-border mobility for affordable and high-quality dental care, identifies the economic, technological, and socio-cultural factors shaping dental tourism, and aims to evaluate the sector's potential to enhance access to healthcare while highlighting areas requiring improvement for its sustainable development.

Chapter 2. Cross-Border Dental Care: Navigating The Landscape Of Dental Tourism

This chapter aims to holistically analyze the causes, consequences, and impacts of cross-border dental care and to emphasize the necessity of coordinated policies to ensure the sustainable and patient-centered development of dental tourism.

Chapter 3. Global Trends in Dental Tourism and Shaping an Optimal Dental Treatment Journey

This chapter aims to examine dental tourism within a comprehensive framework in light of existing research, identify the sector's strengths and weaknesses as well as its opportunities and threats, and provide strategic insights for decision-makers accordingly.

Chapter 4. Sustainable and Smart Destinations for Dental Health Tourism: An Analytical Review

This chapter aims to evaluate the positive effects of integrating environmentally friendly practices with digital health technologies on tourism demand, revisit intention, and operational efficiency, and to emphasize that innovation and environmental responsibility must be addressed together to ensure the sustainable development of dental health tourism.

Chapter 5. Dental Tourism Marketing: Attracting International Patients Strategies For Dental Clinics And Health Tourism Operators To Attr

This chapter aims to examine how the trust perceptions of patients seeking cross-border dental treatment are shaped by online reviews, testimonials, and digital promotional tools, and to reveal the impact of these factors on clinics' competitiveness and patient preferences.

Chapter 6. Dental Tourism Marketing

This chapter aims to analyze how factors such as high healthcare costs, long waiting times, limited insurance coverage, and the globalization of healthcare services in developed countries have contributed to the expansion of dental tourism, and to emphasize the growing importance of this phenomenon within the global healthcare system.

Chapter 7. Deep Learning in Dental Radiology: Enhancing Diagnosis and Decision-Making in Modern Dentistry

This chapter aims to evaluate the potential of CNN-based artificial intelligence systems to enhance diagnostic accuracy by analyzing dental imaging data, accelerate clinical processes, and expand access to healthcare, while also drawing attention to critical issues such as ethics, privacy, and transparency.

Chapter 8. AI-Driven Personalization in Dental Health Tourism: Smart Diagnostics, Virtual Consultations, and Treatment Optimization

This chapter aims to analyze the role of AI-based technologies in establishing personalized, efficient, and cross-border care models in dental health tourism, and to comprehensively examine their impacts on patient experience, service quality, and continuity of care.

Chapter 9. Deep Learning for Caries Detection and Diagnosis

This chapter aims to evaluate the development, implementation, and clinical implications of AI-based systems for the automated detection of dental caries from radiographic images, emphasizing their potential to enhance diagnostic accuracy and improve the effectiveness of healthcare delivery, particularly within the context of dental health tourism.

CONCLUSION

This volume offers both a thorough examination of the present landscape and a forward-looking analysis of the innovations and destination strategies that will define the next era of dental health tourism. It brings together the voices of health management scholars, dental practitioners, artificial intelligence researchers, legal experts, and tourism strategists, creating a multidimensional resource for understanding an industry that is growing not only in economic scale but also in technological sophistication and regulatory complexity.

As the editors of Next-Generation Treatment Methods and Destinations in Dental Health Tourism, we take great pride in presenting this work as a substantive contribution to the scholarly and professional communities dedicated to advancing dental health tourism. We are deeply grateful to each contributing author for their rigorous scholarship, original insights, and unwavering commitment to expanding the frontiers of knowledge in this dynamic field. Our appreciation also extends to the reviewers, colleagues, and institutions whose support made this publication possible, and to all readers who will carry these findings forward into practice, policy, and future research.

Ömer Faruk Şarkbay
İstanbul Gelişim University, Turkey

Aslı Kaya
İstanbul Gelişim University, Turkey

Acknowledgement

We would like to express our deepest gratitude to our families who have been my greatest supporters and sources of inspiration throughout our life journey.

We would also like to extend my sincere thanks to the esteemed authors;

Dr. Mohammad Badruddoza Talukder

Mr. Shivansu Sachan

Dr. Sanjeev Kumar

Dr. Narendra Kumar

Dr. Kartal Doğukan Çıkı

Mr. Suraj Jaywant Yadav

Dr. Velmurugan R

Dr. Bhuvaneswari R.

Dr. Ravi Thirumalaisamy

Dr. Selvakumar P,

Mr. Affaan Shaikh

Mr. Varun Prasanna. D.

Mr. Ravi Teja Kothuru

Ms. Muskan Kumari

Dr. Heba Talal Saeed

Dr. Amro Yaser Hmedan

Dr. Padmaja Kadiri

Ms. Sura Bhuvaneswari,

Ajay Kumar

Mr. Vangara Teja Venkata Sainath

Ms. Siddavatam Yashaswini

Dr. Prakash Putta

who contributed to the preparation of this book, as well as to our Scientific Committee and Editorial Advisory Board for their valuable support in reviewing the content of the studies.

We would like to express our sincere gratitude to the IGI Global family for their unwavering support in the preparation of our book.

Dr. Ömer Faruk ŞARKBAY & Dr. Aslı KAYA

İstanbul Gelişim University

01.03.2026

Chapter 1
The Rise of Dental Tourism:
A Comprehensive Overview of the Global Landscape

Mohammad Badruddoza Talukder
http://orcid.org/0009-0008-1662-9221
International University of Business Agriculture and Technology, Bangladesh

Shivansu Sachan
http://orcid.org/0000-0002-9893-8018
CSJM University, India

Sanjeev Kumar
http://orcid.org/0000-0002-7375-7341
Lovely Professional University, India

ABSTRACT

Dental tourism, the practice of traveling abroad to access affordable and high-quality dental care, has emerged as a significant trend in global healthcare. Driven by escalating costs, long wait times, and limited insurance coverage in developed nations, patients are increasingly seeking treatments in countries such as Mexico, Hungary, Thailand, and India. This paper provides a comprehensive overview of the dental tourism industry, exploring its economic, cultural, and technological drivers through four detailed case studies. The study highlights key trends shaping the industry's future, including advancements in teledentistry, 3D-printed implants, sustainable practices, personalized travel packages, insurance integration, and the

DOI: 10.4018/979-8-3373-4114-9.ch001

rise of emerging markets. This chapter underscores the transformative potential of dental tourism in making dental care more accessible while identifying areas for improvement to ensure patient safety and satisfaction.

INTRODUCTION

Dental tourism, a rapidly expanding subset of medical tourism, refers to traveling across international borders to receive dental care, often at significantly lower costs than in one's home country (Lubowiecki-Vikuk, 2018). This phenomenon has surged in popularity over the past two decades, driven by escalating healthcare costs, limited insurance coverage, long waiting times, and the appeal of combining dental treatments with travel experiences. Patients from high-income countries such as the United States, Canada, Australia, and Western Europe increasingly seek affordable, high-quality dental care in destinations like Mexico, Thailand, India, Hungary, and Costa Rica. These countries offer advanced dental facilities, internationally trained professionals, and competitive pricing, making dental tourism a viable option for millions (Adams et al., 2018).

This chapter provides a comprehensive exploration of dental tourism, delving into its historical roots, market size and growth, key drivers, major destinations, procedures in demand, challenges, ethical considerations, and future trends. By examining the global landscape through data, case studies, and expert insights, this overview aims to offer a nuanced understanding of why dental tourism has become a transformative force in global healthcare and what lies ahead for this dynamic industry (Badruddoza et al., 2024a).

HISTORICAL CONTEXT AND EVOLUTION

The concept of dental tourism emerged in the late 20th century as globalization and affordable international travel made cross-border healthcare feasible (Ozbek & Hassan, 2022). Early forms of medical tourism focused on elective surgeries and wellness treatments, but dental care quickly became a prominent segment due to its high costs in developed nations and the universal need for oral health services. By the early 2000s, countries like Hungary and Mexico began marketing themselves as dental tourism hubs, capitalizing on their proximity to Western markets and lower operational costs (Swenson & Bansal, 2024).

The rise of the internet and digital marketing further accelerated the growth of dental tourism. Online platforms allowed clinics to showcase their services, accreditations, and patient testimonials, building trust among prospective patients

(Talukder, Hossain, Ferdous, et al., 2025). Social media and review sites like Yelp and Google Reviews also played a pivotal role, enabling patients to share experiences and compare providers. By the 2010s, dental tourism had evolved into a structured industry, with travel agencies offering all-inclusive packages that combined dental treatments with accommodations, transportation, and sightseeing (Tsekouropoulos et al., 2024).

Today, dental tourism is a multi-billion-dollar industry, supported by advancements in dental technology, international accreditations (e.g., Joint Commission International), and a growing acceptance of cross-border healthcare. The World Health Organization (WHO) estimates that oral diseases affect over 3.5 billion people globally, with untreated dental caries impacting 2.5 billion and severe periodontal disease affecting 1 billion. This immense burden of oral health issues, coupled with economic disparities in healthcare access, has positioned dental tourism as a practical solution for millions.

Market Size and Growth

The global dental tourism market has witnessed remarkable growth, fueled by a combination of affordability, accessibility, and the rising global demand for dental care. Valued at approximately USD 7.1–8.8 billion in 2023–2024, the market is projected to expand significantly, reaching USD 21.5–62.65 billion by 2031–2034, with compound annual growth rates (CAGRs) ranging from 13.6% to 22.3%. This robust growth trajectory underscores the increasing acceptance of dental tourism as a viable alternative to costly domestic dental care, supported by the expansion of infrastructure in key destinations and growing consumer awareness (Ahmadimanesh et al., 2021).

Key Statistics

- **Cost Disparities**: One of the primary drivers of dental tourism is the significant cost savings offered by developing countries, where dental procedures are typically 60–85% cheaper than in developed nations (Anjalin et al., 2025). For instance, a dental implant in the United States can cost between USD 3,000 and USD 5,000, whereas in countries like Mexico, India, or Thailand, the same procedure ranges from USD 600 to USD 1,200. Similarly, a porcelain crown, which costs USD 1,000–2,000 in the U.S., is priced at USD 100–300 in India or Thailand.
- **Patient Volume**: The scale of dental tourism is substantial. Over 1.2 million Americans travel abroad annually for dental care, with similar trends observed in Canada, Australia, and the United Kingdom (Lovelock et al., 2018).

Mexico alone attracts 800,000–1 million dental tourists each year, primarily from the U.S., due to its proximity and affordability. In Europe, Hungary sees over 100,000 dental tourists annually, while Thailand and India collectively serve millions of international patients.

- **Market Share**: The Asia-Pacific region dominates the dental tourism market, holding a 45–54.7% share in 2023–2024, driven by countries like India, Thailand, and Malaysia. Europe follows with a 25–30% share, led by Hungary, Poland, and Turkey. Latin America, particularly Mexico and Costa Rica, accounts for 15–20% of the market, benefiting from proximity to North America (Oltean et al., 2020).

Growth Drivers

Several interconnected factors contribute to the rapid expansion of the dental tourism market, reflecting economic, social, and technological trends:

1. **Rising Dental Costs in High-Income Countries**: Dental care in developed nations is often prohibitively expensive, particularly for procedures not covered by standard health insurance plans. For example, a full mouth reconstruction in the U.S. can cost between USD 50,000 and USD 100,000, while the same procedure in India or Costa Rica ranges from USD 10,000 to USD 20,000. These disparities make dental tourism an attractive option for patients seeking complex treatments like implants, crowns, or full mouth restorations (Garner, 2019).
2. **Limited Insurance Coverage**: In countries like the U.S. and UK, dental insurance often covers only basic procedures such as cleanings or fillings, leaving patients to bear the full cost of advanced treatments like orthodontics, implants, or cosmetic procedures. For instance, dental implants are rarely covered by insurance in the U.S., pushing patients to seek more affordable options abroad. In the UK, private dental care costs for procedures like veneers or root canals can be exorbitant, further driving demand for dental tourism (Papakoca & Petrovski, 2021).
3. **Long Waiting Times in Public Healthcare Systems**: In countries with publicly funded healthcare systems, such as the UK and Canada, patients often face long waiting lists for non-emergency dental procedures. In the UK, NHS dental waiting times can exceed six months, and access to specialists is limited, prompting patients to seek faster treatment abroad. For example, a root canal that might take months to schedule through the NHS can be completed in days in Poland or Hungary (Białk-Wolf, 2025).

4. **High-Quality Care in Destination Countries**: Many dental tourism hubs boast state-of-the-art facilities, internationally trained dentists, and accreditations from reputable organizations like the Joint Commission International (JCI) or the International Organization for Standardization (ISO). Clinics in Thailand, Hungary, and Mexico often use the same materials, technologies, and techniques as those in Western countries, ensuring comparable quality at a fraction of the cost (Mandagi & Tappy, 2024). For instance, dental clinics in Bangkok and Budapest frequently employ dentists trained in the U.S., UK, or Australia, and many are equipped with advanced tools like 3D imaging and CAD/CAM systems for precise restorations (Hyder et al., 2019).
5. **Tourism Appeal and Cultural Experiences**: The opportunity to combine dental care with a vacation in exotic or culturally rich destinations adds significant appeal to dental tourism. Countries like Thailand and Costa Rica offer tropical getaways, with pristine beaches and eco-tourism opportunities, while Hungary and Poland provide access to historic European cities like Budapest and Krakow. Dental clinics and travel agencies often partner to offer all-inclusive packages that include treatment, accommodations, transportation, and guided tours, making the experience seamless and attractive (Talukder, 2025).
6. **Globalization and Digital Connectivity**: The rise of the internet and digital marketing has made it easier for patients to research and book dental treatments abroad. Online platforms, clinic websites, and review sites like Yelp, Google Reviews, and Trustpilot allow patients to compare providers, read testimonials, and verify accreditations. Social media also plays a critical role, with clinics showcasing before-and-after photos and patient experiences to build trust. Additionally, virtual consultations via telehealth platforms enable patients to discuss treatment plans with dentists before traveling (Talukder & Hoque, 2025).
7. **Economic Disparities and Currency Advantages**: The lower cost of living and favorable exchange rates in developing countries allow clinics to offer competitive pricing without compromising quality. For example, a strong U.S. dollar or euro gives patients from high-income countries greater purchasing power in countries like Mexico, India, or Thailand, amplifying cost savings (Talukder, Khan, Kumar, & Singh, 2025).
8. **Aging Populations and Cosmetic Dentistry Trends**: The global aging population and growing demand for cosmetic dentistry are also driving dental tourism. Older adults often require complex procedures like implants or bridges, which are costly in their home countries. Meanwhile, younger patients seek cosmetic treatments like veneers or teeth whitening to enhance their appearance, further boosting demand for affordable options abroad.

Major Dental Tourism Destinations

Dental tourism is concentrated in specific regions known for their affordability, quality, and robust infrastructure. Below is a detailed overview of the leading destinations, their unique strengths, and their contributions to the global dental tourism market (Zolfagharian et al., 2018).

1. Asia-Pacific

The Asia-Pacific region is the largest and fastest-growing dental tourism market, commanding a 45–54.7% share in 2023–2024. Countries like India, Thailand, Malaysia, and the Philippines have emerged as global leaders due to their cost-effective services, high-quality care, and vibrant tourism industries.

- **India**: India is a powerhouse in dental tourism, with over 170,000 dental surgeons and a reputation for delivering high-quality care at significantly lower costs. Cities like Delhi, Mumbai, Bangalore, and Chennai host JCI-accredited clinics equipped with cutting-edge technology . A dental crown in India costs USD 100–300, compared to USD 1,000–2,000 in the U.S., while a full mouth restoration ranges from USD 10,000 to USD 20,000, versus USD 50,000–100,000 in Western countries. India's appeal is enhanced by its large English-speaking workforce, internationally trained dentists, and a well-developed medical tourism infrastructure. The country's cultural diversity, historic landmarks, and wellness tourism options, such as Ayurveda retreats, further attract patients .
- **Thailand**: Known as the "Land of Smiles," Thailand has positioned itself as a premier dental tourism destination, combining world-class dental care with a vibrant tourism industry. Bangkok and Phuket are home to advanced clinics accredited by international bodies like JCI and ISO. A dental implant in Thailand costs USD 800–1,500, significantly less than the USD 3,000–5,000 charged in the U.S. or UK. Patients often combine treatments with beach vacations, cultural tours, or wellness retreats, with clinics offering packages that include accommodations and guided excursions. Thailand's government actively promotes medical tourism, ensuring high standards and patient satisfaction.
- **Malaysia**: Malaysia's dental tourism sector benefits from strong government support, modern facilities, and a reputation for excellent patient care. Kuala Lumpur and Penang are key hubs, offering competitive pricing (e.g., USD 1,000 for dental implants) and a multicultural environment that appeals to international patients. Malaysia's clinics are known for their patient-centric ap-

proach, with many providing English-speaking staff and personalized treatment plans. The country's affordability, combined with its vibrant food scene and tourist attractions, makes it a growing player in the market (Talukder, Kabir, & Jibon, 2025).

- **Philippines**: The Philippines is an emerging dental tourism destination, particularly for patients from Australia and the U.S. Manila and Cebu offer dental procedures at 60–70% lower costs than in Western countries. For example, a dental implant costs USD 800–1,200, and teeth whitening is priced at USD 50–100. The country's English-speaking population and proximity to Asia-Pacific markets enhance its appeal.

2. Europe

Europe is a major dental tourism hub, particularly for patients from Western Europe, North America, and the Middle East. Hungary, Poland, and Turkey lead the region, offering high-quality care at a fraction of Western prices.

- **Hungary**: Often referred to as the "dental capital of Europe," Hungary attracts over 100,000 dental tourists annually, primarily to Budapest. Hungarian clinics offer treatments at 50–70% lower costs than in Western Europe, with dental implants priced at USD 800–1,200 and crowns at USD 200–400. Many dentists in Hungary are trained in Western countries, and clinics are equipped with advanced technologies like laser dentistry and 3D imaging. The country's ISO-certified clinics and proximity to Western Europe make it a top choice for UK and German patients. Budapest's rich history, thermal baths, and cultural attractions further enhance its appeal.
- **Poland**: Poland's dental tourism industry is rapidly growing, with cities like Warsaw, Krakow, and Gdansk offering affordable care and cultural attractions. A root canal in Poland costs USD 100–200, compared to USD 800–1,500 in the UK, while dental implants range from USD 700–1,200. Polish clinics are known for their high standards, with many holding ISO or JCI accreditations. The country's vibrant history, affordable accommodations, and proximity to Western Europe make it an attractive destination for dental tourists.
- **Turkey**: Turkey's dental tourism market is projected to reach USD 5 billion by 2025, with 70% driven by international patients. Istanbul and Antalya are popular for their blend of dental care and tourism, offering procedures like veneers at USD 200–400 per tooth, compared to USD 1,500–2,500 in the U.S. Turkey's clinics are equipped with modern facilities, and many dentists are trained internationally. The country's rich cultural heritage, Mediterranean

climate, and affordable travel options make it a favorite among European and Middle Eastern patients.

3. Latin America

Latin America, particularly Mexico and Costa Rica, is a top choice for North American dental tourists due to its proximity, affordability, and high-quality care.

- **Mexico**: Mexico is the leading dental tourism destination for U.S. and Canadian patients, with border towns like Tijuana, Los Algodones (nicknamed "Molar City"), and Cancun hosting hundreds of dental clinics. A dental implant in Mexico costs USD 600–1,200, offering savings of 60–80% compared to U.S. prices. Los Algodones alone has over 350 dental clinics, catering to thousands of patients daily. Proximity to the U.S. border allows for same-day or short trips, making Mexico a convenient option. Many clinics are JCI-accredited and employ English-speaking staff, ensuring a seamless experience.
- **Costa Rica**: Known for its eco-tourism and natural beauty, Costa Rica offers high-quality dental care in San José and coastal areas like Jaco and Tamarindo. A full mouth restoration costs USD 10,000–15,000, compared to USD 50,000–100,000 in the U.S. Costa Rican clinics cater to English-speaking patients and often provide all-inclusive packages that include accommodations, transportation, and guided tours. The country's reputation for safety, modern facilities, and tropical attractions makes it a top choice for North American patients.

4. Emerging Destinations

Several emerging destinations are gaining traction in the dental tourism market due to competitive pricing and improving infrastructure:

- **Vietnam**: Vietnam offers dental implants for as low as USD 700 and crowns for USD 100–200. Cities like Ho Chi Minh City and Hanoi are investing in modern dental facilities to attract international patients, particularly from Australia and Southeast Asia. The country's affordability, cultural attractions, and growing medical tourism infrastructure make it a rising star.
- **Philippines**: As mentioned, the Philippines is emerging as a cost-effective destination, with dental care costs 60–70% lower than in Western countries. Its English-speaking population and proximity to Asia-Pacific markets enhance its appeal.

- **Croatia**: Croatia combines affordable dental care with Mediterranean tourism, attracting European patients to cities like Zagreb and Split. A dental implant in Croatia costs USD 800–1,200, and the country's scenic coastline and historic sites add to its allure.
- **Colombia**: Colombia is gaining popularity for its affordable dental care and vibrant tourism industry. Bogotá and Medellín offer dental implants for USD 800–1,500, and patients can combine treatments with cultural experiences or cosmetic surgery, another growing sector in the country.

Popular Dental Procedures

Dental tourism encompasses a wide range of procedures, from routine care to complex reconstructions. The affordability of these treatments abroad is a key driver of the industry's growth. Below are the most sought-after procedures and their cost comparisons:

1. **Dental Implants**: Dental implants are among the most expensive procedures in developed countries, making them a primary driver of dental tourism. A single implant in Mexico, India, or Thailand costs USD 600–1,200, compared to USD 3,000–5,000 in the U.S. or UK. Implants require advanced expertise and materials, and many dental tourism clinics use the same high-quality titanium implants as Western providers.
2. **Crowns and Bridges**: Porcelain crowns, used to restore damaged teeth, cost USD 100–300 in dental tourism hubs, versus USD 1,000–2,000 in Western countries. Bridges, which replace missing teeth, are similarly affordable, with costs ranging from USD 300–600 per unit abroad, compared to USD 2,000–4,000 in the U.S. These procedures are popular due to their durability and aesthetic appeal.
3. **Veneers**: Cosmetic procedures like porcelain veneers are in high demand, particularly in Turkey and Thailand, where they cost USD 200–400 per tooth, compared to USD 1,500–2,500 in the U.S. or UK. Veneers are sought after for their ability to enhance smiles, making them a favorite among younger patients and those seeking cosmetic improvements.
4. **Teeth Whitening**: Teeth whitening is a routine procedure that costs USD 50–100 abroad, versus USD 500–1,000 in developed nations. Its affordability and quick recovery time make it a popular add-on for dental tourists.
5. **Orthodontics**: Braces and clear aligners like Invisalign are increasingly sought after in countries like India and Mexico, where costs are 50–70% lower than in Western countries. For example, Invisalign treatment in India costs USD 1,500–3,000, compared to USD 5,000–8,000 in the U.S.

6. **Full Mouth Restorations**: Complex procedures involving multiple implants, crowns, or bridges are significantly cheaper abroad, attracting patients with extensive dental needs. A full mouth restoration in Costa Rica or India costs USD 10,000–20,000, compared to USD 50,000–100,000 in the U.S. These procedures often require multiple visits, which dental tourism clinics accommodate through flexible scheduling.
7. **Root Canals**: A root canal in Poland or Mexico costs USD 100–200, compared to USD 800–1,500 in the UK or U.S. The procedure's affordability and the availability of skilled endodontists abroad make it a common choice for dental tourists.
8. **Dentures**: Full or partial dentures are significantly cheaper abroad, with costs ranging from USD 200–500 in Mexico or India, versus USD 1,500–3,000 in the U.S. High-quality materials and custom fittings ensure patient satisfaction.

Challenges and Risks

While dental tourism offers significant benefits, it also presents challenges and risks that patients must navigate:

1. **Quality Variability**: Not all clinics abroad meet international standards. Patients must research accreditations (e.g., JCI, ISO) and dentist qualifications to ensure quality care.
2. **Follow-Up Care**: Post-treatment complications may require follow-up visits, which can be difficult for patients returning to their home countries. For example, implant failures or infections may necessitate costly revisions.
3. **Language Barriers**: Communication issues can arise in countries where English is not widely spoken, potentially leading to misunderstandings about treatment plans.
4. **Travel Risks**: Long flights, unfamiliar environments, and recovery periods abroad can pose logistical and health challenges, particularly for complex procedures.
5. **Legal Recourse**: Patients may have limited legal options if malpractice occurs in a foreign country, as regulations and consumer protections vary widely.
6. **Ethical Concerns**: Some critics argue that dental tourism exploits economic disparities, with wealthy patients from developed nations benefiting from lower wages in developing countries. Additionally, the influx of foreign patients can strain local healthcare systems (Demonja & Uglješić, 2020).

Ethical and Regulatory Considerations

The rise of dental tourism raises important ethical and regulatory questions. From an ethical standpoint, the industry highlights global inequalities in healthcare access. While patients from high-income countries benefit from affordable care, local populations in destination countries may face limited access to the same facilities due to prioritization of foreign clients. This dynamic has sparked debates about the commodification of healthcare and the need for equitable access (Lina & Talukder, 2025).

Regulatory frameworks also vary significantly. In countries like Thailand and Hungary, governments have implemented strict standards for dental clinics catering to international patients, including mandatory accreditations and licensing. However, in less regulated markets, patients face risks from unqualified practitioners or substandard facilities. Organizations like the International Medical Travel Journal advocate for global standards to ensure patient safety and quality care (Mohammad & Iva, 2024).

Patients are advised to:

- Verify clinic accreditations (e.g., JCI, ISO).
- Confirm dentist credentials, including international training or certifications.
- Review patient testimonials and third-party ratings.
- Consult with their home-country dentist for pre- and post-treatment planning.

CASE STUDIES AND FUTURE TRENDS

Dental tourism, the practice of traveling abroad to receive dental care at a lower cost, has grown into a global phenomenon, driven by rising healthcare costs, long wait times, and the increasing availability of high-quality dental services in developing countries (Talukder, Huda, Kumar, et al., 2025). Patients from developed nations, such as the United States, Canada, the United Kingdom, and Australia, are increasingly seeking affordable, high-quality dental care in countries like Mexico, Hungary, Thailand, and India. This report explores four detailed case studies of individuals who pursued dental tourism, highlighting their motivations, experiences, challenges, and outcomes. Additionally, it examines the future trends shaping the dental tourism industry, including technological advancements, sustainability efforts, personalized travel packages, insurance integration, and emerging markets. By analyzing these case studies and trends, this report aims to provide a comprehensive understanding of the opportunities and challenges within the dental tourism sector (Talukder, Rahman, & Khan, 2025).

Case Studies

Case Study 1: American Patient in Mexico

John, a 45-year-old software engineer from San Diego, California, faced a significant dental health challenge. After years of neglecting routine dental care due to a demanding work schedule, he required four dental implants and a full mouth restoration to address severe tooth decay and missing teeth. In the United States, John received quotes averaging USD 60,000 for the procedure, a cost far beyond his financial means, even with dental insurance covering only a fraction of the expenses. Frustrated but determined, John began researching alternatives online and discovered dental tourism as a viable option.

Through online forums and patient reviews, John identified a Joint Commission International (JCI)-accredited dental clinic in Tijuana, Mexico, just a short drive from his home in San Diego. The clinic offered the same treatment plan—four dental implants and a full mouth restoration—for USD 12,000, representing a savings of over 80%. The clinic's website showcased state-of-the-art facilities, English-speaking staff, and board-certified dentists trained in the U.S. and Europe. Intrigued, John contacted the clinic and was impressed by their prompt response, which included a detailed treatment plan, cost breakdown, and a virtual consultation with the lead dentist.

John decided to combine his dental treatment with a week-long trip to Tijuana. The clinic provided a comprehensive package that included airport transfers, accommodation at a nearby hotel, and a dedicated patient coordinator to assist with logistics. During his stay, John underwent the dental procedures over five days, with each session lasting a few hours. The clinic used advanced technology, such as computer-guided implant placement, to ensure precision and minimize recovery time. John was particularly impressed by the professionalism of the staff and the cleanliness of the facility, which rivaled the best dental offices he had visited in the U.S.

Beyond the dental care, John took advantage of his time in Tijuana to explore local attractions, including the vibrant food scene and cultural landmarks like the Tijuana Cultural Center. The clinic provided a one-year follow-up plan, which included virtual check-ins and the option to return for in-person evaluations if needed. Upon returning to California, John reported high satisfaction with the outcome of his treatment. His implants were successful, and he experienced no complications. The significant cost savings allowed him to invest in other areas of his life, such as paying off debt and planning a family vacation.

John's experience highlights the appeal of dental tourism for Americans, particularly those living near the U.S.-Mexico border. The proximity of Tijuana, combined with high-quality care and significant cost savings, makes it an attractive destination. However, John's success was partly due to his thorough research and selection of a JCI-accredited clinic, underscoring the importance of due diligence when choosing a provider (Ramos & Cuamea, 2023).

Case Study 2: UK Patient in Hungary

Sarah, a 32-year-old graphic designer from London, faced a different set of challenges. She required a root canal and crown to address a painful tooth infection but was frustrated by the six-month waiting list for treatment through the UK's National Health Service (NHS). Private dental care in the UK quoted her USD 2,000 for the procedures, a cost she found exorbitant given her freelance income. After discussing her situation with a friend who had traveled to Budapest, Hungary, for dental work, Sarah decided to explore dental tourism.

Sarah found a reputable dental clinic in Budapest that was ISO-certified and had glowing reviews from international patients. The clinic offered a root canal and crown for USD 400, a fraction of the UK price. Encouraged by the potential savings, Sarah booked a four-day trip to Budapest, combining her dental appointments with a weekend exploring the city's historic sites, such as Buda Castle and the thermal baths. The clinic provided a seamless experience, with English-speaking staff, modern equipment, and a comfortable environment. Sarah completed her treatment in two visits, with the root canal performed on the first day and the crown fitted on the third.

While Sarah was thrilled with the quality of care and the affordability of the treatment, she encountered challenges upon returning to the UK. Her local NHS dentist was hesitant to provide follow-up care for work done abroad, citing differences in treatment protocols and a lack of familiarity with the materials used. Sarah eventually found a private dentist willing to assist, but the experience highlighted a key challenge of dental tourism: coordinating post-treatment care. Despite this hurdle, Sarah's overall experience was positive, and she recommended dental tourism to her colleagues, emphasizing the importance of discussing follow-up plans with both the overseas clinic and local providers before traveling.

Sarah's case illustrates the growing popularity of dental tourism in Europe, where countries like Hungary have established themselves as hubs for affordable, high-quality dental care. The combination of low costs, accredited facilities, and the opportunity to explore a culturally rich destination makes cities like Budapest appealing. However, her experience also underscores the need for better integration between international clinics and local healthcare systems to ensure continuity of care (Lubowiecki-Vikuk & Dryglas, 2019).

Case Study 3: Canadian Patient in Thailand

Emily, a 60-year-old retiree from Vancouver, Canada, needed extensive dental work, including multiple crowns, bridges, and teeth whitening to restore her smile after years of wear and tear. In Canada, her dentist quoted CAD 25,000 (approximately USD 18,500) for the procedures, which was unaffordable on her fixed pension. After researching online, Emily discovered Thailand's reputation as a leading dental tourism destination, known for its world-class clinics and tropical appeal. She chose a clinic in Bangkok that was accredited by the International Organization for Standardization (ISO) and had partnerships with Canadian dental associations.

The clinic offered Emily's treatment plan for USD 4,500, including all procedures and a complimentary teeth-whitening session. The package also included airport transfers, a week's stay in a four-star hotel, and a guided tour of Bangkok's Grand Palace. Emily booked a 10-day trip, allowing time for both dental care and leisure. The clinic's staff were fluent in English, and the facility was equipped with cutting-edge technology, including digital X-rays and laser dentistry. Emily completed her treatment over six days, with appointments spaced to allow her to enjoy Thailand's vibrant culture, from street markets to Buddhist temples.

Emily's experience was overwhelmingly positive. The clinic provided detailed post-treatment instructions and a six-month virtual follow-up plan via teledentistry, which allowed her to consult with her Bangkok dentist from Canada. Upon returning home, Emily's Canadian dentist was impressed with the quality of the work and agreed to monitor her progress during routine check-ups. Emily saved over 75% compared to Canadian prices and described the trip as a "life-changing" blend of healthcare and adventure. Her only regret was not exploring dental tourism sooner.

Emily's case highlights the appeal of combining dental care with an exotic vacation. Thailand's established dental tourism industry, with its focus on patient experience and affordability, makes it a top destination. The use of teledentistry for follow-up care also demonstrates how technology can address one of the primary challenges of dental tourism, ensuring patients feel supported after returning home (Chongthanavanit & Kheokao, 2018).

Case Study 4: Australian Patient in India

Michael, a 28-year-old teacher from Sydney, Australia, needed orthodontic treatment to correct misaligned teeth. In Australia, the cost of Invisalign braces was quoted at AUD 8,000 (approximately USD 5,300), which was beyond his budget as a young professional. After reading about India's growing reputation in medical and dental tourism, Michael researched clinics in New Delhi and found one accredited by the National Accreditation Board for Hospitals & Healthcare Providers (NABH).

The clinic offered Invisalign treatment for USD 1,800, including consultations and follow-up aligners .

Michael booked a two-week trip to New Delhi, where the clinic arranged airport transfers and accommodation in a nearby guesthouse. The treatment process began with a 3D scan of his teeth, followed by a customized Invisalign plan. The clinic's orthodontist, who had trained in the UK, provided clear instructions and a timeline for wearing the aligners. Michael completed his initial fittings in three visits, with the clinic shipping subsequent aligners to Australia for ongoing treatment. During his stay, Michael explored New Delhi's rich history, visiting sites like the Red Fort and India Gate, and enjoyed the city's diverse cuisine.

The clinic's use of teledentistry for remote monitoring ensured Michael could continue his treatment seamlessly after returning to Sydney. His Australian dentist agreed to oversee the process, as the Indian clinic provided detailed records and aligner schedules. Michael saved over 65% on his treatment and was delighted with the professionalism of the clinic and the cultural experience of his trip. However, he noted that navigating New Delhi's bustling environment required some adjustment, and he advised future dental tourists to plan for logistical challenges in unfamiliar cities .

Michael's experience showcases India's rising prominence in dental tourism, driven by competitive pricing, accredited facilities, and skilled professionals. The integration of teledentistry and international shipping of aligners highlights how clinics are adapting to meet the needs of global patients, making dental tourism more accessible and convenient (Marcus et al., 2022).

Future Trends and Outlook

The dental tourism industry is poised for significant growth, with projections estimating a global market value exceeding USD 12 billion by 2030. This expansion is driven by a combination of economic pressures, technological advancements, and evolving consumer preferences. Below, we explore five key trends shaping the future of dental tourism, drawing on insights from the case studies and broader industry developments (Das et al., 2024).

1. Technological Advancements

Technology is transforming dental care, making it more efficient, precise, and accessible for international patients. Innovations such as 3D-printed dental implants, laser dentistry, and computer-aided design/computer-aided manufacturing (CAD/CAM) systems are becoming standard in top dental tourism destinations. For example, John's clinic in Tijuana used computer-guided implant placement to ensure accuracy, while Emily's Bangkok clinic employed digital X-rays and laser dentistry for enhanced outcomes (Talukder & Afchar, 2025).

Teledentistry is a particularly transformative trend, as seen in Emily and Michael's cases. Remote consultations and follow-ups allow patients to maintain contact with their overseas dentists, addressing concerns about post-treatment care. Artificial intelligence (AI) is also playing a growing role, with clinics using AI-powered tools to analyze patient data, predict treatment outcomes, and personalize care plans (Badruddoza et al., 2024b). By 2030, AI-driven diagnostics and virtual reality simulations may enable patients to preview their results before traveling, further boosting confidence in dental tourism.

Blockchain technology is another emerging tool, offering secure storage and transfer of patient records across borders. This ensures continuity of care and builds trust between patients, international clinics, and local providers. As technology continues to advance, dental tourism destinations that invest in cutting-edge equipment and digital solutions will likely attract more patients seeking high-quality, efficient care (Talukder, 2024).

2. Sustainability and Ethical Practices

As dental tourism grows, so do concerns about its impact on local communities. Some critics argue that prioritizing foreign patients can strain local healthcare systems and limit access for residents. In response, leading clinics are adopting sustainable and ethical practices. For instance, some facilities in Thailand and India allocate a portion of their profits to provide free or subsidized dental care for underserved local populations. Others are implementing eco-friendly practices, such as reducing waste and using sustainable materials in dental procedures (Talukder et al., 2025).

Regulatory frameworks are also evolving to balance the needs of foreign and local patients. Countries like Hungary and Mexico are introducing guidelines to ensure clinics maintain high standards for both groups. Patients like Sarah, who faced challenges coordinating follow-up care, would benefit from such regulations, which could standardize treatment protocols and facilitate collaboration between international and local providers. By prioritizing ethical practices, dental tourism destinations can enhance their reputation and appeal to socially conscious travelers (Sanjeev et al., 2024).

3. Personalized Packages

The integration of dental care with tourism is a hallmark of the industry, as demonstrated by all four case studies. Clinics and travel agencies are increasingly offering personalized packages that combine dental treatments with wellness retreats, cultural tours, or adventure travel. For example, Emily's Bangkok clinic included a guided tour of the Grand Palace, while Michael's New Delhi trip incorporated visits to historic sites. These tailored experiences cater to a broader audience, including younger travelers like Michael, who seek both affordable care and memorable travel experiences (Piya et al., 2023).

By 2030, personalized packages are expected to become more sophisticated, with options for wellness-focused retreats (e.g., yoga and meditation alongside dental care) or adventure-based itineraries (e.g., trekking in Costa Rica or diving in Thailand). Data analytics will play a key role in customizing these packages, allowing providers to match treatments and activities to patients' preferences and health needs. This trend will likely attract a more diverse demographic, including families and retirees, further expanding the dental tourism market (Kopmaz et al., 2019).

4. Insurance Integration

One of the barriers to dental tourism is the lack of insurance coverage for treatments performed abroad. However, some insurance providers in developed countries are beginning to explore partnerships with international clinics to offer partial or full coverage for dental tourism. This trend could significantly reduce costs for patients like John, who saved 80% but still faced a substantial out-of-pocket expense (Stackpole et al., 2021).

For example, some U.S. and Canadian insurers are piloting programs with accredited clinics in Mexico and Thailand, allowing patients to claim reimbursements for specific procedures. In Europe, insurers are collaborating with clinics in Hungary and Poland to offer bundled packages for common treatments like implants and crowns. These partnerships require rigorous quality assurance, as insurers demand evidence of accreditation, patient outcomes, and follow-up care protocols.

By 2030, insurance integration could become a standard feature of dental tourism, making it more accessible to middle-income patients. This would also encourage clinics to maintain high standards and transparency, as seen in the JCI- and ISO-accredited facilities chosen by John, Sarah, and Emily (Badri & Yarmohamadi, 2022).

5. Emerging Markets

While established destinations like Mexico, Hungary, and Thailand dominate the dental tourism market, emerging markets are gaining traction. Countries such as Vietnam, Colombia, and Albania are investing heavily in healthcare infrastructure to attract international patients. Vietnam, for instance, offers dental treatments at costs up to 70% lower than in Western countries, with cities like Hanoi and Ho Chi Minh City developing modern clinics and tourism-friendly amenities (Dang et al., 2020).

Colombia is emerging as a hub for Latin American dental tourism, with Medellín and Bogotá offering high-quality care and vibrant cultural experiences. Albania, known for its affordability and proximity to Europe, is also attracting patients from the UK and Germany. These emerging markets are leveraging competitive pricing, skilled professionals, and government support to capture a share of the growing market.

However, these destinations face challenges, such as building trust with international patients and ensuring consistent quality. Accreditation from organizations like JCI or NABH, as seen in the case studies, will be critical for emerging markets to compete with established players (Talukder et al., 2025).

CHALLENGES AND CONSIDERATIONS

Despite its growth, dental tourism is not without challenges. The case studies highlight several key considerations for patients and providers:

- **Quality Assurance**: Patients must thoroughly research clinics to ensure they are accredited and staffed by qualified professionals. John's success in Tijuana was due to his choice of a JCI-accredited clinic, while Sarah's follow-up issues in the UK underscore the risks of choosing providers without robust post-treatment plans (Nexhipi, 2018).
- **Post-Treatment Care**: Coordinating follow-up care remains a significant hurdle, as seen in Sarah's case. Clinics that offer teledentistry or partnerships with local providers, as in Emily and Michael's cases, are better positioned to address this challenge (Fahim et al., 2022).
- **Cultural and Logistical Barriers**: Navigating unfamiliar cities, as Michael experienced in New Delhi, can be daunting. Clinics that provide comprehensive support, such as airport transfers and patient coordinators, enhance the patient experience (Ashiti & Moshkun, 2021).
- **Ethical Concerns**: The industry must address concerns about prioritizing foreign patients over local communities. Sustainable practices, as discussed in the trends section, can mitigate these issues (Saxena et al., 2023).

CONCLUSION

Dental tourism has emerged as a transformative force in global healthcare, offering affordable, high-quality dental care to millions while addressing the challenges of cost, access, and waiting times in developed nations. With a market valued at billions and projected to grow significantly, destinations like India, Thailand, Hungary, and Mexico are leading the charge, combining advanced dental care with appealing travel experiences. However, challenges such as quality variability, follow-up care, and ethical concerns underscore the need for careful planning and regulation.

As the industry evolves, technological advancements, sustainable practices, and innovative business models will shape its future (Huda et al., 2024). For patients, dental tourism offers a compelling solution to the high costs and inaccessibility of dental care, provided they conduct thorough research and prioritize quality. For destination countries, it presents an opportunity to boost economies and showcase their healthcare and tourism potential. The rise of dental tourism reflects the broader trends of globalization and healthcare democratization, making it a phenomenon worth watching in the years to come.

REFERENCES

Adams, K., Snyder, J., Crooks, V. A., & Berry, N. S. (2018). A critical examination of empowerment discourse in medical tourism: The case of the dental tourism industry in Los Algodones, Mexico. *Globalization and Health, 14*(1), 70. DOI: 10.1186/s12992-018-0392-3 PMID: 30029610

Ahmadimanesh, F., Pourmehdi, M., & Paydar, M. M. (2021). Evaluation and prioritisation of potential locations for investment in dental tourism. *Soft Computing, 25*(24), 15313–15333. DOI: 10.1007/s00500-021-06124-2

Anjalin, U., Sohel-Uz-Zaman, A. S. M., Mazumdar, A., & Khan, M. I. (2025). The Prospects and Intricacies of Dental Tourism in South Asia. In Hamdan, R. K. (Ed.), *Sustainable Data Management: Navigating Big Data, Communication Technology, and Business Digital Leadership* (Vol. 2, pp. 461–469). Springer Nature Switzerland., DOI: 10.1007/978-3-031-83915-3_37

Ashiti, S., & Moshkun, C. (2021). Dental tourists: Treat, re-treat or do not treat? *British Dental Journal, 230*(2), 73–76. DOI: 10.1038/s41415-020-2591-6 PMID: 33483660

Badri, S. A., & Yarmohamadi, N. (2022). A game theory–based model for dental centers in a competitive market of dental tourism under government intervention. *Journal of Applied Research on Industrial Engineering, 9*(1), 78–94. DOI: 10.22105/jarie.2021.300196.1370

Badruddoza, T. Mohammad, Sanjeev, K., & Kumar, T., Pankaj. (2024a). *Impact of AI and Tech-Driven Solutions in Hospitality and Tourism*. IGI Global.

Badruddoza, T. Mohammad, Sanjeev, K., & Kumar, T., Pankaj. (2024b). *Impact of AI and Tech-Driven Solutions in Hospitality and Tourism*. IGI Global.

Białk-Wolf, A. (2025). Developments in the medical tourism market in Poland from the perspective of international factors. *Worldwide Hospitality and Tourism Themes, 17*(2), 261–272. DOI: 10.1108/WHATT-01-2025-0020

Chongthanavanit, P., & Kheokao, J. (2018). Factors Influencing the Use of Dental Services by Foreign Tourists in Thailand. *Asian Journal for Public Opinion Research, 5*(2), 63–83. DOI: 10.15206/AJPOR.2018.5.2.63

Dang, H.-S., Nguyen, T.-M.-T., Wang, C.-N., Day, J.-D., & Dang, T. M. H. (2020). Grey System Theory in the Study of Medical Tourism Industry and Its Economic Impact. *International Journal of Environmental Research and Public Health, 17*(3), 961. DOI: 10.3390/ijerph17030961 PMID: 32033177

Das, I. R., Talukder, M. B., & Kumar, S. (2024). Implication of Artificial Intelligence in Hospitality Marketing. In Kumar, S., Talukder, M. B., & Pego, A. (Eds.), *Advances in Hospitality, Tourism, and the Services Industry* (pp. 291–310). IGI Global., DOI: 10.4018/979-8-3693-1978-9.ch014

Demonja, D., & Uglješić, N. (2020). Dental Tourism and Business Risks: The Example of the Republic of Croatia. *Interdisciplinary Description of Complex Systems : INDECS, 18*(4), 425–445. DOI: 10.7906/indecs.18.4.3

Fahim, A., Saleem, Z., Malik, K. A., Atta, K., Mahmood, R., Alam, M. K., & Sethi, A. (2022). Exploring challenges and mitigation strategies towards practicing teledentistry. *BMC Oral Health, 22*(1), 658. DOI: 10.1186/s12903-022-02685-2 PMID: 36585644

Garner, R. (2019). Implications of dental tourism Examining US patients travelling to Mexico for dental care. *BDJ In Practice, 32*(10), 20–23. DOI: 10.1038/s41404-019-0182-5

Huda, Md. N., Talukder, M. B., & Kumar, S. (2024). Securing Healthcare AI: Applied Federal Learning. In P. Bhattacharya, H. Liu, P. K. Dutta, J. J. P. C. Rodrigues, & G. Sethi (Eds.), *Revolutionizing Healthcare 5.0: The Power of Generative AI: Advancements in Patient Care Through Generative AI Algorithms* (pp. 255–272). Springer Nature Switzerland. DOI: 10.1007/978-3-031-75771-6_17

Hyder, A. S., Rydback, M., Borg, E., & Osarenkhoe, A. (2019). Medical tourism in emerging markets: The role of trust, networks, and word-of-mouth. *Health Marketing Quarterly, 36*(3), 203–219. DOI: 10.1080/07359683.2019.1618008 PMID: 31210584

Kopmaz, B., Kitapci, N. S., Kitapci, O. C., Bulu, S. B., Aksu, P. K., Koksal, L., & Mumcu, G. (2019). Dental Websites as New Media Tools for Patients in Dental Health Tourism. *Acta Informatica Medica, 27*(2), 128–132. DOI: 10.5455/aim.2019.27.128-132 PMID: 31452572

Lina, F. Y., & Talukder, M. B. (2025). AI in Tourism: Business and Economic Perspectives. In *Innovation Management for a Resilient Digital Economy* (pp. 81–104). IGI Global Scientific Publishing. DOI: 10.4018/979-8-3693-8357-5.ch004

Lovelock, B., Lovelock, K., & Lyons, K. (2018). The impact of outbound medical (dental) tourism on the generating region: New Zealand dental professionals' perspectives. *Tourism Management, 67*, 399–410. DOI: 10.1016/j.tourman.2018.02.001

Lubowiecki-Vikuk, A. (2018). Consumption of dental services: Medical tourism in CEE. *European Journal of Service Management, 27*(3/1), 135–142.

Lubowiecki-Vikuk, A., & Dryglas, D. (2019). Medical tourism services and medical tourism destinations in Central and Eastern Europe—The opinion of Britons and Germans. *Economic Research -. Ekonomska Istrazivanja*, *32*(1), 1256–1274. DOI: 10.1080/1331677X.2019.1627892

Mandagi, D. W., & Tappy, Y. P. (2024). Determinants of Health Tourism Destination Attractiveness: A Comprehensive Systematic Review. *Jurnal Studi Perhotelan Dan Pariwisata*, *2*(2), 57–69. DOI: 10.35912/jspp.v2i2.3261

Marcus, K., Balasubramanian, M., Short, S. D., & Sohn, W. (2022). Dental diaspora: Oral health care attitudes and experiences in culturally and linguistically diverse mothers in Australia. *BMC Health Services Research*, *22*(1), 1314. DOI: 10.1186/s12913-022-08708-6 PMID: 36329526

Mohammad, B. T., & Iva, R. D. (2024). The technology impacts and AI solutions in hospitality. *I-Manager's Journal on Artificial Intelligence &. Machine Learning*, *2*(1), 56. DOI: 10.26634/jaim.2.1.20291

Nexhipi, O. (2018). Medical Tourism Management Challenges—The Case of Dental Tourism in Albania. *European Journal of Interdisciplinary Studies*, *10*(1), 80. DOI: 10.26417/ejis.v10i1.p80-86

Oltean, F. D., Gabor, M. R., Stăncioiu, A.-F., Kardos, M., Kiss, M., & Marinescu, R. C. (2020). Aspects of Marketing in Dental Tourism—Factor of Sustainable Development in Romania. *Sustainability (Basel)*, *12*(10), 4320. DOI: 10.3390/su12104320

Ozbek, O., & Hassan, A. (2022). Medical Tourism and the Application of Technology. In *Handbook of Technology Application in Tourism in Asia* (pp. 607–627). Springer., DOI: 10.1007/978-981-16-2210-6_28

Papakoca, K., & Petrovski, M. (2021). Dental tourism -our perspectives. *Knowledge –. International Journal (Toronto, Ont.)*, *48*(3), 479–482.

Piya, S., Triki, C., Al Maimani, A., & Mokhtarzadeh, M. (2023). Optimization model for designing personalized tourism packages. *Computers & Industrial Engineering*, *175*, 108839. DOI: 10.1016/j.cie.2022.108839

Ramos, K., & Cuamea, O. (2023). Dental tourism: Factors influencing travelers' revisit intention to the Mexican border. *International Journal of Tourism Cities*, *9*(3), 806–831. DOI: 10.1108/IJTC-03-2023-0046

Sanjeev, K., & Badruddoza, T. Mohammad, & Ana, P. (2024). *Utilizing Smart Technology and AI in Hybrid Tourism and Hospitality*. IGI Global.

Saxena, V., Deheriya, M., & Datla, A. (2023, June 1). *Bibliometric Analysis of Dental Tourism: A Global Perspective. | EBSCOhost*. DOI: 10.30491/IJT-MGH.2023.387742.1349

Stackpole, I., Ziemba, E., & Johnson, T. (2021). Looking around the corner: COVID-19 shocks and market dynamics in US medical tourism. *The International Journal of Health Planning and Management*, *36*(5), 1407–1416. DOI: 10.1002/hpm.3259 PMID: 34096092

Swenson, M. S., & Bansal, A. (2024). *Medical, Dental, and Wellness Tourism: A Post-Pandemic Perspective*. Apple Academic Press., DOI: 10.1201/9781003433569

Talukder, M. B. (2024). Implementing Artificial Intelligence and Virtual Experiences in Hospitality. In *Innovative Technologies for Increasing Service Productivity* (pp. 145–160). IGI Global Scientific Publishing., DOI: 10.4018/979-8-3693-2019-8.ch009

Talukder, M. B. (2025). Current Trends and Future Research Directions of Eco-Friendly Steps of Hotel Industry. *RPER*, *71*(71), 7–18. DOI: 10.59072/rper.vi71.695

Talukder, M. B., & Afchar, M. N. (2025). Vision Hotels: Shaping the Future of Hospitality Through Innovation, Sustainability, and Technology. In *Global Practices and Innovations in Sustainable Homestay Tourism* (pp. 269–294). IGI Global Scientific Publishing. DOI: 10.4018/979-8-3373-0427-4.ch012

Talukder, M. B., & Hoque, M. (2025). Navigating the Digital Horizon: Transforming Travel Agencies in the Digital Era. In *Perspectives on Digital Transformation in Contemporary Business* (pp. 383–410). IGI Global Scientific Publishing. DOI: 10.4018/979-8-3693-5966-2.ch014

Talukder, M. B., Hossain, S. E., Ferdous, F. A., & Khan, M. R. (2025). Exploring the Rise of Wellness Tourism: Trends, Benefits, and Market Potential. In *AI Technologies and Advancements for Psychological Well-Being and Healthcare* (pp. 351–378). IGI Global Scientific Publishing. DOI: 10.4018/979-8-3693-9158-7.ch013

Talukder, M. B., Huda, M. N., Kumar, S., & Hasan, M. M. (2025). Metaverse Future of Digital Medical Tourism. In *Revolutionizing Healthcare Experience With Digital Medical Tourism* (pp. 173–198). IGI Global Scientific Publishing., DOI: 10.4018/979-8-3693-7888-5.ch007

Talukder, M. B., Kabir, F., & Jibon, F. A. (2025). AI-Driven Personalized Room Management in the Modern Hotel Industry. In *AI Technologies for Personalized and Sustainable Tourism* (pp. 59–82). IGI Global Scientific Publishing., DOI: 10.4018/979-8-3693-5678-4.ch003

Talukder, M. B., Khan, M. R., & Haghi, A. K. (2025). Redefining Hospital Waste Management: Circular Economy Strategies for Reducing Toxicity. In *Sustainable Business Ecosystems and Social Perspectives* (pp. 335–358). IGI Global Scientific Publishing. DOI: 10.4018/979-8-3693-8437-4.ch015

Talukder, M. B., Khan, M. R., Kumar, S., & Singh, K. (2025). Blockchain and Tourism: Enhancing Community Participation and Sustainability. In *Open Innovation and Technology in Tourism and Hospitality* (pp. 279–302). IGI Global Scientific Publishing. DOI: 10.4018/979-8-3693-8633-0.ch015

Talukder, M. B., Khan, M. R., Kumar, S., Singh, K., & Lina, F. Y. (2025). AI Strategies for Tourism Development in Emerging Markets. In *Practical Strategies and Case Studies for Online Marketing 6.0* (pp. 117–138). IGI Global Scientific Publishing., DOI: 10.4018/979-8-3373-2058-8.ch007

Talukder, M. B., Rahman, M. Z., & Khan, M. R. (2025). Enhancing Guest Experience Through Smart Hotel Technologies. In *Adapting to Evolving Consumer Experiences in Hospitality and Tourism* (pp. 301–324). IGI Global Scientific Publishing., DOI: 10.4018/979-8-3693-7021-6.ch011

Tsekouropoulos, G., Vasileiou, A., Hoxha, G., Dimitriadis, A., & Zervas, I. (2024). Sustainable Approaches to Medical Tourism: Strategies for Central Macedonia/ Greece. *Sustainability (Basel)*, *16*(1), 121. DOI: 10.3390/su16010121

Zolfagharian, M., Rajamma, R. K., Naderi, I., & Torkzadeh, S. (2018). Determinants of medical tourism destination selection process. *Journal of Hospitality Marketing & Management*, *27*(7), 775–794. DOI: 10.1080/19368623.2018.1444527

Chapter 2
Cross-Border Dental Care:
Navigating the Landscape of Dental Tourism

Narendra Kumar
http://orcid.org/0000-0002-3325-3448
Amity Institute of Travel & Tourism, Amity University, Noida, India

ABSTRACT

Dental tourism reflects the increasing movement of patients across borders seeking affordable, high-quality dental care. This study explores the conceptual foundation, global trends, economic impacts, and policy implications of cross-border dental care. Key destinations such as Hungary, Thailand, Mexico, and India have become leading hubs due to cost advantages, skilled professionals, and advanced technology. While the industry contributes significantly to host economies through employment, infrastructure, and foreign exchange, it also raises ethical and socio-cultural challenges, including inequality, resource allocation, and cultural homogenization. The chapter concludes that sustainable growth in dental tourism requires coordinated policies, ethical governance, and digital innovation to ensure equitable and patient-centered global healthcare mobility.

INTRODUCTION

In the era of globalization, healthcare has transcended borders, enabling individuals to access medical and dental services beyond their home countries. Among the many segments of medical tourism, *dental tourism* (the practice of traveling internationally to seek dental care) has witnessed exponential growth. High dental

DOI: 10.4018/979-8-3373-4114-9.ch002

costs in developed countries, advancements in dental technology, improved connectivity, and increasing awareness through digital media are among the factors that are fuelling the growth of dental tourism. As patients become more cost-conscious and health-aware, they actively explore global options for procedures ranging from routine checkups and cosmetic treatments to complex oral surgeries. Consequently, dental tourism has evolved into a distinct component of the global healthcare tourism industry, contributing significantly to both source and destination economies. Thus, this book chapter aligns with the theme of the book and offers insights about dental tourism worldwide. The global dental tourism market, valued in billions of dollars, continues to expand each year. Countries such as Mexico, Thailand, Hungary, Turkey, Costa Rica, and India have emerged as key destinations, offering affordable yet high-quality dental services. According to recent estimates, more than 15 million patients travel abroad annually for medical purposes, and dental treatments constitute a substantial portion of this movement. The convergence of healthcare and tourism industries has resulted in a hybrid experience, where patients not only seek treatment but also combine it with travel, leisure, and cultural exploration. This merging of *healthcare needs with touristic desires* gives dental tourism its distinctive appeal in the global marketplace.

In an age of digital communication, the accessibility of information has empowered potential patients. Online reviews, social media groups, and health tourism platforms have democratized knowledge, allowing individuals to compare costs, assess clinic reputations, and even consult specialists online before making a decision. This digital transformation has reduced information asymmetry between patients and providers, thereby promoting transparency and fostering confidence in cross-border dental care. Moreover, the emergence of dental tourism facilitators—intermediary agencies that coordinate travel, treatment, and accommodation—has professionalized the sector and made it more accessible to international patients.

LITERATURE REVIEW

Dental tourism represents a specialized and rapidly expanding segment within the broader domain of medical tourism, encompassing the intentional travel of individuals across national borders to obtain dental care services. Conceptually, it lies at the intersection of healthcare, economics, and tourism, reflecting both the globalization of medical services and the commodification of health. Unlike domestic dental care, which is often constrained by local costs, insurance policies, and healthcare systems, dental tourism offers patients the flexibility to seek treatment in countries where high-quality services are available at comparatively lower prices. It includes a wide range of procedures such as preventive (cleaning, scaling), restorative (fillings, crowns, bridges), cosmetic (veneers, whitening), and surgical (implants, extractions, maxillofacial surgeries) treatments. The defining characteristic of dental tourism is that it combines healthcare consumption with travel and leisure experiences, thereby blending the roles of a patient and a tourist(Milosevic, 2009). This dual identity underpins its conceptual distinctiveness from conventional healthcare delivery systems.

At a theoretical level, dental tourism can be understood through several academic lenses. From an economic perspective, it aligns with the theory of *comparative advantage*, whereby patients choose destinations that offer the optimal balance between cost, quality, and accessibility. This economic rationality is reinforced by wide disparities in healthcare pricing between developed and developing countries. From a consumer behavior viewpoint, it resonates with the *push–pull model* of tourism motivation: patients are "pushed" by high domestic costs, long waiting times, or lack of specialized expertise at home, and "pulled" by the promise of affordability, advanced technology, personalized service, and the allure of combining treatment with tourism in appealing destinations(Lubowiecki-Vikuk, 2018). Moreover, the service marketing paradigm highlights the experiential and trust-based nature of dental tourism, where patients evaluate intangible attributes such as reputation, professionalism, and care quality, often through online reviews and word-of-mouth recommendations before making a purchase decision.

The conceptual foundation of dental tourism is also deeply embedded in the phenomenon of *global healthcare mobility*. Advances in transportation, digital communication, and international accreditation have made it easier for patients to transcend national boundaries in search of better healthcare outcomes(Gupta et al., 2015). The proliferation of internet platforms and tele-dentistry consultations enables patients to connect directly with providers abroad, compare treatment packages, and plan their travel and procedures in detail. This digitalization of health-related decision-making democratizes information and empowers consumers, contributing to what scholars describe as the "patient-as-consumer" paradigm. Additionally, *social exchange theory* offers insight into the relational dimension of dental tourism, where trust, reputation, and interpersonal interaction between providers and patients influence satisfaction and repeat visits.

In essence, dental tourism is not merely a functional response to cost disparities but a manifestation of globalization's impact on healthcare consumption. It reflects a broader societal shift where individuals exercise autonomy over their health choices, blending clinical needs with lifestyle aspirations. As a multidisciplinary construct, it involves dimensions of economics, culture, technology, and policy, making it a dynamic field for scholarly inquiry. Its conceptual foundation thus rests on the interplay between *economic rationality, experiential motivation, and transnational mobility*, positioning dental tourism as both a healthcare service and a tourism experience in the 21st-century global landscape(Leggat & Kedjarune, 2009; Sterle et al., 2009).

Dental tourism has emerged as one of the most dynamic and rapidly expanding segments of the global healthcare tourism industry, reflecting the increasing movement of patients across borders in search of affordable, high-quality dental care. Over the past two decades, globalization, technological progress, and improved air connectivity have transformed the way patients access dental services, reshaping traditional healthcare systems and fostering an interconnected network of cross-border providers. The global dental tourism market has seen exponential growth, with millions of patients traveling annually to countries offering competitive pricing, superior clinical expertise, and an appealing tourism environment. A fundamental driver of this trend is the stark disparity in treatment costs between developed and developing nations. For example, procedures such as dental implants or cosmetic veneers that may cost between USD 3,000 and 6,000 in the United States can often be obtained for less than USD 1,000 in destinations such as Mexico, India, or Thailand, without compromising on quality or technology. Furthermore, in many Western countries, dental care—particularly cosmetic or elective treatments—is often excluded from public health insurance or private coverage, leading patients to seek alternative, affordable solutions abroad. As a result, global dental tourism has evolved from a niche phenomenon to a mainstream component of international travel. This transformation has been catalyzed by the convergence of health services, hospitality, and technology, with many destinations adopting a business model that integrates professional dental care with cultural and leisure experiences, positioning themselves as holistic healthcare destinations rather than purely medical providers. The growing influence of digital technologies, such as online consultations, teledentistry, 3D imaging, and social media marketing, has further democratized information and empowered patients to make informed choices. Reviews, testimonials, and treatment videos available online have enhanced transparency, building global trust in cross-border dental practices. As travel restrictions eased post-pandemic, the revival of health-focused tourism has accelerated further, with dental services playing a key role due to their elective and short-duration nature, making them ideally suited for international travelers seeking quick, high-quality interventions.

Geographically, global dental tourism exhibits a diverse and regionally specialized pattern(Lubowiecki-Vikuk, 2018). In Europe, Hungary, Poland, and Turkey have emerged as leading dental tourism hubs, attracting patients primarily from Western and Northern Europe. Hungary, often referred to as the "Dental Capital of Europe," has developed a strong reputation for excellence in prosthodontics and implantology. Cities like Budapest and Mosonmagyaróvár host hundreds of internationally accredited clinics staffed by English- and German-speaking professionals trained at globally recognized institutions. The country's proximity to Western Europe, competitive prices, and advanced infrastructure make it a preferred destination for patients from the United Kingdom, Ireland, Germany, and Austria. Poland has similarly established itself as a reliable destination for cost-effective dental care, emphasizing hygiene, efficiency, and EU-compliant standards. Turkey, on the other hand, represents one of the most rapidly expanding markets in this field, combining advanced technology, aesthetic dentistry, and a world-class tourism environment. Istanbul, Antalya, and Izmir have become magnets for European and Middle Eastern dental tourists, particularly those seeking cosmetic procedures such as veneers, crowns, and teeth whitening. Turkish clinics are often bundled with luxury tourism services, including accommodation in resort hotels, private transportation, and guided excursions, creating an integrated experience of healthcare and hospitality. The Middle East has also witnessed growing intra-regional dental tourism, particularly within the Gulf Cooperation Council (GCC) countries, where high-income patients frequently travel to Lebanon, Jordan, or Turkey for specialized dental treatments(Felkai et al., 2021; Iqbal, 2023). Moreover, emerging economies in Eastern Europe—such as Romania, Bulgaria, and Serbia—are capitalizing on the growing demand for affordable but high-quality dental care, leveraging their integration with European Union regulatory standards to build credibility and attract international clientele. This intra-European mobility demonstrates a regional pattern of proximity-based health travel, where patients prefer destinations that are accessible, culturally familiar, and linguistically compatible, thereby minimizing the stress and uncertainty associated with overseas treatment.

In the Americas and Asia-Pacific regions, the patterns of dental tourism are shaped by distinct economic and cultural dynamics but share the common objective of combining affordability with quality and tourism appeal. In the Western Hemisphere, Mexico and Costa Rica have positioned themselves as dominant players, particularly catering to the North American market. Border cities like Los Algodones, commonly known as "Molar City," are almost entirely dependent on dental tourism, offering hundreds of clinics that cater specifically to U.S. and Canadian patients. These clinics often feature bilingual staff, U.S.-trained dentists, and modern equipment comparable to American standards, yet at a fraction of the cost. The proximity of Mexico to the United States provides a logistical advantage, enabling short visits and even same-day treatments for cross-border travelers. Costa Rica, in contrast, emphasizes a more upscale approach, targeting wellness-oriented and eco-conscious tourists who value both healthcare quality and the natural environment(Charati et al., 2024). The country's strong healthcare reputation, political stability, and focus on sustainable tourism make it one of the top choices for North American patients seeking implantology, full-mouth restoration, or cosmetic dentistry. In South America, Colombia and Brazil have also entered the global dental tourism arena, leveraging their expertise in cosmetic dentistry and orthodontics along with vibrant cultural and leisure attractions. Moving to Asia, Thailand remains one of the world's premier destinations for dental tourism, offering state-of-the-art facilities, internationally accredited clinics, and competitive prices. Bangkok, Phuket, and Chiang Mai are well-known for their "dental spas" that combine treatment with relaxation and luxury hospitality. India has followed a similar trajectory, becoming a preferred destination for patients from the Middle East, Africa, and Western countries. Indian cities such as New Delhi, Mumbai, Bengaluru, and Chennai are home to internationally certified clinics equipped with cutting-edge technology and staffed by English-speaking dentists trained abroad(Gupta et al., 2015; Ravneet Sandhu, 2018). India's advantage lies in its strong base of medical education, affordability, and hospitality culture. The Philippines and Malaysia have also developed robust dental tourism sectors, capitalizing on their English proficiency, tropical appeal, and government-led initiatives to promote medical travel. In Australia and New Zealand, the trend moves in the opposite direction: patients from these high-cost countries often travel to Southeast Asian nations for affordable care, reinforcing regional healthcare interdependence.

The global landscape of dental tourism reflects a series of broader structural shifts in international healthcare and tourism economies. First, the sector's evolution illustrates how developing and middle-income countries have leveraged their comparative advantage in labor costs and medical expertise to compete globally, thereby turning healthcare into a tool for economic diversification and soft power projection. Second, the emergence of specialized dental clusters—such as Los Algodones in Mexico or Budapest in Hungary—demonstrates the importance of clustering effects in enhancing competitiveness, standardizing service quality, and building brand recognition. Third, the integration of accreditation mechanisms, such as Joint Commission International (JCI) or ISO certifications, has elevated patient confidence and established international benchmarks for quality assurance. These certifications have become crucial marketing assets for clinics competing in a global marketplace. Moreover, the convergence of healthcare and tourism policies has led governments to invest in medical infrastructure, improve visa facilitation for patients, and promote dental tourism through targeted campaigns. For example, Thailand's "Medical Hub Policy," India's "Heal in India" initiative, and Turkey's national health tourism strategy have significantly enhanced their global standing as healthcare destinations. Technological advancements also continue to reshape the sector, with innovations like digital impressions, CAD/CAM restorations, and 3D-printed prosthetics improving efficiency and outcomes, thereby making international treatment more appealing. The global dental tourism industry is also increasingly influenced by sustainability and ethics, with some destinations focusing on eco-friendly clinics, patient safety standards, and community-based healthcare integration. However, despite its immense potential, the industry faces challenges such as regulatory inconsistencies, post-treatment complications, and the absence of standardized international insurance frameworks. As dental tourism continues to expand, the global trend is moving toward consolidation and professionalization—creating formal networks of accredited clinics, digital platforms for patient engagement, and policy frameworks to ensure quality and accountability. Overall, the worldwide expansion of dental tourism represents not merely a consumer trend but a structural transformation in how healthcare is delivered, experienced, and globalized. It signifies the growing interdependence of nations in health and tourism sectors and highlights the shift toward a borderless world of medical mobility, where patients exercise global choice in pursuit of wellness, beauty, and affordability.

ANALYSIS OF GLOBAL CONTEXT AND EMERGING TRENDS

Dental tourism has developed into a competitive global industry characterized by regional specialization and cross-border collaboration. In Europe, countries like Hungary, Poland, and Turkey have positioned themselves as leaders in restorative and cosmetic dentistry. Their proximity to Western Europe, advanced clinical infrastructure, and skilled dental professionals attract thousands of patients annually. Hungary, in particular, is often referred to as the "Dental Capital of Europe," hosting a network of internationally accredited clinics catering to foreign patients. In the Americas, Mexico and Costa Rica dominate the market. Mexican border cities such as Los Algodones—popularly known as "Molar City"—cater almost exclusively to American and Canadian patients seeking low-cost treatments. Costa Rica, with its reputation for sustainable tourism, combines top-tier dental care with tropical wellness experiences, appealing to eco-conscious medical tourists. Similarly, in the Asia-Pacific region, Thailand, India, and the Philippines are rising stars in the field. Thailand's globally renowned dental clinics offer comprehensive services alongside a world-class tourism infrastructure, while India's combination of affordability, technological advancement, and English-speaking professionals attracts an increasing number of foreign patients. These patterns highlight not only the economic potential of dental tourism but also its strategic role in national healthcare diplomacy and tourism policy. Many governments actively promote dental tourism as part of their health tourism strategies, offering incentives for clinic accreditation, international marketing, and infrastructure development. Such initiatives underscore the growing recognition of healthcare travel as a driver of foreign exchange earnings and soft power.

Drivers of Cross-Border Dental Care

Economic Drivers

The most significant driver of cross-border dental care is the stark economic disparity in dental treatment costs between developed and developing nations. In countries such as the United States, Canada, the United Kingdom, and Australia, dental services—especially cosmetic, prosthodontic, and implant procedures—are often prohibitively expensive and not fully covered by insurance schemes. As a result, patients are motivated to seek affordable alternatives abroad, where procedures may cost between 50% and 80% less, even after accounting for travel and accommodation expenses. For example, a single dental implant that costs around USD 3,000 in the U.S. may be performed for less than USD 800 in countries like India, Mexico, or Thailand, using comparable materials and technologies. Additionally, favorable currency exchange rates, flexible payment options, and package-based pricing models enhance the cost-effectiveness of overseas dental care. This financial advantage is further reinforced by long waiting times in public health systems, driving patients toward private clinics abroad that offer immediate services. Consequently, economic rationality and price sensitivity remain central motivators, positioning dental tourism as an attractive global alternative for patients seeking both affordability and value-based care.

Quality and Professional Expertise Drivers

Beyond cost considerations, the perceived and actual quality of care serves as a major driver for patients seeking cross-border dental services. Many dental tourism destinations have invested heavily in modern infrastructure, advanced technology, and international accreditation to ensure clinical excellence. Dentists in countries like Hungary, Thailand, Turkey, and India often receive training from prestigious Western universities and maintain memberships in global professional associations, reinforcing their credibility. Clinics are equipped with digital imaging systems, CAD/CAM technology, and 3D printing tools that enable precision, customization, and superior aesthetic outcomes. Moreover, international accreditation bodies such as Joint Commission International (JCI) and ISO have established standardized frameworks that assure patients of adherence to global safety and hygiene standards. Personalized service, efficient scheduling, and one-on-one consultations further enhance patient confidence. Importantly, many patients perceive that the attention and hospitality they receive abroad surpass the rushed or impersonal experiences common in domestic healthcare systems(Arends, 2011; Ní Ríordáin & McCreary, 2009). Hence, the combination of professional expertise, modern equipment, and patient-centered care ensures that global destinations can successfully compete with, and often surpass, the quality standards of developed countries.

Technological and Informational Drivers

Rapid advancements in information and communication technologies have revolutionized the way patients engage with healthcare providers abroad, serving as a key driver of cross-border dental care. Tele-dentistry, virtual consultations, and digital diagnostic sharing allow prospective patients to interact directly with dentists before traveling, reducing uncertainty and facilitating pre-procedure planning. The widespread use of the internet and social media has democratized access to information, enabling patients to compare prices, treatment options, and clinic reputations in real time. Online forums, patient testimonials, and video reviews on platforms like YouTube and Facebook have become vital tools in shaping perceptions and building trust. Digital marketing and reputation management strategies adopted by clinics further enhance their global visibility, while mobile applications streamline booking, payment, and post-treatment follow-up. The integration of emerging technologies such as artificial intelligence, 3D printing, and augmented reality in treatment planning also appeals to tech-savvy patients seeking innovation and precision. In this digital era, information transparency reduces information asymmetry between patients and providers, empowering consumers to make confident, data-driven decisions about cross-border dental care.

Sociocultural and Psychological Drivers

Sociocultural and psychological factors play an equally influential role in motivating individuals to pursue dental care abroad. Many patients perceive dental tourism not merely as a medical necessity but as a transformative life experience that combines self-improvement with adventure. The opportunity to travel, explore new cultures, and enjoy hospitality while addressing one's dental needs creates a strong emotional appeal. In several cases, patients prefer to undergo procedures in destinations where privacy is maintained, allowing them to recover away from social or professional circles(Kovacs & Szocska, 2013). Word-of-mouth recommendations from family, friends, and online communities also carry significant persuasive power, creating social validation and reducing anxiety about seeking care overseas. Cultural affinity, linguistic familiarity, and perceptions of empathy and warmth among healthcare providers further enhance comfort levels. For example, Indian and Filipino clinics are often preferred by Western patients for their English proficiency and compassionate approach, while European patients value cultural similarity and proximity in destinations like Hungary or Turkey. Thus, emotional reassurance, cultural compatibility, and the aspiration for positive self-transformation collectively form the sociocultural and psychological foundation of dental tourism.

Tourism and Leisure Appeal Drivers

One of the defining features of dental tourism is its fusion of healthcare with leisure, making the *tourism appeal* a distinct and powerful driver. Patients increasingly view dental care abroad as part of a holistic travel experience—an opportunity to combine treatment with rest, rejuvenation, and cultural exploration. Destinations such as Thailand, Turkey, Costa Rica, and India have successfully packaged dental services with sightseeing tours, wellness retreats, and luxury accommodation options, thereby transforming medical trips into mini-vacations. This approach not only alleviates the anxiety associated with dental procedures but also enhances the overall value proposition of the journey. For many travelers, the chance to recover in a scenic, stress-free environment accelerates healing and enhances satisfaction(Orlic et al., 2023). Governments and private operators in key destinations actively promote "smile and holiday" campaigns to position dental tourism as a lifestyle experience rather than a medical necessity. Furthermore, the symbolic appeal of returning home with both a new smile and new memories amplifies the psychological and aesthetic value of the trip. Consequently, tourism-driven incentives—supported by hospitality excellence and destination branding—have become central to the success and sustainability of cross-border dental care.

The phenomenon of dental tourism has evolved into a dynamic segment of the global health tourism industry, exerting multifaceted economic and socio-cultural impacts on host destinations. As individuals increasingly travel across borders to access affordable, high-quality dental care, host nations experience both tangible and intangible effects that extend beyond clinical settings. These impacts manifest through economic stimulation, employment generation, infrastructure development, and foreign exchange earnings, as well as through transformations in social attitudes, cultural exchanges, and community identity(Dhama et al., 2016). While the benefits of this form of tourism are widely acknowledged, there also exist concerns related to cultural commodification, social inequality, and dependency on volatile international markets. The complex interplay between economic opportunity and cultural adaptation thus defines the broader implications of dental tourism for host destinations around the world.

Economically, dental tourism represents a significant source of revenue generation for host countries. Nations such as Thailand, Hungary, Mexico, Costa Rica, and India have emerged as prominent hubs, attracting tens of thousands of international patients annually. Each dental tourist not only spends money on medical services but also contributes to the local economy through accommodation, dining, transport, and recreation. The multiplier effect of such expenditures enhances the circulation of income within communities, benefiting sectors that are indirectly linked to healthcare. For instance, in Thailand, dental tourism is closely integrated with the hospitality and wellness industries, generating revenue that sustains hotels, restaurants, travel agencies, and ancillary service providers. Similarly, in Hungary, which is often termed the "dental capital of Europe," the towns of Budapest and Mosonmagyaróvár have witnessed revitalization through dental clinics that cater predominantly to British, German, and Austrian patients. This has led to the creation of micro-economies centered on dental care, where even local taxi operators, interpreters, and real estate agents benefit from the flow of medical tourists.

The economic impact of dental tourism also extends to employment generation and human capital development. As the industry expands, it creates a diverse range of jobs—not only for dental professionals such as dentists, hygienists, and technicians but also for support staff in administration, hospitality, logistics, and marketing. The demand for multilingual employees and culturally sensitive staff has further encouraged skill development and professional training. In destinations like India and the Philippines, where English-speaking professionals are abundant, the global appeal of dental services has been amplified by the workforce's ability to communicate effectively with foreign patients. Moreover, competition among clinics has driven investments in technology, research, and innovation, elevating the overall standard of dental care within the country. This has a spillover effect on domestic patients, who gain access to advanced dental technologies that may otherwise have been unaffordable or unavailable.

Foreign exchange earnings represent another vital economic dimension. As dental tourists typically pay in strong foreign currencies such as the U.S. dollar, euro, or pound sterling, host countries benefit from increased inflows of hard currency. This contributes to a favorable balance of payments and strengthens the tourism sector's contribution to national GDP. In small economies like Costa Rica, dental and medical tourism have become essential sources of foreign income, second only to traditional tourism. The government and private sector collaborate to promote the country as a "smile destination," linking oral healthcare services with eco-tourism and wellness experiences. The same is observed in Turkey and Mexico, where dental tourism is recognized as a high-value niche segment capable of generating sustainable income with relatively low environmental impact compared to mass tourism. Such diversification of economic activity reduces dependence on seasonal tourist flows and promotes year-round revenue stability.

Infrastructure development is another critical economic impact associated with dental tourism. To attract international patients, host destinations often invest heavily in upgrading healthcare facilities, transportation networks, and urban amenities. The construction of state-of-the-art dental clinics equipped with modern diagnostic and treatment technologies contributes not only to patient satisfaction but also to the overall healthcare capacity of the region. This infrastructural improvement often spills into other areas such as airport modernization, road connectivity, and hospitality enhancement, which further stimulate local economies. For instance, in Indian cities like Delhi, Chennai, and Mumbai, the growth of dental tourism has encouraged the establishment of specialized dental hubs with integrated hospitality services, including recovery lounges and wellness centers. These developments strengthen the destination's competitiveness and enhance its international reputation for medical and dental excellence.

However, while the economic benefits of dental tourism are substantial, they are accompanied by several challenges that require careful management. One of the most significant concerns is the uneven distribution of wealth generated by the industry(Dhama et al., 2016; Gupta et al., 2015). High-end dental clinics often cater to affluent foreign patients and are typically located in urban centers or tourist hotspots, leaving rural and low-income communities with limited access to these economic gains. This spatial concentration can exacerbate regional inequalities and create healthcare dualism, wherein elite private clinics thrive while public dental facilities remain underfunded. Additionally, the dependence on foreign clientele makes host economies vulnerable to external shocks such as currency fluctuations, global recessions, or pandemics. The COVID-19 crisis, for instance, severely disrupted international travel and exposed the fragility of tourism-dependent healthcare businesses, many of which suffered significant financial losses during prolonged border closures.

Beyond the economic sphere, dental tourism exerts profound socio-cultural influences on host destinations. The movement of patients across borders facilitates intercultural interaction, encouraging dialogue and understanding between individuals from diverse cultural backgrounds. For many local residents, encounters with foreign patients provide opportunities to learn new languages, adopt global communication norms, and expand their worldview. This cross-cultural exposure often results in the enrichment of local hospitality traditions, as service providers adapt their behavior, etiquette, and aesthetic preferences to meet the expectations of international clientele(Collins, 2022). In countries like Thailand and the Philippines, where hospitality is deeply embedded in cultural identity, the integration of healthcare and tourism has reinforced the image of these nations as warm, caring, and service-oriented societies.

The cultural exchange facilitated through dental tourism also influences lifestyle aspirations and social behaviors within host communities. Exposure to foreign patients who emphasize dental aesthetics, oral hygiene, and preventive care has contributed to changing local perceptions of oral health. In many developing nations, dental care was historically perceived as secondary to general health, but the growing influx of international patients seeking advanced cosmetic and restorative procedures has elevated dentistry's social status. As a result, local populations have become more aware of dental aesthetics and more inclined to invest in orthodontics, whitening, and implants—procedures once considered luxuries. This diffusion of dental awareness represents a positive socio-cultural spillover that enhances the overall health consciousness of the community.

At the same time, the socio-cultural impacts of dental tourism are not uniformly positive. The influx of foreign patients and investors can sometimes lead to cultural homogenization or the commodification of local identities. In destinations that aggressively market themselves as global dental hubs, there is a risk that local traditions and aesthetics may be overshadowed by Westernized standards of beauty and professionalism. For instance, the adoption of Western clinic designs, English-only signage, and foreign branding strategies may inadvertently erode indigenous cultural expressions. This cultural adaptation, while economically beneficial, raises questions about authenticity and long-term sustainability. Furthermore, interactions between locals and foreign patients may occasionally generate tension or misunderstanding if cultural differences in communication styles, expectations, or social norms are not managed sensitively.

Another socio-cultural concern relates to the ethical dimensions of resource allocation. As dental tourism becomes more profitable, there is a tendency for skilled practitioners to prioritize foreign patients over local ones, particularly when the latter cannot afford high-end private care. This "brain drain within borders" may reduce access to quality dental services for domestic populations, particularly in rural or marginalized communities. Moreover, the commercialization of dental care risks transforming health into a commodity, where treatment decisions are driven more by profit motives than by medical necessity(Demonja & Uglješic, 2020; Felkai et al., 2023). This raises ethical dilemmas about the social responsibility of healthcare providers and the equitable distribution of healthcare benefits. Host governments and regulatory bodies must therefore ensure that policies governing dental tourism balance economic growth with social justice and public health equity.

On the positive side, dental tourism can strengthen social cohesion and pride by positioning destinations as centers of excellence and innovation. Communities often take pride in their international reputation as providers of world-class care, and this recognition can enhance local morale and civic engagement. The rise of dental tourism can also stimulate community-based entrepreneurship, as small and medium enterprises (SMEs) develop complementary services such as home stays, cultural tours, or traditional healing experiences. These localized ventures foster inclusive growth and help distribute the benefits of tourism more equitably. Moreover, by promoting cross-cultural understanding, dental tourism contributes to soft diplomacy, improving the host nation's image and fostering goodwill among international visitors who return home as informal ambassadors.

The integration of cultural and spiritual dimensions into dental tourism experiences also offers opportunities for differentiation and sustainable development. In India, for instance, several clinics combine dental treatments with yoga, meditation, or Ayurvedic wellness programs, creating a holistic approach that reflects the nation's cultural heritage. Such models align with the growing trend toward wellness-oriented healthcare and attract patients seeking both physical restoration and emotional rejuvenation(Ramos & Cuamea, 2023). These hybrid experiences demonstrate how dental tourism can serve as a platform for cultural preservation rather than erasure, if designed thoughtfully and ethically.

In examining the broader socio-cultural landscape, it becomes evident that dental tourism also influences gender dynamics and professional identities. The industry has created new career pathways for women, who often occupy key roles as dental assistants, clinic managers, and hospitality coordinators. Their participation not only contributes to family incomes but also challenges traditional gender roles in societies where female employment was previously constrained. Similarly, the increasing presence of international patients has encouraged dental professionals to engage in continuous education, intercultural communication training, and global networking, thereby fostering a more cosmopolitan professional community. These transformations signify the potential of dental tourism to catalyze social modernization and empowerment at multiple levels.

Nevertheless, maintaining socio-cultural harmony requires continuous ethical vigilance and policy regulation. Governments and tourism boards must establish standards for patient safety, transparency, and cultural sensitivity. Community participation should be encouraged in decision-making processes to ensure that local residents benefit from tourism development rather than being marginalized by it. Strategies such as community-based tourism models, fair-trade healthcare certification, and responsible marketing can help mitigate negative cultural and social impacts. Furthermore, integrating dental tourism into broader frameworks of sustainable development can ensure that economic growth is accompanied by cultural respect and social inclusion.

In conclusion, the economic and socio-cultural impacts of dental tourism on host destinations are profound, complex, and multidimensional. Economically, the industry contributes significantly to national income, employment, and infrastructural modernization, while simultaneously enhancing global competitiveness in healthcare services. Socio-culturally, it fosters intercultural exchange, elevates health awareness, and reshapes community identities through exposure to global values and aesthetics. Yet, these benefits are accompanied by challenges such as inequality, ethical dilemmas, and cultural commodification. The sustainability of dental tourism therefore depends on the capacity of host destinations to balance economic ambition with social equity and cultural integrity. A holistic approach—integrating economic planning, community engagement, ethical governance, and cultural preservation—can transform dental tourism into a catalyst for inclusive and sustainable development. Ultimately, the success of this growing phenomenon will not be measured solely by the number of patients treated or the revenue generated, but by the extent to which it enriches both local lives and global understanding in a truly human-centered manner.

ETHICAL AND REGULATORY CONCERNS

While dental tourism offers economic and personal benefits, it also raises ethical and legal questions. Cross-border treatments complicate issues of medical liability—patients may struggle to pursue legal redress in case of malpractice due to differing jurisdictional frameworks. Ethical concerns also arise around informed consent, transparency of costs, and post-treatment accountability. Moreover, the commercialization of healthcare may risk prioritizing profit over patient welfare(-Jaapar et al., 2017).

To address these concerns, international accreditation and regulatory frameworks have been introduced. Organizations like the *Joint Commission International (JCI)* and *Temos International* certify clinics based on safety, quality, and patient care standards. However, enforcement remains inconsistent across countries. Therefore, collaborative policies, bilateral agreements, and standardized guidelines are essential to ensure patient protection and sustainable industry growth.

DISCUSSION

The economic contribution of dental tourism extends beyond the dental clinics themselves. It stimulates demand in related sectors such as hospitality, transportation, insurance, and local tourism services. Host destinations benefit from foreign exchange earnings, job creation, and infrastructure development. For instance, the dental tourism industry in Thailand and Hungary has catalyzed the growth of dental technology suppliers, translator services, and wellness hotels(Barrowman et al., 2010). However, there are potential socio-economic challenges as well. In some developing nations, catering to foreign patients may divert healthcare resources from local populations, creating inequality in access. Balancing commercial profitability with social responsibility remains a critical policy challenge. From a cultural standpoint, dental tourism fosters intercultural interaction and knowledge exchange. Patients engage with local communities, traditions, and hospitality, often developing positive perceptions that enhance destination branding. This integration of health and cultural tourism strengthens the host country's image as both a healthcare and leisure hub.

The Role of Technology and Innovation

Innovation lies at the heart of modern dental tourism. Digital dentistry, 3D printing, computer-aided design (CAD/CAM), and AI-based diagnostic tools have transformed dental care into a precise, patient-centric service. Tele-dentistry allows initial assessments before travel and facilitates remote follow-up care, thereby enhancing continuity and trust. Furthermore, blockchain technologies are being explored for secure medical record storage and data sharing between providers across borders. Social media marketing, virtual clinic tours, and influencer-driven testimonials have also reshaped the way patients perceive and select dental destinations. Destinations leveraging technology for transparent communication, online booking, and reputation management enjoy higher patient inflow and brand credibility.

CHALLENGES AND RISK CONSIDERATIONS

Despite its potential, dental tourism presents inherent risks. Medical risks include postoperative complications, infection, or dissatisfaction with aesthetic results. Travel-related risks such as long flights, language barriers, or cultural misunderstandings can further complicate the experience. Financial risks also exist due to hidden costs, exchange rate fluctuations, or absence of reimbursement mechanisms. Moreover, the lack of continuity in care after returning home may pose long-term health challenges. Addressing these risks requires coordinated efforts from governments, industry bodies, and healthcare institutions. Implementation of patient safety protocols, clear cost disclosure, standardized insurance policies, and post-treatment support systems are essential to sustain the industry's credibility.

FUTURE DIRECTIONS AND POLICY IMPLICATIONS

As dental tourism continues to evolve as a distinct component of global health and travel systems, it is entering a new phase defined by technological innovation, policy realignment, and ethical consciousness. The future of cross-border dental care will be shaped by how nations, industries, and international organizations collaborate to address emerging challenges and harness new opportunities. While dental tourism offers clear economic and healthcare benefits, its long-term sustainability depends on the development of coherent policy frameworks, robust quality assurance mechanisms, and equitable access models. Future directions must therefore focus on integrating dental tourism into broader health, tourism, and trade policies while ensuring that ethical standards, patient safety, and cultural sensitivity remain central to its growth.

One of the most significant future directions involves the institutionalization and regulation of dental tourism(Ahmadimanesh et al., 2019; Lwin et al., 2021). Currently, the global dental tourism market operates in a largely fragmented regulatory environment. There is a lack of universally accepted standards governing treatment quality, cross-border insurance coverage, accreditation of clinics, and malpractice liability. This absence of harmonized regulations can create uncertainty and risk for patients while undermining trust in the sector. To address this, governments and professional bodies should collaborate to establish transnational accreditation systems, similar to those developed by Joint Commission International (JCI) or the International Society for Quality in Health Care (ISQua). A global registry of certified dental tourism providers could enhance transparency, allowing patients to verify credentials, clinical outcomes, and ethical practices before travel. Moreover, bilateral or regional agreements between countries—especially within blocs like the European Union, ASEAN, and SAARC—can facilitate standardized protocols for cross-border healthcare delivery, thereby improving patient mobility and safety.

Technological innovation will also play a defining role in the future landscape of dental tourism(Adams et al., 2018; Kaur & Hira, 2021). The integration of digital dentistry, tele-dentistry, and artificial intelligence (AI) will reshape how patients interact with dental professionals across borders. Virtual consultations can enable pre-treatment planning, remote diagnostics, and postoperative follow-ups, reducing the logistical and emotional barriers associated with international care. AI-assisted imaging and predictive analytics can enhance precision, while blockchain-based patient records can ensure data integrity and security across different jurisdictions. Governments and professional councils must therefore develop legal and ethical frameworks for the cross-border exchange of medical data to safeguard patient privacy. Investment in digital infrastructure and training programs will be essential to prepare clinics for a technology-driven, patient-centric future. As digitalization progresses, the ability to offer hybrid care—where diagnosis and follow-up occur remotely and procedures are conducted in-person—will become a defining feature of competitive destinations.

The future of dental tourism will also be closely tied to the principles of sustainability and responsible tourism. While the industry's carbon footprint is lower than that of mass tourism, increased global mobility inevitably raises environmental concerns(Akbar et al., 2021; Lovelock et al., 2018). Policymakers should encourage eco-conscious practices, such as sustainable clinic design, waste reduction, and the use of biocompatible and recyclable dental materials. Clinics could adopt green certifications or participate in sustainability rating systems that assess their environmental performance. On a broader scale, integrating dental tourism into sustainable destination management frameworks ensures that economic benefits are balanced with ecological preservation and social equity. Local governments can incentivize community-based enterprises—such as homestays, craft markets, or wellness centers—that complement dental tourism, ensuring that local populations share in the economic benefits. The future model of dental tourism must thus evolve from profit-centric growth to a "shared value" approach that aligns healthcare excellence with environmental stewardship and community empowerment.

Another critical policy implication concerns human resource development and capacity building. As the demand for high-quality dental care grows, there is a risk that professionals in host countries will prioritize international patients at the expense of local populations. Policymakers must therefore design frameworks that balance global competitiveness with domestic accessibility. This may include mandatory service provisions in public clinics, incentives for rural practice, or revenue-sharing models that channel a portion of tourism income into strengthening national oral health programs. Universities and vocational institutes should also update their curricula to include global health diplomacy, intercultural communication, and medical tourism management, ensuring that the future workforce is globally competent and ethically aware. Furthermore, the inclusion of continuous professional development (CPD) requirements tied to international standards can help sustain the quality of care and reinforce the credibility of host destinations.

The development of cross-border insurance and financing mechanisms represents another frontier for policy innovation. Most dental tourists currently pay out of pocket, which limits participation to middle- and upper-income groups. Governments and insurers could collaborate to design portable dental insurance schemes or reimbursement models that recognize accredited foreign providers. Such mechanisms would democratize access to dental tourism while maintaining accountability and cost control. Additionally, partnerships with global health organizations could support the establishment of international dispute resolution mechanisms, ensuring that patients have legal recourse in the event of malpractice. Strengthening consumer protection laws will be crucial to maintaining trust and encouraging long-term growth.

Marketing and destination branding will continue to shape the competitiveness of dental tourism destinations. Future strategies should move beyond cost-based promotion toward value-driven branding that emphasizes safety, transparency, innovation, and cultural uniqueness. Governments, tourism boards, and professional associations should jointly promote national dental tourism clusters under a unified identity—for example, "Smile Thailand," "Hungary: The Dental Capital of Europe," or "Incredible India Dental Care." These campaigns should highlight quality assurance, technological capabilities, and ethical standards rather than merely low prices. Digital storytelling through patient testimonials, virtual tours, and influencer collaborations can enhance global visibility, particularly among younger demographics who are increasingly seeking aesthetic and preventive dental treatments. However, policies must regulate marketing claims to prevent misinformation or overpromising, ensuring that promotional content aligns with verified clinical outcomes.

From a socio-cultural perspective, the future of dental tourism requires policies that protect cultural integrity while promoting inclusivity. The influx of international patients often brings cultural adaptation pressures that may lead to homogenization of clinic aesthetics or professional practices. Policymakers should encourage cultural integration rather than imitation by promoting local design, language, and hospitality traditions within clinic environments. Additionally, community engagement should be institutionalized in tourism planning processes to ensure that local residents benefit from and participate in the industry's development. Initiatives such as local employment quotas, cultural orientation programs for healthcare providers, and ethical training modules can foster mutual respect and minimize cultural friction. The creation of community-based dental tourism cooperatives—where profits are reinvested in local education or public health—can also enhance social cohesion and trust.

At a global governance level, there is a growing need for multilateral cooperation in the regulation of medical and dental tourism. International organizations such as the World Health Organization (WHO), the World Tourism Organization (UNWTO), and the International Dental Federation (FDI) can play a coordinating role in establishing global guidelines for patient safety, ethical marketing, and professional mobility. Joint research initiatives could facilitate the collection of standardized data on dental tourism flows, patient satisfaction, and economic impact, enabling evidence-based policymaking. Furthermore, global forums and conferences dedicated to medical tourism can serve as platforms for dialogue, knowledge exchange, and capacity building among policymakers, practitioners, and researchers. The future of dental tourism governance must therefore be multilevel—combining local innovation with international collaboration.

Finally, the long-term sustainability of dental tourism will depend on how effectively policies address ethical, equity, and resilience considerations. Ethical governance requires transparent pricing, informed consent, and accountability in treatment outcomes. Equity entails ensuring that the growth of the sector does not marginalize local patients or exacerbate healthcare disparities. Resilience demands preparedness for global disruptions—such as pandemics, climate-related crises, or economic downturns—that can abruptly halt cross-border mobility. Policies must therefore promote adaptive strategies, including digital service continuity, domestic patient diversification, and flexible business models. Governments could establish emergency support schemes for healthcare enterprises dependent on international tourism, safeguarding livelihoods and maintaining system stability during global shocks.

In essence, the future of cross-border dental care lies in its ability to evolve from an informal market-driven activity into a structured, ethical, and inclusive global industry. Policymakers, practitioners, and academic institutions must collaborate to design frameworks that integrate dental tourism into national development agendas while aligning with global standards of care and sustainability. The next decade will likely witness increased convergence between healthcare, technology, and tourism, creating a hybrid ecosystem that transcends traditional boundaries. If guided by thoughtful policy interventions and a commitment to human well-being, dental tourism can emerge not only as a driver of economic growth but also as a model for equitable and culturally sensitive global healthcare exchange.

CONCLUSION

The phenomenon of cross-border dental care has emerged as one of the most dynamic and rapidly expanding dimensions of global health tourism. Driven by economic disparities in healthcare costs, the pursuit of high-quality and timely dental services, and the desire to combine medical care with leisure, dental tourism has transformed from a niche activity into a mainstream global industry. Countries across Asia, Europe, and Latin America have strategically positioned themselves as leading dental tourism destinations by leveraging comparative advantages in cost, expertise, and hospitality. As a result, this sector now represents a significant contributor to national economies, supporting employment generation, foreign exchange inflows, and infrastructural modernization while reshaping the contours of international healthcare mobility.

Yet, the true significance of dental tourism extends beyond its economic value. It symbolizes a broader reconfiguration of how individuals perceive healthcare, travel, and wellness in the age of globalization. Patients are increasingly empowered as global consumers, exercising choice and agency in seeking care that aligns with their financial, cultural, and emotional preferences. This shift has redefined traditional patient-provider relationships and has encouraged destinations to adopt patient-centered approaches, combining technological sophistication with personalized hospitality. At the same time, it has stimulated knowledge exchange, professional innovation, and intercultural understanding, reinforcing the interdependence between healthcare and human mobility.

However, the rapid growth of cross-border dental care also poses complex challenges that demand careful governance. Issues such as uneven wealth distribution, ethical dilemmas in prioritizing foreign patients, inconsistent quality standards, and potential cultural homogenization must be addressed through comprehensive policy frameworks. Host destinations face the dual responsibility of maintaining competitiveness while ensuring equitable access for their local populations. The sustainability of dental tourism will therefore hinge on the ability of governments and industry stakeholders to balance profit motives with principles of fairness, accountability, and social inclusivity. This requires strong regulatory oversight, transparent accreditation systems, and continuous investment in education, research, and professional development.

Looking ahead, the future of dental tourism will be profoundly influenced by technology, sustainability, and global collaboration. The integration of digital dentistry, tele-dentistry, and artificial intelligence will reshape treatment delivery and cross-border communication, while sustainability imperatives will push clinics and destinations to adopt environmentally responsible practices. At the policy level, international cooperation—through frameworks developed by organizations such as WHO, UNWTO, and FDI—can harmonize standards, enhance patient safety, and foster ethical growth. Moreover, embedding dental tourism within broader sustainable development agendas will ensure that its benefits extend beyond economic gain to include cultural preservation, social equity, and community empowerment.

In conclusion, cross-border dental care represents both an opportunity and a responsibility. It offers the promise of affordable, high-quality oral healthcare to millions while serving as a catalyst for innovation, diplomacy, and sustainable development. Yet, its continued success will depend on the collective efforts of policymakers, practitioners, educators, and patients to create a globally integrated system that prioritizes safety, integrity, and human well-being. The challenge moving forward is not merely to expand the market but to shape it into a model of ethical globalization—one where every smile restored reflects not only dental excellence but also the shared values of care, respect, and inclusivity that define a truly global society.

REFERENCES

Adams, K., Snyder, J., Crooks, V. A., & Berry, N. S. (2018). A critical examination of empowerment discourse in medical tourism: The case of the dental tourism industry in Los Algodones, Mexico. *Globalization and Health*, *14*(1), 70. Advance online publication. DOI: 10.1186/s12992-018-0392-3 PMID: 30029610

Ahmadimanesh, F., Paydar, M. M., & Asadi-Gangraj, E. (2019). Designing a mathematical model for dental tourism supply chain. *Tourism Management*, *75*, 404–417. DOI: 10.1016/j.tourman.2019.06.001

Akbar, F. H., Rivai, F., Abdullah, A. Z., & Awang, A. H. (2021). Relationship between information access, service quality, costs saving, cultural similarity and supporting service towards medical (dental) tourism patients' satisfaction. *Journal of Dentomaxillofacial Science*, *6*(1), 31. DOI: 10.15562/jdmfs.v6i1.1106

Arends, B. (2011). Inward dental tourism. *British Dental Journal*, *211*(12), 584. DOI: 10.1038/sj.bdj.2011.1062 PMID: 22193468

Barrowman, R. A., Grubor, D., & Chandu, A. (2010). Dental implant tourism. *Australian Dental Journal*, *55*(4), 441–445. DOI: 10.1111/j.1834-7819.2010.01267.x PMID: 21133945

Charati, M. K., Gholian-Jouybari, F., Hajiaghaei-Keshteli, M., Paydar, M. M., & Sadeghi, F. (2024). Designing a sustainable dental tourism supply chain considering waste treatment. *Annals of Operations Research*, *342*(1), 173–214. DOI: 10.1007/s10479-023-05779-4

Collins, L. (2022). The burden of dental tourism. *British Dental Journal*, *233*(7), 516–516. DOI: 10.1038/s41415-022-5109-6 PMID: 36241780

Demonja, D., & Uglješic, N. (2020). Dental Tourism and Business Risks: The Example of the Republic of Croatia. *Interdisciplinary Description of Complex Systems*, *18*(4), 425–445. DOI: 10.7906/indecs.18.4.3

Dhama, K., Patthi, B., Singla, A., Gupta, R., Niraj, L. K., Ali, I., Kumar, J. K., & Prasad, M. (2016). Global tourist guide to oral care - A systematic review. *Journal of Clinical and Diagnostic Research : JCDR*, *10*(9). Advance online publication. DOI: 10.7860/JCDR/2016/19438.8408 PMID: 27790595

Felkai, P. P., Flaherty, G., & Felkai, T. (2021). International dental tourism in a post-COVID era: Pre-travel advice. *Journal of Travel Medicine*, *28*(7), taab108. Advance online publication. DOI: 10.1093/jtm/taab108 PMID: 34272850

Felkai, P. P., Nakdimon, I., Felkai, T., Levin, L., & Zadik, Y. (2023). Dental tourism and the risk of barotrauma and barodontalgia. *British Dental Journal*, *234*(2), 115–117. DOI: 10.1038/s41415-023-5449-x PMID: 36707585

Gupta, M., Mishra, P., Srivastava, R., & Jyoti, B. (2015). Holistic oral health care in India: A corporate perspective. *Journal of Indian Academy of Oral Medicine and Radiology*, *27*(2), 237–240. DOI: 10.4103/0972-1363.170144

Iqbal, M. A. (2023). Dental Tourism in Bangladesh: A Growing Opportunity. *Update Dental College Journal*, *13*(2), 1–2. DOI: 10.3329/updcj.v13i2.69143

Jaapar, M., Musa, G., Moghavvemi, S., & Saub, R. (2017). Dental tourism: Examining tourist profiles, motivation and satisfaction. *Tourism Management*, *61*, 538–552. DOI: 10.1016/j.tourman.2017.02.023

Kaur, R., & Hira, J. K. (2021). Enquiring the dental practitioners' perceptions about dental tourism: A phenomenological viewpoint. *World Review of Entrepreneurship, Management and Sustainable Development*, *17*(2/3), 323. DOI: 10.1504/WREMSD.2021.114438

Kovacs, E., & Szocska, G. (2013). Vacation for your teeth' - Dental tourists in Hungary from the perspective of Hungarian dentists. *British Dental Journal*, *215*(8), 415–418. DOI: 10.1038/sj.bdj.2013.995 PMID: 24157766

Leggat, P., & Kedjarune, U. (2009). Dental health, "dental tourism" and travellers. *Travel Medicine and Infectious Disease*, *7*(3), 123–124. DOI: 10.1016/j.tmaid.2009.02.001 PMID: 19411039

Lovelock, B., Lovelock, K., & Lyons, K. (2018). The impact of outbound medical (dental) tourism on the generating region: New Zealand dental professionals' perspectives. *Tourism Management*, *67*, 399–410. DOI: 10.1016/j.tourman.2018.02.001

Lubowiecki-Vikuk, A. (2018). Consumption of dental services: Medical tourism in CEE. *European Journal of Service Management*, *27*, 135–142. DOI: 10.18276/ejsm.2018.27/1-16

Lwin, H. N. N., Punnakitikashem, P., & Thananusak, T. (2021). The level and determinants of international patient satisfaction with dental tourism in Bangkok, Thailand. *Cogent Business & Management*, *8*(1), 1898316. Advance online publication. DOI: 10.1080/23311975.2021.1898316

Milosevic, A. (2009). DENTAL TOURISM—A GLOBAL ISSUE? *Journal of Esthetic and Restorative Dentistry*, *21*(5), 289–291. DOI: 10.1111/j.1708-8240.2009.00277.x PMID: 19796293

Ní Ríordáin, R., & McCreary, C. (2009). Dental patients' use of the Internet. *British Dental Journal, 207*(12), 583–586. DOI: 10.1038/sj.bdj.2009.1137 PMID: 20019727

Orlic, E., Spalj, S., Ivancic Jokic, N., Bakarcic, D., Cicvaric, O., & Grzic, R. (2023). Pandemic Financial Stress in Dental Medicine in Croatia. *Dentistry Journal, 11*(1), 9. Advance online publication. DOI: 10.3390/dj11010009 PMID: 36661546

Ramos, K., & Cuamea, O. (2023). Dental tourism: Factors influencing travelers' revisit intention to the Mexican border. *International Journal of Tourism Cities, 9*(3), 806–831. DOI: 10.1108/IJTC-03-2023-0046

Sandhu, R. (2018). Dental Tourism: A Review. *International Healthcare Research Journal, 2*(3), 55–58. DOI: 10.26440/IHRJ/02_03/172

Sterle, A., Balázs, P., & Delgado, J. (2009). Travelling for teeth: Characteristics and perspectives of dental care tourism in Hungary. *British Dental Journal, 206*(8), 425–428. DOI: 10.1038/sj.bdj.2009.308 PMID: 19396208

Chapter 3
Global Trends in Dental Tourism and Shaping an Optimal Dental Treatment Journey

Kartal Doğukan Çıkı
http://orcid.org/0000-0002-8307-8561
İstanbul Gelişim University, Turkey

ABSTRACT

The increase in demand for cross-border dental treatment reflects not only individual patient preferences but also the transformation of global healthcare delivery models. To understand the multi-layered nature of this transformation, this book chapter aims to examine the dimensions of dental tourism—service delivery, organizational operations, and patient experience—using a holistic approach. In this context, the aim of this chapter is to examine the dynamics of dental tourism within a comprehensive framework by utilizing bibliometric analysis, document analysis, and SWOT analysis methods, based on existing research in the literature. To achieve the objective of the research, 70 studies retrieved from WoS were first examined using bibliometric analysis. Of these studies, the 10 most cited studies were subjected to document analysis. In the final stage of the research, a SWOT analysis was performed based on the studies examined. The findings of the research may provide insights for strategic planning in the dental tourism market.

DOI: 10.4018/979-8-3373-4114-9.ch003

1. INTRODUCTION

The growth trend in medical tourism is directly related not only to the increase in patient numbers but also to how this field is managed, which actors steer it, and the normative frameworks that shape it (Béland and Zarzeczny, 2018). Positioned outside national health systems, this sector often develops under private sector initiative and progresses within a structure where public oversight is weak (Basu et al., 2012). This situation reduces the patient-service provider relationship to a mere "consumer-seller" equation, while also blurring the ethical framework. In particular, the promotion of medical tourism by developing countries to generate foreign exchange income produces secondary consequences that could, in the long term, overshadow their own citizens' access to healthcare services (Vijaya, 2010).

On the other hand, the scope of medical tourism is not limited to treatment processes alone (Crooks et al., 2010). The integrated operation of ancillary sectors such as accommodation, transportation, guidance, translation services, and post-operative care demonstrates that this field has acquired a multi-actor and multi-scale structure. This situation separates medical tourism from healthcare in the traditional sense, transforming it into a new economic model based on "service clusters" (Wernz et al., 2014). However, this diversity also brings with it standardization issues; for example, inconsistencies between the quality of services provided by clinics and the quality of accommodation facilities directly affect patient satisfaction (Kesar & Mikulić, 2017). Therefore, medical tourism should be approached not only as an interdisciplinary issue but also as a matter of cross-sectoral balance management (Virani et al., 2020). Dental tourism is one of the important sub-areas of this broad framework. The high costs of dental health services, long waiting times, and limited access to certain treatments push individuals to seek alternatives across borders (Barrowman et al., 2010).

Dental tourism is considered a subset of medical tourism (Kesar & Mikulić, 2017), but over time it has become an independent form of health tourism with its own unique patient profile, service structure, and tourist integration (Gan & Frederick, 2011; Xu et al., 2020). Structural reasons such as dental services being provided by the private sector in many countries, public services being inadequate or out of scope, or limited accessibility due to high costs, drive individuals to seek alternative solutions abroad (Kovacs & Szocska, 2013). In this context, dental tourism is not merely a process where treatment services are provided, but also represents a systematic approach that shapes the competitive strategies of economic destinations and directs the international circulation of healthcare services (Ancy et al., 2020). It is reported that a significant portion of medical tourism revenues in some countries is generated from dental treatments (Crooks et al., 2010). Despite its frequent coverage in the media, this growth has been studied to a limited extent in research areas such as health law, dental ethics, health economics, or tourism (Page, 2009). Therefore, the need to address the phenomenon of dental tourism from a multidimensional perspective is becoming increasingly important (Oltean et al., 2020).

The main purpose of this chapter is to examine the structural characteristics of dental tourism and the service dynamics that shape this field within a conceptual framework. The research aims to examine the components of dental tourism in the context of cross-border health mobility through a theoretical review of the existing literature. Furthermore, this chapter aims to provide an in-depth perspective on the subject, contribute to academic gaps in the field, and establish a theoretical foundation for future studies. Methodologically, a comparative evaluation was conducted through qualitative content analysis of selected sources.

2. THEORETICAL FRAMEWORK

2.1. Medical Tourism

The increasing cost pressure on healthcare systems globally, inequalities in service provision, and technology-driven developments necessitate that medical tourism be addressed not only as a regional but also as a structural phenomenon (Al-Romeedy et al., 2025). When local healthcare services fall short in terms of accessibility, speed, or quality, individuals seeking treatment beyond national borders is no longer seen as an individual choie but rather as a systemic manifestation (Figueiredo et al., 2024). In this context, medical tourism has become an interdisciplinary field of research, woven with multi-layered dynamics on both the supply and demand sides (Hu et al., 2023).

This phenomenon is not based solely on lower costs or shorter waiting times; it also involves service providers' strategic transformations towards accepting international patients, incentive mechanisms supported by public policies, and aggressive marketing activities conducted through digital platforms (Kesar & Mikulić, 2017). In this respect, medical tourism has a complex structure that must be understood not only in terms of healthcare provision (Carrera and Bridges, 2006), but also in terms of the global health economy, patient mobility, regulatory frameworks, and destination brand management (Ancy et al., 2020).

This mobility, which is particularly concentrated in areas such as dental treatment, cosmetic surgery, IVF, and eye health, has become an industry in some countries and has even been placed at the center of regional development policies (Lunt et al., 2016; Tanriverdi et al., 2025). Destination country preferences are not only price-driven; they are also shaped by socio-cultural factors such as linguistic proximity, cultural similarities, geographical accessibility, and diasporic ties (Aydin and Karamehmet,

2017). Therefore, analyzing patient behavior requires evaluation not only through economic logic but also through sociological and cultural codes (Jensen, 2008).

On the other hand, the complex consequences of medical tourism for both patients and service providers cannot be ignored (Snyder et al., 2011). In a structure where clinical outcomes are not standardized, the inability to follow up on services, patients facing a lack of legal protection, or local health professionals being left alone to manage complications demonstrate how fragile this area is. Cross-border health mobility brings with it not only individual but also systemic ethical, financial, and governance risks.

Another prominent factor among all these structural differences is the changing patient decision-making processes that accompany digitalization (Kokshagina, 2021). The proliferation of internet-based information sources, the increasing influence of patient experience-based reviews on treatment preferences, and the ways in which clinics position themselves in digital media have transformed traditional healthcare communication (Zhao et al., 2024). Social media channels, online review platforms, and multilingual web infrastructures, in particular, have become new interfaces that drive international patient traffic (Farsi, 2021).

The new balances that emerged, particularly in the post-pandemic period, have redefined both risk perception and trust relationships in the field of medical tourism (Swenson and Bansal, 2023). Travel restrictions, the inward-looking nature of local systems, and hygiene concerns have temporarily disrupted growth in this sector. However, during the same period, virtual consultations, remotely planned treatment processes, and hybrid care models have developed; therefore, medical tourism has now transformed into not only physical but also digital mobility (Wong and Hazley, 2021).

2.2. Dental Tourism

Dental tourism has increasingly become a phenomenon that is gaining attention as one of the most visible and pragmatic sub-sectors of medical tourism (Wong et al., 2021). Particularly because it can be planned more quickly compared to general healthcare services, involves lower costs, and less invasive procedures, this field carries a significant concentration in the international patient flow. Dental practices are subject to either high-cost private services or long waiting lists within public systems in many countries. This situation is one of the main triggers that push individuals to seek treatment in other countries (Paisi et al., 2020).

Another key feature characterizing dental tourism is the ability to plan treatment and tourism almost simultaneously and in an integrated manner (Ancy et al., 2020). While patients undergo procedures such as implants, zirconium crowns, aesthetic fillings, or orthodontic treatments, they also encounter a multi-component service package that includes accommodation, city tours, gastronomic experiences, or spa services during the same trip (Pérez-Campdesuñer et al., 2025). In this respect, dental tourism is not just treatment-focused mobility, but also transforms into an "experience-based" form of consumption (Lunt et al., 2014).

Technical indicators such as the clinical infrastructure of the destination country, the educational background of physicians, sterilization standards, and whether or not they have international accreditation play an important role in patients' decision-making process (Wang et al., 2023). However, these decisions are based not only on rational comparisons but also on digital reviews, social media representations, experiences shared on patient forums, and the perceived trust created by visual content (Tanriverdi et al., 2025). Therefore, digital visibility and the management of patient reviews have become a strategic necessity for clinics (Khanbhai et al., 2019).

Another dynamic to consider specifically in dental tourism is how this field is regulated in service provider countries. Many destination countries, recognizing the demand in this area, have reviewed their health tourism legislation and developed certification systems and quality control processes to enable clinics to provide international services (Sandberg, 2017). However, in many countries, these processes are still not clearly defined or effectively implemented. This situation leads to ambiguity regarding post-service responsibilities, particularly in cases where complications arise.

From the patient's perspective, cross-border dental treatment is not only an economic choice; it can also be seen as an endeavor that embodies the desire to "access better care" (Turner, 2008) However, it is clear that this choice does not always translate into a smooth experience. In some cases, problems arise such as treatment plans not being properly prepared, insufficient radiological images, or treatment being left incomplete when complications arise (Stefanac and Nesbit, 2006). This situation demonstrates that treatment must be planned not only in the clinic but also before and after.

In many countries, dental tourism has become a significant sector at the macroeconomic level (Ancy et al., 2020). Regions such as Central and Eastern Europe, Latin America, Southeast Asia, and Turkey have positioned themselves as strong destinations in this field with models that combine affordable costs and high service quality (Enache et al., 2013). At the same time, the concentration of dental clinics in tourist areas such as coastal cities and thermal regions, as well as major cities, is important data that also shows how this service is organized geographically (Connell, 2006).

2.3. Global Dental Tourism Trends

Dental tourism stands out as one of the fastest-growing sub-sectors of medical tourism on a global scale (Hall, 2011). Increased international patient mobility in recent years has been shaped primarily by differences in the cost, accessibility, and quality of dental services (Vahdati et al., 2024). Trends in this field influence not only individual patient preferences but also the structural transformation of health-care systems and the strategic planning of destination countries (Yeganeh, 2019).

Recent studies reveal that the regions with the highest concentration of dental tourism are destinations such as Central and Eastern Europe, Asia and Latin America (Barrowman et al., 2010; Jaapar et al 2017; Österle et al., 2009; Kovacs and Szocska, 2013). These regions stand out by combining the advantage of low costs with international accreditations, high-tech investments, and cultural proximity. For example, Hungary, Poland and Croatia have become major centers for dental implants and cosmetic procedures for European patients, while Thailand and Malaysia have gained a leading position in the Asia-Pacific market. Turkey, meanwhile, has positioned itself as a strong dental tourism destination catering to both the European and Middle Eastern markets over the past decade.

Another dimension of global trends is the diversification of patient motivations. While cost advantage has traditionally been at the forefront, today factors such as the ability to complete treatment quickly, service packages integrated with tourist activities, digital consultation options, and meeting aesthetic expectations are also key determinants. With increasing digitalization, online reviews, social media posts, and virtual patient communities are profoundly influencing the decision-making processes of international patients. The quality of clinics' websites, price transparency, and online visibility have become factors that directly shape patient flow.

On the other hand, the development of global dental tourism presents not only opportunities but also risks. Three issues in particular stand out in the literature: (i) lack of aftercare and difficulties in managing complications, (ii) heterogeneity of standards and accreditation processes in different countries, (iii) ethical and legal uncertainties regarding patient safety. These issues are critical in terms of both patient confidence and the international reputation of service providers.

Although the COVID-19 pandemic temporarily disrupted these trends, it also created lasting innovations in the sector. Travel restrictions rapidly popularized tele-health applications and digital pre-assessment processes; hybrid care models (online consultation followed by treatment at the destination) have become one of the new standards in global dental tourism. The recovery observed in the post-pandemic period demonstrates that this field is vulnerable to crises, yet it also highlights its high capacity for adaptation.

At the current stage, global dental tourism is not merely an economic sector; it is also seen as a multidimensional field where health inequalities, cultural preferences, digital technologies, and international regulatory debates intersect. Therefore, understanding current trends should not be limited to patient motivations or price comparisons, but should be approached from an integrated perspective of global health and tourism systems.

3. RESEARCH METHODOLOGY

This study aims to present a comprehensive framework by examining the current state of research on dental tourism using three different approaches. First, articles published on dental tourism were manually extracted from the Web of Science (WoS) database, and then a bibliometric analysis was performed using VOSviewer. Subsequently, the most highly cited studies were examined through document analysis. In the final stage, a SWOT analysis was conducted based on these studies, aiming to identify the strengths, weaknesses, opportunities, and threats of dental tourism. Accordingly, bibliometric analyses were primarily utilized in this research (See Figure 1).

Figure 1. Methodological stages of the research

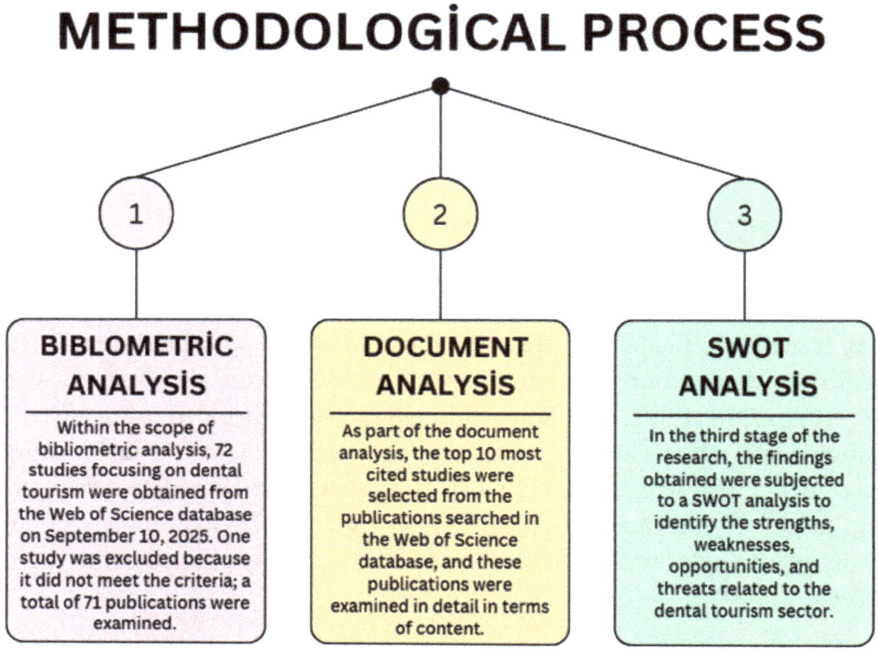

3.1. Bibliometric Analysis and Document Analysis

Using VOSviewer software, questions such as which countries showed the most interest in the subject, which universities and authors stood out, and which keywords were preferred were clarified (Van Eck and Waltman, 2010). Bibliometric analysis is a statistical analysis that reveals the current status of studies conducted during a specific period (Ciki and Tanriverdi, 2023). For bibliometric analysis, the keyword "dental tourism" was searched in the WoS database, and the search was completed to include titles, abstracts, and keywords. The targeted search yielded 72 studies. The studies were manually checked one by one, and one study was excluded from the research because it was outside the scope. The data for the study were obtained from the WoS database on September 10, 2025.

As a result of bibliometric analysis, the 10 most cited studies on dental tourism were examined using document analysis, one of the qualitative research methods. Document analysis provides the opportunity for structured framework analysis based on published documents (Patton, 2002). This analysis allows researchers to gain a comprehensive view of the current state of research in their field of interest.

3.2. SWOT (Strengths, Weaknesses, Opportunities and Threats) Analysis

Finally, based on the research in the body of knowledge obtained, a SWOT (Strengths, Weaknesses, Opportunities, and Threats) analysis was conducted using qualitative research methods to shape an optimal dental tourism trip. With SWOT analysis, a case or process can be examined systematically (Puyt et al., 2023). In this context, the current chapter aims to reveal the opportunities, advantages, and disadvantages that dental tourism offers to patients traveling for this purpose through SWOT analysis. However, this research acknowledges that these aspects of dental tourism may vary depending on the destination and that supporting research is necessary in this context.

4. RESULTS

4.1. Bibliometric Analysis and Document Analysis Findings

Figure 2 shows the distribution of studies on dental tourism published in journals indexed in the Web of Science (WoS) by year. The first study on dental tourism was published in 2007. The years with the highest number of publications were 2009 and 2018 (8 publications each). The years 2023 and 2025 are second in this regard with 7 studies each. The years 2017 and 2021 are the third years with the highest number of publications on dental tourism with 6 publications each (WoS, 2025). In terms of publication distribution, it was determined that a significant portion of the studies were articles (38 documents). When the WoS categories of the publications were examined, 'Dentistry Oral Surgery Medicine' ranked first with 25 publications. 'Hospitality Leisure Sport Tourism' ranked second with 15 publications. The vast majority of studies published on the subject are in English (70 documents).

Figure 2. Distribution of publications by year

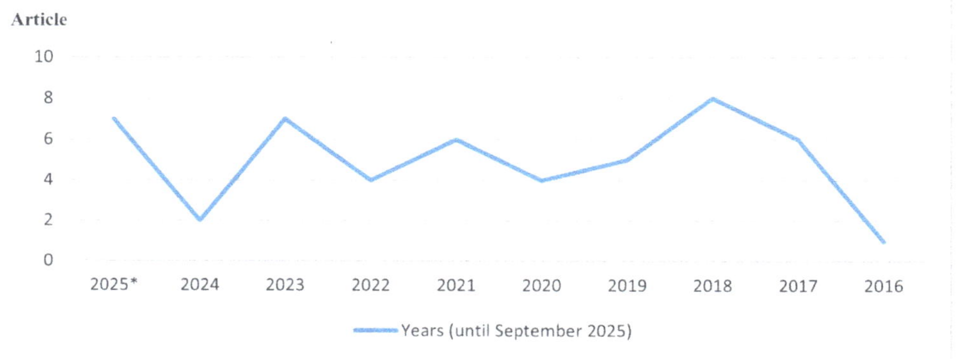

Figure 3 shows international collaborations in academic studies on dental tourism. In terms of the number of publications by authors, Croatia ranks first with 8 documents. Croatia is followed by Australia, Iran, the USA, and Canada with 6 documents each. Hungary follows these three countries with 5 publications.

Figure 3. Map of international collaboration

Figure 4 presents a visual representation of the collaborations among authors with the highest number of publications on dental tourism. According to the analysis results obtained using VOSviewer, Adams Krystyna, Croos Valorie, and Snyder Jeremy are the top three authors who have contributed the most to the dental tourism literature with four publications each. Paydadr Mohammad Mahdir follows the leading researchers with three publications.

Figure 4. Cooperation links between scientists

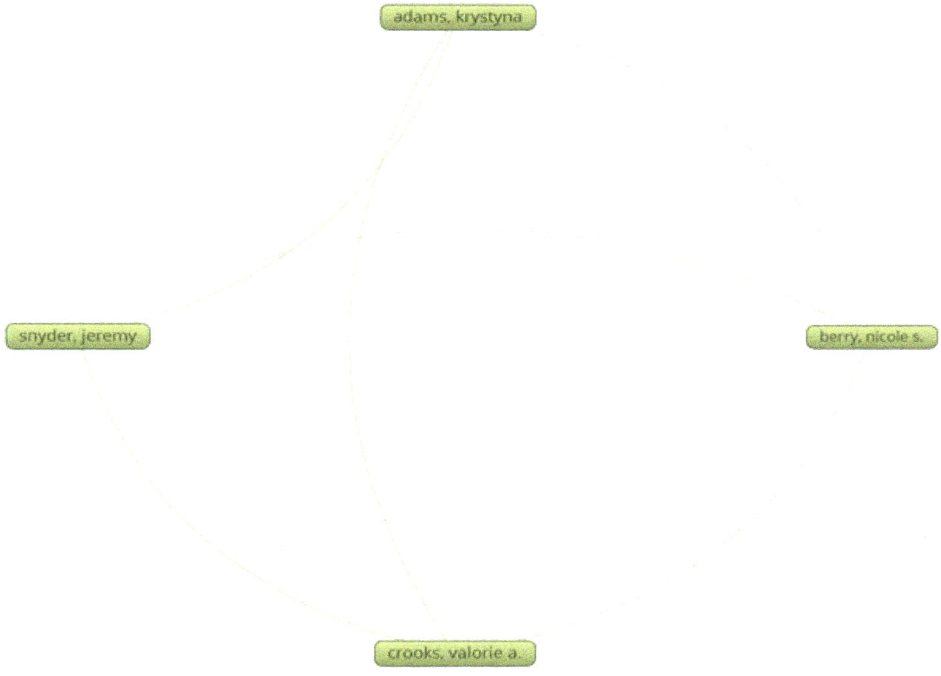

The collaborations of universities contributing most to dental tourism are presented in Figure 5. According to the data obtained from the analysis performed with VOSviewer software, Semmelweis University and Simon Fraser University are at the top of the list of institutions contributing most to dental tourism with 4 documents each. These two universities are followed by James Cook University and Babol Noshirvani University of Technology with 3 documents each.

Figure 5. Top contributing organizations

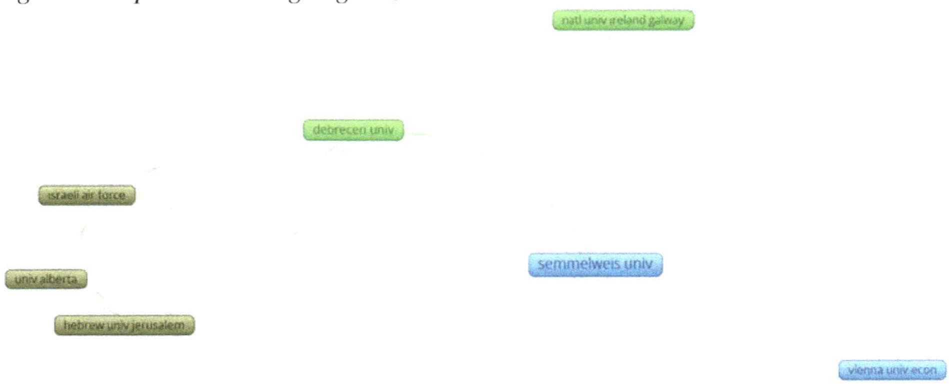

Figure 6 shows the connections between keywords in dental tourism-themed studies. Among the most frequently used keywords in studies on dental tourism is 'dental tourism'. The keyword "dental tourism" appeared 26 times in these studies. This keyword was followed by the keyword "medical tourism," which was used in 19 studies. In third place, with 4 studies each, "health tourism," "dental care," and "Croatia" were among the most frequently recurring keywords.

Figure 6. Keyword links for dental tourism

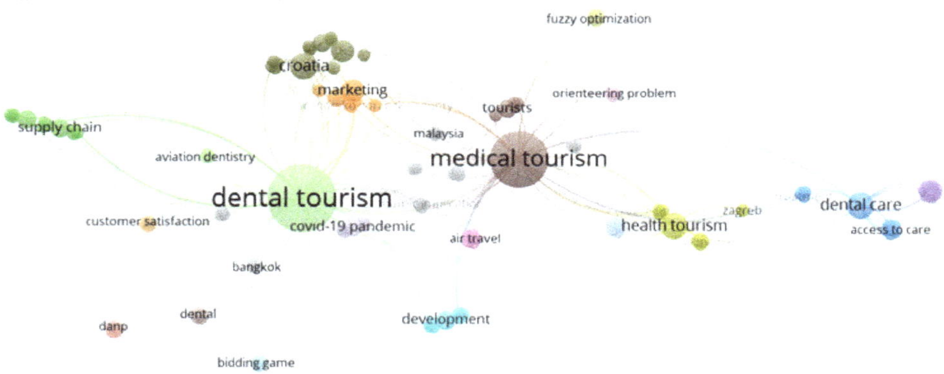

Table 1 presents the top 10 most cited articles on dental tourism published in WoS journals (up to September 2025). According to the table, the most recent article(s) on the list date back to 2019, while the earliest article was published in 2008. Hall's article, published in Tourism Review in 2011, tops the list of most cited dental tourism studies with 145 citations. Second on the list is the article by Hanefeld et al. (2014), published in the Journal of Travel Medicine (with 89 citations). This article is followed by Turner's 2008 article published in Tourism Management with 54 citations. On the other hand, the British Dental Journal tops the list of journals publishing the most cited studies with four articles (analyses conducted in September 2025). Tourism Management follows this journal with three articles.

Table 1. The most cited articles among those published in journals indexed in WoS

	Author(s)	Title	Journals	Citation (WoS)	Year
1	Hall, C.M.	Health and medical tourism: a kill or cure for global public health?	Tourism Review	145	2011
2	Hanefeld, J., Smith, R., Horsfall, D. and Lunt, N.	What Do We Know About Medical Tourism? A Review of the Literature With Discussion of Its Implications for the UK National Health Service as an Example of a Public Health Care System	Journal of Travel Medicine	89	2014
3	Jaapar, M., Musa, G., Moghavvemi, S. and Saub, R.	Dental tourism: Examining tourist profiles, motivation and satisfaction	Tourism Management	63	2017
4	Turner, L.	Cross-border dental care: 'dental tourism' and patient mobility	British Dental Journal	54	2008
5	Ríordáin, R.N. and McCreary, C.	Dental patients' use of the Internet	British Dental Journal	47	2009
6	Österle, A., Balázs, P. and Delgado, J.	Travelling for teeth: characteristics and perspectives of dental care tourism in Hungary	British Dental Journal	33	2009
7	Barrowman, R.A., Grubor, D. and Chandu, A.	Dental implant tourism	Australian Dental Journal	32	2010
8	Ahmadimanesh, F., Paydar, M.M. and Asadi-Gangraj, E.	Designing a mathematical model for dental tourism supply chain	Tourism Management	26	2019
9	Lovelock, B., Lovelock, K. and Lyons, K.	The impact of outbound medical (dental) tourism on the generating region: New Zealand dental professionals' perspectives	Tourism Management	22	2018
10	Kovacs, E. and Szocska, G.	'Vacation for your teeth' – dental tourists in Hungary from the perspective of Hungarian dentists	British Dental Journal	22	2013

4.1.1. Gaps and Limitations in Existing Literature

As a result of the bibliometric analysis, the most cited studies were examined in depth and are presented in Table 2. This revealed the trends in dental tourism-based research, the methods used, and the research gaps, providing clues for future research. Four of the most cited studies were designed using quantitative methods.

Table 2. The scope of the most cited studies

	Author(s), Year, Title	Research Method	The Purpose and Topic of the Research	Data Source
1	Hall, C.M. (2011) Health and medical tourism: a kill or cure for global public health?	Conceptual	To reveal the current state of research conducted on medical and dental tourism.	Literature review
2	Hanefeld, J., Smith, R., Horsfall, D. and Lunt, N. (2014) What Do We Know About Medical Tourism? A Review of the Literature With Discussion of Its Implications for the UK National Health Service as an Example of a Public Health Care System	Conceptual	To reveal the current state of research conducted on medical tourism.	Literature review
3	Jaapar, M., Musa, G., Moghavvemi, S. and Saub, R. (2017) Dental tourism: Examining tourist profiles, motivation and satisfaction	Quantitative	To examine the travel motivation and satisfaction of tourists traveling to Malaysia for dental tourism activities.	Questionnaire application
4	Turner, L. (2008) Cross-border dental care: 'dental tourism' and patient mobility	Conceptual	This article discusses the reasons for the emergence of dental tourism in the context of increasing patient mobility, its potential benefits, and the risks it entails. The study examines the phenomenon of dental tourism as part of global health care mobility and explores the socio-economic factors that drive patients to seek cross-border dental treatment.	Literature review
5	Ríordáin, R.N. and McCreary, C. (2009) Dental patients' use of the Internet	Quantitative	The authors aimed to reveal the participants' interest in using the internet to obtain information before seeking dental treatment in this study.	Questionnaire application
6	Österle, A., Balázs, P. and Delgado, J. (2009) Travelling for teeth: characteristics and perspectives of dental care tourism in Hungary	Quantitative	The authors conducted a survey of dentists practicing in Budapest as part of their research to determine Hungary's dental tourism potential, aiming to reveal the motivations of dental tourists for these trips from the dentists' perspective.	Questionnaire application

continued on following page

Table 2. Continued

	Author(s), Year, Title	Research Method	The Purpose and Topic of the Research	Data Source
7	Barrowman, R.A., Grubor, D. and Chandu, A. (2010) Dental implant tourism	Qualitative	The authors focused on five cases to highlight the problems that tourists traveling abroad (to Australia) for dental implant treatment may encounter.	Case study
8	Ahmadimanesh, F., Paydar, M.M. and Asadi-Gangraj, E. (2019) Designing a mathematical model for dental tourism supply chain	Quantitative	This study aimed to design a supply chain network for dental tourism. To this end, a mathematical model was used and subsequently supported by case studies.	Case study
9	Lovelock, B., Lovelock, K. and Lyons, K. (2018) The impact of outbound medical (dental) tourism on the generating region: New Zealand dental professionals' perspectives	Mixed Method	The aim is to reveal the perspectives of dental health professionals on dental tourism through surveys and interviews.	Questionnaire application and in-depth interviews
10	Kovacs, E. and Szocska, G. (2013) 'Vacation for your teeth' – dental tourists in Hungary from the perspective of Hungarian dentists	Mixed Method	The authors aimed to determine Hungary's current position in dental tourism using a mixed-method approach that included administering a survey to dentists and conducting interviews with representatives of dental professional organizations.	Questionnaire application and in-depth interviews

The most cited quantitative studies focus on dental tourists' travel motivation, satisfaction, and interest in internet use prior to treatment, while qualitative research addresses potential problems that may be encountered. On the other hand, while some quantitative studies focus on the opinions of dentists and dental health professionals, they also focus on their perspectives on dental tourism and their views on the travel motivations of dental tourists. Conceptual studies examine the current state of dental tourism, its potential benefits, and risks.

Other studies in the WoS database have examined satisfaction (Lwin et al., 2021; Ostojic et al., 2025), loyalty (Lwin et al., 2021), dissatisfaction (Kesar & Mikulic, 2017), revisit intention (Ramos and Cuamea, 2023), and service quality (Ramos & Cuamea, 2023). Consequently, while researchers have shown more interest in travel motivation and satisfaction, they have not paid sufficient attention to important variables such as loyalty, behavioral intentions (revisit and/or recommendation), and service quality. In addition, researchers have overlooked many variables such as subjective well-being, recommendation intention, perceived safety, and pre-post travel behaviors.

On the other hand, the data sources of the studies generally include information collected from dental tourists and dental health professionals. However, there is a lack of comprehensive research that also includes other stakeholders. Practices targeting dental health professionals are also quite limited. There is a wide range of research gaps, such as burnout, job satisfaction, and workplace loneliness. Similarly, research on the demographic characteristics of dental tourists is limited. In this context, various studies could be conducted on issues encountered by female patients during their travels and behaviors that vary according to demographic characteristics and destination.

Research in the WoS database shows that applications have been made in countries such as Hungary, Malaysia, Ireland, Australia, and New Zealand. However, research in countries with significant potential for dental tourism, such as Turkey, Romania, and Thailand, is limited. Research conducted in this context could fill an important gap in the literature.

Another significant gap in the dental tourism literature is the lack of long-term research. Similarly, there is a lack of research on the environmental consequences of dental tourism, the carbon footprint of those traveling for dental treatment, and the sustainability dimension. Furthermore, while research is conducted on tourists and destinations in medical tourism, the reasons for the transfer of resources abroad based on the health systems and other factors of the sending countries are not addressed. Another area of research that is lacking is the economic dimensions of dental tourism. Furthermore, there is no research on revealing the dimensions of the dental tourism experience, motivations, and satisfaction levels in the context of comments made by dental tourists on user-generated content-based websites such as Trustpilot.

4.1.2. Tourists' Motivation for Dental Tourism

One of the rising branches of medical tourism, dental tourism, has grown for a variety of reasons. The most important motivation for dental tourists is likely access to good dental care. Many patients believe that the modern technologies and current treatment approaches used in international clinics are equivalent to or more advanced than those in their own countries. In addition, transparent pricing through package programs, the ability to plan the duration of treatment in advance, and comprehensive customer service reinforce the feeling of trust. This is considered a powerful factor influencing patient decisions, especially in complex implant and prosthetic treatments. However, the literature also highlights the mismatch between perceived quality and actual treatment outcomes; while some patients embark on treatment with high expectations, the lack of adequate control mechanisms can increase the risk of complications. Therefore, although perceived quality and trust are central to motivation, they can lead to conflicting outcomes in the patient experience.

However, service quality alone may not always be sufficient, and it is expected to be offered as an integrated service incorporating various factors. In this regard, one of the most prominent motivations is affordable service. Furthermore, the desire to avoid long waiting times and receive faster service is a powerful reason that drives individuals to seek cross-border dental treatment for their dental health. However, motivation is not solely economic or time-related; some destinations are preferred because they offer quality advantages through modern technologies, advanced clinical infrastructure, and a patient-centered service approach. Furthermore, cultural affinity, language ease, or family and social ties for individuals of immigrant origin are also decisive factors in choosing a country. The ability to combine the treatment process with a tourist experience is another factor that increases motivation. Ultimately, the reasons behind dental tourism can be explained by the intersection of economic, time-related, cultural, and experiential dimensions.

The widespread use of the internet in modern society has become a critical factor in strengthening motivations for dental tourism. Patients are no longer solely reliant on their own dentists' recommendations; they can now directly access information from international clinics' websites, social media platforms, and user-generated content-based websites (such as Trustpilot) through patient reviews. This allows for price comparisons, detailed information about treatment processes, and the creation of an environment of trust based on user experiences. In addition, packages offered online by travel agencies and medical tourism companies facilitate the treatment process for patients by integrating it with airline tickets and accommodation. This digital transparency contributes to potential patients viewing treatment not only as a medical necessity but also as a process that can be planned and managed. Thus, ease of access to information and the visibility provided by digital networks significantly increase the motivation of individuals who choose dental tourism.

One of the factors that makes dental tourism attractive is that treatment services are combined not only with clinical quality but also with the overall appeal of the destination. Patients are more strongly drawn to these destinations when they find the opportunity to combine their search for affordable treatment with tourist experiences. For example, countries such as Romania and Croatia offer not only competitive prices and expertise, but also a comprehensive experience supported by historical heritage, sea tourism, or cultural events. Furthermore, factors such as cultural affinity, a common language, or diaspora ties are also important motivators in destination selection. Therefore, the rise of dental tourism is closely linked not only to treatment costs but also to the integrated offering of healthcare and tourism products.

In addition, patients who choose dental tourism have significant concerns alongside their motivations. Differences in clinical regulations, lack of post-treatment care, and legal accountability issues directly affect patients' decision-making processes. Complications seen in implant treatments, in particular, create additional burdens for both patients and dentists in their home countries. A study conducted in New Zealand highlighted that dentists believe patients who have undergone treatment abroad have been victimized due to low quality and fragmented care. In this context, risk perception stands in opposition to motivation and may cause some patients to reconsider their decisions.

4.2. SWOT Analysis Findings

A SWOT analysis was conducted based on research related to dental tourism (see Table 3). The analysis revealed that one of the most significant advantages for patients choosing dental tourism is the availability of affordable pricing options. Implants, prosthetics, or cosmetic treatments, which are quite expensive in regions such as Western Europe, North America, and Australia, are offered at lower prices in countries such as Eastern Europe and Thailand. In addition, the absence of waiting periods that could last for months in their own countries is a particularly important attraction factor for potential tourists. Another appeal of dental tourism is the opportunity to combine the treatment process with a tourist experience; as seen in the example of Croatia, the vacation destination also becomes the treatment center (Peručić, 2019). Furthermore, clinics' investment in modern infrastructure and internationally trained specialists reinforces the perception of trust among tourists. Therefore, the strengths of dental tourism emerge from the combination of economic, time-saving, and experiential advantages.

Table 3. SWOT analysis results

Strengths	*Weaknesses*
• Affordable pricing options • High quality of service • Short waiting times and quick access to treatment • Opportunity to combine treatment with vacation and comprehensive packages • Modern clinic infrastructure and specialist physicians • International communication facilities • Personalized services and pre-treatment personal consultation	• Lack of follow-up after complications • Differences in quality standards • Inadequate insurance coverage • Trust issues and risk perception • Difficulties in seeking legal rights • Communication problems, risk of misunderstanding • Travel fatigue
Opportunities	***Threats***
• Easy access to healthcare centers with developing transportation systems • Online reservations, patient reviews, price comparisons, and easy access to services thanks to digitalization • Competitive prices and variety in treatment packages combined with vacations • Public incentives and healthcare tourism investments in some countries • Increased trust with international accreditation and quality certifications	• The difficulty and cost of tourists continuing treatment in their own country after complications • Intensive procedures due to the short duration of treatment • Unexpected additional costs • The possibility of losing the price advantage due to currency fluctuations

In addition to all these advantages, dental tourism also has significant weaknesses from the tourists' perspective. First and foremost, it is difficult to ensure continuity of treatment abroad in the event of complications. Many patients may require additional interventions upon returning to their home country, but their own dentists may be reluctant to take on these cases (Barrowman, 2010; Lovelock et al., 2018). Furthermore, most national health insurance plans exclude dental procedures performed abroad, creating economic uncertainty (Hanefeld et al., 2014). Treatment protocols compressed into the vacation period also complicate the recovery process and increase the risk of complications (Lovelock et al., 2018). Furthermore, language barriers, difficulties in seeking legal recourse, and quality differences between clinics can also negatively affect patient satisfaction (Demonja and Uglješić, 2020). This points to weaknesses in the dental tourist experience that must be carefully managed.

The growth of dental tourism brings with it various opportunities for tourists. Patient mobility regulations within the European Union facilitate individuals seeking treatment outside their home countries and increase accessibility (Perućić, 2019). Demographically, the aging population's increasing need for dental treatment is expanding the international health tourism market. The integration of wellness tourism, cultural activities, and dental care makes destinations more attractive. Furthermore, the proliferation of online consultation and second opinion services allows tourists to plan their pre-treatment processes more safely (Demonja and

Uglješić, 2020). These opportunities offer significant advantages in optimal travel planning for dental tourists.

However, there are also some threats faced by tourists who choose dental tourism. Global health crises such as the COVID-19 pandemic can disrupt treatment plans by restricting freedom of travel. Currency fluctuations and political instability carry the risk of eliminating cost advantages in destinations (Peručić, 2019). Furthermore, regulatory gaps and differences in hygiene standards in some countries can undermine tourists' perception of safety (Lovelock et al., 2018). The rapid spread of negative patient experiences on digital platforms is also a factor that threatens the image of destinations (Demonja and Uglješić, 2020). This situation shows that opportunities in dental tourism are balanced by serious threats.

In conclusion, while the strengths of dental tourism offer significant opportunities to tourists, its weaknesses and threats necessitate careful management of the process. An optimal dental tourism trip should focus on maximizing cost and quality advantages while minimizing complications, insurance, and legal risks. This is because the most decisive factor in shaping the dental tourism industry is the expectations, experiences, and perceptions of tourists seeking treatment.

5. CONCLUSIONS AND RECOMMENDATIONS

This book chapter follows a three-stage process to reveal the current state of dental tourism. First, bibliometric analysis was used to determine the structure of the literature, prominent actors, and thematic concentrations. In the second stage, the most cited studies were examined using a document analysis approach, and theoretical and methodological trends in the field were discussed. Finally, a SWOT analysis was conducted to systematically evaluate the strengths and weaknesses of dental tourism, along with the opportunities it presents and the threats it faces. This resulted in the development of a multidimensional framework that can guide both the body of knowledge and sectoral applications.

Bibliometric analyses show that dental tourism has rapidly become an academic field of research since 2007, with a particular increase between 2009 and 2018. The findings reveal that this field is not limited to dentistry alone, but is also studied in disciplines such as tourism, health economics, and destination management. The majority of publications are in English. However, it is noteworthy that publications from countries with high dental tourism potential, such as Turkey, Romania, and Thailand, are limited. This suggests that there is insufficient regional diversity in the literature and that the experiences of certain countries have led to a one-sided academic knowledge production.

When examining international cooperation networks, countries such as Croatia, Australia, and Canada are seen to be at the forefront of dental tourism research. This can be attributed to both these countries being destinations with a high patient influx and having research infrastructure supported by international funding. In contrast, the relatively weak position of countries such as Mexico and Turkey, which play an important role in global patient flows, in research collaborations reflects the uneven distribution of the literature. This finding shows that, despite dental tourism being a global phenomenon, research production is still concentrated in certain geographical areas and that different experiences are not sufficiently visible.

The examination of the most cited studies has provided important insights into the theoretical orientations of the literature. Conceptual studies such as Hall (2011) and Hanefeld et al. (2014) have discussed medical and dental tourism within a broader healthcare system context, highlighting the ethical, economic, and governance dimensions of this field. On the other hand, quantitative studies such as Jaapar et al. (2017) and Österle et al. (2009) have produced more micro-level results by focusing on patient profiles, motivations, and satisfaction dimensions. This diversity shows that the literature addresses both macro-level policy and regulation issues and micro-level patient experiences. However, the bridges between these two approaches appear weak, meaning that individual motivations are not sufficiently linked to systemic outcomes.

Furthermore, it is noteworthy that the most cited studies are methodologically based primarily on literature reviews, surveys, and case analyses. This indicates that dental tourism has been examined more at a descriptive level, with experimental or long-term studies lacking. Indeed, while variables such as satisfaction, travel motivation, loyalty, intention to revisit, or digital experience are addressed in some studies, broader impacts such as patients' quality of life, health inequalities, or sustainability are largely overlooked. In this context, it is expected that the literature will deepen methodologically and move towards more comprehensive research designs.

The findings of the SWOT analysis indicate that dental tourism has strengths such as affordable pricing options for individuals, short waiting times, modern clinic infrastructure, and integration with the tourist experience. However, significant weaknesses include a lack of follow-up after complications, legal uncertainties, and quality differences between clinics. Opportunities include easy access to transportation and services, competitive pricing and variety in treatment packages combined with vacation, and other such factors. Threats have been identified as currency fluctuations, intensive procedures due to the short treatment duration, and unexpected additional costs. This analysis reveals that dental tourism has both high potential and a fragile structure.

The research indicates that, from a theoretical perspective, dental tourism should be more strongly linked to the concepts of "patient mobility" and "global health networks." In the future of this field, it is important to establish more comprehensive theoretical frameworks incorporating health geography, service quality theories, and consumer behavior models. In particular, holistic models that combine micro-level analysis of patient experiences with macro-level examination of destination competitiveness can contribute to overcoming the fragmented structure in the literature.

At a practical level, it appears critical to establish regulations that will ensure the flow of international patients. Differences in standards and lack of oversight pose a significant risk for tourists, making it necessary to strengthen international accreditation systems and ensure transparent oversight of clinics. Furthermore, health insurance policies covering overseas treatment to a certain extent will both reduce tourists' perception of risk and contribute to the sector's sustainable growth. For political actors, this area should be approached not only as a tourism segment that generates foreign exchange but also as a policy tool that will strengthen global health equity.

From the perspective of clinics, designing services that meet international patient expectations is becoming increasingly critical. In particular, developing post-treatment follow-up mechanisms, implementing guarantee policies, and providing continuous support through digital communication channels will increase patient satisfaction. Furthermore, adopting environmentally conscious practices in line with sustainable tourism principles can strengthen the destination's image. In this context, clinics must move beyond being merely "low-cost treatment providers" and become international players that build long-term patient relationships.

5.1. Future Research Directions and Limitations

This chapter of the book has certain limitations. One of the most significant limitations of this research is methodological. While bibliometric analysis and document analysis are useful for understanding the salient points of the literature, these methods naturally carry a certain selectivity. On the other hand, the fact that bibliometric analysis is limited to the journals covered by the databases used has led to the exclusion of studies published in certain regions but not included in international indexes. Furthermore, the selection of articles based on citation counts for document analysis has overlooked some innovative but not yet sufficiently visible studies. Therefore, the results obtained reflect the "mainstream" research perspective rather than the entire global literature. Although the SWOT analysis used in the study allowed for the systematic categorization of the strengths and weaknesses of dental tourism, the fact that this approach inherently involves subjective assessments should be considered a limitation. The SWOT analysis was based on findings derived from the literature and was not supported by direct patient experiences or field studies.

Finally, since this research presents a literature-based framework, it is not possible to generalize the results obtained to all tourist groups or all destinations.

REFERENCES

Ahmadimanesh, F., Paydar, M. M., & Asadi-Gangraj, E. (2019). Designing a mathematical model for dental tourism supply chain. *Tourism Management*, *75*, 404–417. DOI: 10.1016/j.tourman.2019.06.001

Al-Romeedy, B. S., Emam, M. E., Hussein, H., Singh, A., & Tyagi, P. K. (2025). Digital passports to wellness: How technology is shaping medical tourism. In Ezzat, R. E. R., & Ali, M. F. (Eds.), *Revolutionizing healthcare experience with digital medical tourism*. IGI Global., DOI: 10.4018/979-8-3693-7888-5.ch004

Ancy, R. J., Shenoy, R. P., Jodalli, P. S., & Pasha, I. M. (2020). Benefits of medical and dental tourism–a review. *IOSR Journal of Dental and Medical Sciences*, *19*(3), 26–31.

Aydin, G., & Karamehmet, B. (2017). Factors affecting health tourism and international health-care facility choice. *International Journal of Pharmaceutical and Healthcare Marketing*, *11*(1), 16–36. DOI: 10.1108/IJPHM-05-2015-0018

Barrowman, R. A., Grubor, D., & Chandu, A. (2010). Dental implant tourism. *Australian Dental Journal*, *55*(4), 441–445. DOI: 10.1111/j.1834-7819.2010.01267.x PMID: 21133945

Basu, S., Andrews, J., Kishore, S., Panjabi, R., & Stuckler, D. (2012). Comparative performance of private and public healthcare systems in low- and middle-income countries: A systematic review. *PLoS Medicine*, *9*(6), e1001244. DOI: 10.1371/journal.pmed.1001244 PMID: 22723748

Béland, D., & Zarzeczny, A. (2018). Medical tourism and national health care systems: An institutionalist research agenda. *Globalization and Health*, *14*(1), 68. DOI: 10.1186/s12992-018-0387-0 PMID: 30012218

Carrera, P. M., & Bridges, J. F. P. (2006). Globalization and healthcare: Understanding health and medical tourism. *Expert Review of Pharmacoeconomics & Outcomes Research*, *6*(4), 447–454. DOI: 10.1586/14737167.6.4.447 PMID: 20528514

Ciki, K. D., & Tanriverdi, H. (2023). Self-determination theory in the field of tourism: A bibliometric analysis. Tourism. *Tourism (Zagreb)*, *71*(4), 769–781. DOI: 10.37741/t.71.4.8

Connell, J. (2006). Medical tourism: Sea, sun, sand and … surgery. *Tourism Management*, *27*(6), 1093–1100. DOI: 10.1016/j.tourman.2005.11.005

Crooks, V. A., Kingsbury, P., Snyder, J., & Johnston, R. (2010). What is known about the patient's experience of medical tourism? *BMC Health Services Research, 10*(1), 266. DOI: 10.1186/1472-6963-10-266 PMID: 20825667

Demonja, D., & Uglješić, N. (2020). Dental tourism and business risks: The example of the Republic of Croatia. *Interdisciplinary Description of Complex Systems, 18*(4), 425–445. DOI: 10.7906/indecs.18.4.3

Enache, E. N., Gabor, M.-R., & Morozan, C. (2013). Considerations about dental tourism development and its specific marketing in Romania. *Management Strategies Journal, 22*(Special), 420–426.

Farsi, D. (2021). Social media and health care, Part I: Literature review of social media use by health care providers. *Journal of Medical Internet Research, 23*(4), e23205. DOI: 10.2196/23205 PMID: 33664014

Figueiredo, N., Abrantes, J. L., & Costa, S. (2024). Mapping the sustainable development in health tourism: A systematic literature review. *Sustainability (Basel), 16*(5), 1901. DOI: 10.3390/su16051901

Gan, L. L., & Frederick, J. R. (2011). Medical tourism facilitators: Patterns of service differentiation. *Journal of Vacation Marketing, 17*(3), 165–183. DOI: 10.1177/1356766711409181

Hall, C. M. (2011). Health and medical tourism: A kill or cure for global public health? *Tourism Review, 66*(1-2), 4–15. DOI: 10.1108/16605371111127198

Hanefeld, J., Smith, R., Horsfall, D., & Lunt, N. (2014). What do we know about medical tourism? A review of the literature with discussion of its implications for the UK National Health Service as an example of a public health care system. *Journal of Travel Medicine, 21*(6), 410–417. DOI: 10.1111/jtm.12147 PMID: 25156070

Hu, F., Wen, J., Zheng, D., & Wang, W. (2023). Travel medicine in hospitality: An interdisciplinary perspective. *International Journal of Contemporary Hospitality Management, 35*(9), 3134–3153. DOI: 10.1108/IJCHM-05-2022-0574

Jaapar, M., Musa, G., Moghavvemi, S., & Saub, R. (2017). Dental tourism: Examining tourist profiles, motivation and satisfaction. *Tourism Management, 61*, 538–552. DOI: 10.1016/j.tourman.2017.02.023

Jensen, C. B. (2008). Sociology, systems and (patient) safety: Knowledge translations in healthcare policy. *Sociology of Health & Illness, 30*(1), 100–114. DOI: 10.1111/j.1467-9566.2007.01035.x PMID: 18290938

Kesar, O., & Mikulić, J. (2017). Medical tourist satisfaction and dissatisfaction with dental care services: An exploratory case study. In Tourism in Southern and Eastern Europe 2017: Tourism and Creative Industries: Trends and Challenges (pp. 243-258). University of Rijeka, Faculty of Tourism and Hospitality Management. DOI: 10.20867/tosee.04.41

Khanbhai, M., Flott, K., Darzi, A., & Mayer, E. (2019). Evaluating digital maturity and patient acceptability of real-time patient experience feedback systems: Systematic review. *Journal of Medical Internet Research*, *21*(1), e9076. DOI: 10.2196/jmir.9076 PMID: 31344680

Kokshagina, O. (2021). Managing shifts to value-based healthcare and value digitalization as a multi-level dynamic capability development process. *Technological Forecasting and Social Change*, *172*, 121072. DOI: 10.1016/j.techfore.2021.121072

Kovacs, E., & Szocska, G. (2013). 'Vacation for your teeth'—Dental tourists in Hungary from the perspective of Hungarian dentists. *British Dental Journal*, *215*(8), 415–418. DOI: 10.1038/sj.bdj.2013.995 PMID: 24157766

Lovelock, B., Lovelock, K., & Lyons, K. (2018). The impact of outbound medical (dental) tourism on the generating region: New Zealand dental professionals' perspectives. *Tourism Management*, *67*, 399–410. DOI: 10.1016/j.tourman.2018.02.001

Lunt, N., Horsfall, D., & Hanefeld, J. (2016). Medical tourism: A snapshot of evidence on treatment abroad. *Maturitas*, *88*, 37–44. DOI: 10.1016/j.maturitas.2016.03.001 PMID: 27105695

Lunt, N., Jin, K. N., Horsfall, D., & Hanefeld, J. (2014). Insights on medical tourism: Markets as networks and the role of strong ties. *Korean Social Science Journal*, *41*(1), 19–37. DOI: 10.1007/s40483-014-0012-7

Lwin, H. N. N., Punnakitikashem, P., & Thananusak, T. (2021). The level and determinants of international patient satisfaction with dental tourism in Bangkok, Thailand. *Cogent Business & Management*, *8*(1), 1898316. DOI: 10.1080/23311975.2021.1898316

Oltean, F. D., Gabor, M. R., Stăncioiu, A.-F., Kardos, M., Kiss, M., & Marinescu, R. C. (2020). Aspects of marketing in dental tourism—Factor of sustainable development in Romania. *Sustainability (Basel)*, *12*(10), 4320. DOI: 10.3390/su12104320

Österle, A., Balázs, P., & Delgado, J. (2009). Travelling for teeth: Characteristics and perspectives of dental care tourism in Hungary. *British Dental Journal*, *206*(8), 425–428. DOI: 10.1038/sj.bdj.2009.308 PMID: 19396208

Ostojic, B., Bajramovic, D., & Cvjetkovic, M. (2025). The impact of digital marketing on customer satisfaction in dental tourism in Serbia. Menadžment u hotelijerstvu i turizmu, 13(1), 131–144. DOI: 10.5937/menhottur2500008O

Page, S. J. (2009). Current issue in tourism: The evolution of travel medicine research: A new research agenda for tourism? *Tourism Management*, *30*(2), 149–157. DOI: 10.1016/j.tourman.2008.04.011 PMID: 32287728

Paisi, M., Baines, R., Burns, L., Plessas, A., Radford, P., Shawe, J., & Witton, R. (2020). Barriers and facilitators to dental care access among asylum seekers and refugees in highly developed countries: A systematic review. *BMC Oral Health*, *20*(1), 337. DOI: 10.1186/s12903-020-01321-1 PMID: 33238954

Patton, M. Q. (2002). *Qualitative research and evaluation methods* (3rd ed.). Sage Publications.

Pérez-Campdesuñer, R., Sánchez-Rodríguez, A., García-Vidal, G., Martínez-Vivar, R., Valdés-Alarcón, M. E., & De Miguel-Guzmán, M. (2025). Demographic capital and the conditional validity of SERVPERF: Rethinking tourist satisfaction models in an emerging market destination. *Administrative Sciences*, *15*(7), 272. DOI: 10.3390/admsci15070272

Peručić, D. (2019). Limitations and development opportunities of dental tourism: The case of Croatia. Ekonomski vjesnik/Econviews - Review of Contemporary Business. *Entrepreneurship and Economic Issues*, *32*(1), 93–104.

Puyt, R. W., Lie, F. B., & Wilderom, C. P. M. (2023). The origins of SWOT analysis. *Long Range Planning*, *56*(3), 102304. DOI: 10.1016/j.lrp.2023.102304

Ramos, K., & Cuamea, O. (2023). Dental tourism: Factors influencing travelers' revisit intention to the Mexican border. *International Journal of Tourism Cities*, *9*(3), 806–831. DOI: 10.1108/IJTC-03-2023-0046

Ríordáin, R. N., & McCreary, C. (2009). Dental patients' use of the Internet. *British Dental Journal*, *207*(12), 583–586. DOI: 10.1038/sj.bdj.2009.1137 PMID: 20019727

Sandberg, D. S. (2017). Medical tourism: An emerging global healthcare industry. *International Journal of Healthcare Management*, *10*(4), 281–288. DOI: 10.1080/20479700.2017.1296213

Snyder, J., Dharamsi, S., & Crooks, V. A. (2011). Fly-by medical care: Conceptualizing the global and local social responsibilities of medical tourists and physician voluntourists. *Globalization and Health*, *7*(1), 6. Advance online publication. DOI: 10.1186/1744-8603-7-6 PMID: 21470415

Stefanac, S. J., & Nesbit, S. P. (2006). *Treatment planning in dentistry* (2nd ed.). Elsevier.

Swenson, M. S., & Bansal, A. (2023). *Medical, dental, and wellness tourism: A post-pandemic perspective* (1st ed.). Apple Academic Press., DOI: 10.1201/9781003433569

Tanriverdi, H., Çiki, K. D., Uygun, N., & Çiki, S. (2025). Narratives of medical tourists travelling for hair transplant: A case of Turkiye. *Tourism Recreation Research*, 1–13. Advance online publication. DOI: 10.1080/02508281.2025.2471484

Turner, L. (2008). Cross-border dental care: 'Dental tourism' and patient mobility. *British Dental Journal, 204*(10), 553–554. DOI: 10.1038/sj.bdj.2008.403 PMID: 18500297

Vahdati, A., Khadivi, G., Ghorbani, Z., Vahdati Helan, E., Ranjbar, A., & Azimi, S. (2024). Accessibility of special care dentistry across countries: A scoping review. *Health Care, 12*(23), 2376. DOI: 10.3390/healthcare12232376 PMID: 39684998

Van Eck, N. J., & Waltman, L. (2010). Software survey: VOSviewer, a computer program for bibliometric mapping. *Scientometrics, 84*(2), 523–538. DOI: 10.1007/s11192-009-0146-3 PMID: 20585380

Vijaya, R. M. (2010). Medical tourism: Revenue generation or international transfer of healthcare problems? *Journal of Economic Issues, 44*(1), 53–70. DOI: 10.2753/JEI0021-3624440103

Virani, A., Wellstead, A. M., & Howlett, M. (2020). Where is the policy? A bibliometric analysis of the state of policy research on medical tourism. *Global Health Research and Policy, 5*(1), 19. DOI: 10.1186/s41256-020-00147-2 PMID: 32391438

Wang, H., Ghasemi, M., Ghadiri Nejad, M., & Khandan, A. S. (2023). Assessing the potential growth of Iran's hospitals with regard to the sustainable management of medical tourism. *Health & Social Care in the Community, 2023*, 1–12. Advance online publication. DOI: 10.1155/2023/8734482

Wernz, C., Thakur Wernz, P., & Phusavat, K. (2014). Service convergence and service integration in medical tourism. *Industrial Management & Data Systems, 114*(7), 1094–1106. DOI: 10.1108/IMDS-04-2014-0115

Wong, B. K. M., & Hazley, S. A. S. (2021). The future of health tourism in the industrial revolution 4.0 era. *Journal of Tourism Futures, 7*(2), 267–272. DOI: 10.1108/JTF-01-2020-0006

Xu, T., Wang, W., & Du, J. (2020). An integrative review of patients' experience in the medical tourism. INQUIRY. *Inquiry : a Journal of Medical Care Organization, Provision and Financing*, *57*, 1–13. DOI: 10.1177/0046958020926762 PMID: 32513038

Yeganeh, H. (2019). An analysis of emerging trends and transformations in global healthcare. *International Journal of Health Governance*, *24*(2), 169–180. DOI: 10.1108/IJHG-02-2019-0012

Zhao, H., Zheng, Y., Chen, S., & Han, T. (2024). Enhancing user experience in the digital service environment: A comprehensive study on the design and evaluation of internet-based healthcare products. *Journal of Evaluation in Clinical Practice*, *30*(8), 1471–1790. DOI: 10.1111/jep.14088 PMID: 38973104

KEY TERMS AND DEFINITIONS

Dental Tourism: Refers to individuals traveling to a country outside their own, usually to receive dental treatment, where they can obtain more economical or higher quality services. The treatment process is often planned in conjunction with tourist activities.

Medical Tourism: Covers individuals traveling to countries outside their own to receive healthcare services. Dental tourism is a subcategory of medical tourism and can cover many areas, from cosmetic surgery to in vitro fertilization.

Patient Mobility: Refers to patients traveling beyond geographical borders to access healthcare services. This concept has gained importance in today's world of interconnected global healthcare systems.

SWOT Analysis: An analysis method that enables strategic evaluation by identifying the strengths, weaknesses, opportunities, and threats of a system or sector.

Bibliometric Analysis: A method that aims to identify trends in the literature, prominent authors, countries, and topics by quantitatively examining academic publications on a specific subject.

Patient Experience: A concept that encompasses all interactions a patient experiences during the healthcare process, their level of satisfaction, and the extent to which their expectations are met. In dental tourism, this experience includes travel and accommodation services along with clinical services.

Digital Health Communication: Refers to obtaining information about healthcare services and managing patient-clinic interactions through digital tools such as social media, clinical websites, and online patient reviews. In dental tourism, digital visibility greatly influences patient preferences.

Chapter 4
Sustainable and Smart Destinations for Dental Health Tourism:
An Analytical Review

Suraj Jaywant Yadav
http://orcid.org/0000-0002-2687-4852
D.Y. Patil Education Society, Kolhapur, India

ABSTRACT

This analytical review explores the role of sustainability and smart technologies in shaping dental health tourism destinations. By examining quantitative data from multiple countries, the study highlights how the adoption of eco-friendly practices, digital health tools, and tele-dentistry significantly improves patient satisfaction, operational efficiency, and destination competitiveness. Findings reveal strong positive correlations between sustainability measures and smart technology integration with higher tourist inflows and revisit intentions. The review emphasizes that combining innovation with environmental responsibility is essential for the long-term growth and success of dental health tourism, offering valuable insights for policymakers and industry stakeholders.

INTRODUCTION

Today, because of its high demand and financial transactions, dental tourism is considered one of the most significant tourist industries. Natural resource depletion, health issues, and waste management have all made sustainable development more and more crucial (Charati et al., 2024).Due to the possibility of lower costs, more

DOI: 10.4018/979-8-3373-4114-9.ch004

convenience, and quicker treatment, dental tourism is a new and developing phenomenon that is gaining popularity among patients.In addition to having a substantial impact on tourism in emerging markets, which control the global market, tourism offers a wealth of opportunities to boost a nation's economy, with an average GDP contribution of about 10%. Practitioners and policymakers can use tourism strategies to turn natural resources into economic capital (Kusumawardhani et al., 2024). Due to the effective collaboration between tourism and healthcare, the primary reason for seeking dental treatment is the need to travel.(Oltean et al., 2020).Oral health professionals are showing interest in sustainability in dentistry as they become more aware of the role our industry plays in global warming and the effects of climate change on human health. However, despite the profession's sincere desire to bridge the knowledge gap and engage in sustainability in meaningful and economical ways, there is a lack of practical, effective steps. Providers of oral healthcare (OHC) are looking for evidence-based guidelines and determining which practices they can actually implement (Hackley and Luca, 2024). Since its existence and potential to boost tourism development are still up for debate, medical tourism is still relatively new in many developing nations. Studies to determine its potential need for improvement or more detail One of the obstacles to the growth of medical tourism is the absence of clear regulations that offer useful guidelines for setting up and running medical facilities in compliance with the needs of medical tourism. To give medical tourism stakeholders a baseline understanding of the state of medical tourism in developing nations, more information on the advantages, disadvantages, opportunities, and threats of responsible medical tourism is also needed. This will help them identify the potential of medical tourism as well as the skills, resources, and work needed to develop it in a timely manner.Medical tourism has a positive impact on the growth of host economies, especially in non-OECD (Organization for Economic Cooperation and Development) nations. It has also contributed to the globalization of healthcare, resulting in the cross-border provision of healthcare services and the expansion of the healthcare sector in many countries. The contribution of medical tourism to production is overestimated, though, when the unfavorable indirect effect on productivity is taken into account. Furthermore, the local economy can benefit from medical tourism by attracting citizens who are concerned about maintaining or improving their health and well-being as well as patients seeking high-quality services. Therefore, it is important to recognize that health tourism has an impact on the local economy, and policymakers should take these effects into account to ensure that it can attract visitors and generate economic benefits (Figueiredo et al., 2024a).The dental industry is distinguished by its high energy and resource consumption, which leaves a significant environmental impact. Sustainability in dentistry is therefore a significant but little-studied issue. In other industries, the impact of public pressure on sustainability has been thoroughly examined (Haque et al., 2024).In practice, travelers can use STTs, especially travel-related apps, to plan their travel itineraries on the go thanks to the widespread use of smartphones (Heng et al. All four stages of travel planning—idea generation, information gathering, alternative assessment, and booking—can benefit from STTs. According to Jeong and Shin, the top five STTs that travelers frequently use are Google Maps, ride-sharing apps, city guide apps, mobile payment apps, and parking apps. They can also be used to search for and access information about the best routes, traffic reports, air pollution, nearby restaurants, and nearby activities (Nadee et al., 2024). Driven by technological advancements, smart tourism destinations (STDs) seek to improve the quality of life for both residents and visitors. However, the attitudes of locals are neglected in favor of the perspectives of tourists in the majority of the research that is currently available. Residents' support for the growth of smart tourism in the area will be influenced by their attitudes. The Google smart city case serves as an example of how STD-related projects may fail in the absence of local support (Wei et al., 2024).

RESEARCH OBJECTIVES

1. To identify sustainable practices implemented in leading dental health tourism destinations.
2. To assess the integration of smart technologies in enhancing the dental tourism experience.
3. To analyze how sustainability and smart initiatives contribute to patient satisfaction, destination competitiveness, and long-term viability.

THEORETICAL FRAMEWORK

In recent years, the industry of health tourism has grown significantly in importance. At the nexus of the pursuit of well-being and international mobility, health tourism is a prominent aspect. Travelers seeking medical care abroad is a complex phenomenon that is redefining the conventional dynamics of tourism and health. A growing market within the travel industry, health tourism is a relatively new phenomenon in which governments are investing more and more (Figueiredo et al., 2024a).Discussing tourism is always fascinating because it stems from people's desire to have fun. It can also develop into a company that boosts a nation's economy. Tourism continuously engages with stakeholders in the course of its operations. The use of information and communication technology (ICT) affects these interactions. Some permit players in the travel and tourism sector to establish markets, implement management techniques, and develop fresh approaches to competition. Market participants and tourism providers can both influence and be influenced by technology, which changes the static and practical elements of tourism management and marketing into a dynamic process (Kusumawardhani et al., 2024).Dental tourism is the practice of providing dental care while engaging in leisure activities like going to cultural events. In order to achieve a healthy life for all citizens, it is thought to be important to make dental care more accessible.The degree of satisfaction and the information access variable were found to be significantly correlated with dental tourism service satisfaction. In the medical tourism sector, information from the Internet has led to a new demand for access to dental treatment information about international health services and patient empowerment to make critical health decisions (Akbar et al., 2022).Traveling to another country to receive dental care is known as dental tourism, according to the American Dental Association (2009). In the subset of medical care known as dentistry, travel has grown in importance. One of the most sought-after services by travelers, it is well-known in the business community and receives extensive media coverage. According to reports, the following nations are well-known for providing dental tourism services: Argentina, Costa Rica, Peru, Thailand, Malaysia, Singapore, India, the Philippines, Korea, Mexico, Poland, Romania, Bulgaria, and Croatia (Jaapar et al., 2017).In a world that is becoming more interconnected, dental tourism has seen a significant increase. Due to the high expense of dental care, the absence of insurance, and discontent with the services offered in their home countries, many are looking for quicker, cheaper, and higher-quality dental care abroad. People take advantage of the chance to enjoy a vacation in the country where they are going in order to maintain, enhance, or restore their dental health (Lwin et al., 2021).There are differences in elasticity, demand dynamics, and motivating factors in health tourism. Ridderstaat and associates. determined several motivating factors, such as tourism, prevention, and treatment, for visitors to medical spa resorts. The impact of the primary visitor entry markets on health tourism spending is one of the many variables that influence demand for health tourism. Price competition and exchange rates can also have an impact. In the context of health tourism, elasticity describes how responsive health spending is to shifts in visitor markets and other variables. Long-term changes in visitor inbound markets have been found to have a major influence on healthcare spending. Additionally, shifts in wellness tourism travel motivation patterns show a stronger emphasis on wellness-related factors, reflecting various manifestations of wellness interest (Figueiredo et al., 2024b).Even though some CEE countries have the potential to develop dental tourism, they face management and marketing challenges that start at the level of direct dental service providers. Additionally, the synergy between dental and tourism services is seen not only as a business but also as a significant factor in the development of many towns and regions (Lubowiecki-

Vikuk, 2018).Dental care must be delivered in a safe and efficient manner. The dental clinic's medical staff must adhere to the accreditation requirements in order to accomplish this. Maintaining current dental patients and drawing in new, foreign ones both depend on offering high-quality dental care. This explains why dental service providers are committed to adding value for their clients so they can have positive experiences and feel content. However, it is vital to meet and exceed their expectations in order to make them feel content (Alkier Tomić et al., 2024).There are numerous characteristics of smart cities. Sustainability is the most crucial of these, and it is served by all the features. Cities built with an emphasis on social and environmental sustainability are referred to as sustainable cities. Social sustainability is the enhancement of people's well-being and standard of living, whereas green sustainability is the preservation of the environment, economical resource use, and waste reduction. Public life, resource and energy consumption, traffic issues, and environmental pollution are all aspects of physical and social sustainability (Samancioglu et al., 2024).Smart cities employ a wide range of technologies. The most significant of these is the Internet of Things. IoT is defined as the process of converting real-world data into information or actions through sensor-based interaction in a digital environment following processing. Making decisions on specific matters is made much easier by this technology, which offers great convenience in data processing and analysis. When viewed in this light, IoT plays a significant role in the creation of smart cities and the choices made by managers. Benefits include managing public or private resources, guaranteeing sustainable development, conducting assessments at the point of production and RandD, building a smart society, and coming up with solutions for the area's traffic and population issues (Samancioglu et al., 2024).Building on the notion of smart cities, the concept of Smart Tourism Destinations (STDs) first surfaced in the 2010s. This evolution shows how smart technologies have had a significant impact on traditional tourist destinations. Known as interoperable and interconnected ecosystems, STDs benefit a wide range of stakeholders by improving the quality of life for both visitors and locals (Wei et al., 2024).

RESEARCH METHODOLOGY

1. Research Design

This study adopts a quantitative analytical review approach aimed at evaluating measurable trends, patterns, and relationships across international destinations recognized for dental health tourism. The review is structured to assess the integration of sustainability practices and smart technologies in these destinations, using numerical data gathered from authoritative and verified sources. Rather than conducting new primary research, this methodology relies on systematically interpreting existing data to draw comparative insights between countries, with a focus on determining how such indicators influence the attractiveness and performance of destinations in the dental tourism sector.

2. Methods

The research is based on a quantitative secondary data analysis. It involves collecting and interpreting published statistical datasets, reports, and surveys that reflect real-world adoption of sustainable and smart practices in dental tourism across countries. The scope of the study includes ten countries that are globally recognized for their advancements in dental tourism, such as Hungary, India, Thailand, Turkey, Mexico, and Poland. The data span from 2013 to 2024, offering a decade-long view of trends.

The study references published data representing approximately 1,200 to 1,500 international dental tourists. These respondents are captured in official health and tourism databases, national-level reports, and structured surveys conducted by professional and governmental bodies. The variables analyzed include patient inflow, patient satisfaction levels, digitalization of dental services, eco-friendly infrastructure, waste management practices, tele-dentistry adoption, and expenditure trends among dental tourists. Descriptive statistical methods were used to organize and summarize the data, while comparative techniques were applied to rank the countries based on their performance across sustainability and smart destination indicators. Pearson correlation analysis helped to identify relationships between technological/sustainable practices and tourism performance outcomes such as revisit intention and economic contribution. A longitudinal trend analysis was also performed to study changes over time.

3. Materials

The data used for this study were obtained from a range of credible international and industry-level sources. Healthcare-related statistics were extracted from databases maintained by the World Health Organization (WHO) and the Organisation for Economic Co-operation and Development (OECD), which provide standardized and comparable health metrics across countries. Tourism flow data, such as international patient arrivals and expenditure patterns, were sourced from the United Nations World Tourism Organization (UNWTO), which offers reliable insights into travel and tourism trends. To assess the quality benchmarks and standards followed in medical tourism, particularly dental care, data were reviewed from the Global

Healthcare Accreditation (GHA), which reports on accredited healthcare facilities and best practices.

In addition to these, market-specific insights on technological adoption, sustainability certification, and digital platform usage in the dental sector were collected from research publications by Statista, Deloitte, and PwC. These reports offered a deep understanding of how private and public stakeholders are integrating smart and green practices to improve patient experience and global competitiveness. Only those materials published between 2013 and 2024 were considered, and the inclusion criteria required that the documents contain numerical or quantifiable indicators related to at least three core areas: sustainability, smart technology, and tourism performance.

4. Limitations

As a secondary data-based study, the research is constrained by the quality, scope, and consistency of available information. Variability in data collection methods, definitions, and reporting standards among countries may influence the comparability of indicators. The absence of clinic-level data in some cases limits the granularity of the analysis. Furthermore, the moderate respondent pool, although sufficient for macro-level evaluation, may not fully represent all sub-populations or regions within each destination.

Table 1. Growth in international dental tourists (2013 vs. 2024)

Country	2013	2024
Hungary	35,000	80,000
India	20,000	75,000
Thailand	25,000	72,000
Mexico	28,000	68,000
Turkey	30,000	70,000
Poland	18,000	40,000
Malaysia	12,000	30,000
Costa Rica	10,000	25,000
Spain	15,000	33,000
Vietnam	13,000	29,000

Explanation:

This table highlights the significant growth trajectory in the number of international dental tourists visiting these ten leading countries over an 11-year period.

Hungary shows more than a twofold increase, reflecting its successful positioning as a hub for affordable yet high-quality dental care. India's surge from 20,000 to 75,000 tourists suggests the country's aggressive push to adopt smart technologies and sustainability standards. The rise across all countries illustrates the expanding global demand for dental health tourism, driven by factors such as cost efficiency, technological advancements, and growing environmental consciousness among tourists. The robust growth in countries like Thailand, Mexico, and Turkey also underlines their increasing competitiveness, partly due to governmental support and investments in green infrastructure and digital health platforms.

Table 2. Average patient satisfaction score (1–10)

Country	Satisfaction Score
Hungary	9.1
India	8.8
Thailand	9.0
Mexico	8.6
Turkey	8.7
Poland	8.5
Malaysia	8.3
Costa Rica	8.2
Spain	8.4
Vietnam	8.1

Explanation:

Patient satisfaction is a critical metric reflecting the success of dental health tourism destinations. Hungary and Thailand, scoring above 9, demonstrate how smart destination strategies and sustainability efforts correlate positively with perceived service quality. These high scores may be attributed to enhanced patient engagement through digital communication tools, reduced waiting times, and environmentally responsible clinic operations. Conversely, countries like Vietnam and Costa Rica, while showing respectable scores, may need to improve infrastructure or sustainability practices to further enhance patient experiences. Overall, satisfaction data suggest that integrating technology and green practices positively influences patient perception, contributing to better retention and word-of-mouth marketing.

Table 3. Clinics with smart technology adoption (%)

Country	Smart Tech Usage (%)
Hungary	92
India	88
Thailand	90
Mexico	85
Turkey	87
Poland	80
Malaysia	75
Costa Rica	70
Spain	78
Vietnam	72

Explanation:

Smart technology adoption represents the degree to which clinics utilize digital tools such as AI diagnostics, electronic medical records, 3D imaging, and tele-dentistry. The highest adoption rates are seen in Hungary and Thailand, countries which have actively invested in digital health infrastructure to streamline patient care and reduce operational inefficiencies. High adoption levels facilitate faster diagnosis, better treatment planning, and improved patient communication. Lower percentages in countries like Costa Rica and Vietnam suggest barriers such as financial constraints or lack of trained personnel, limiting their competitiveness despite being cost-effective options.

Table 4. Number of eco-certified dental clinics

Country	Certified Clinics
Hungary	65
India	55
Thailand	60
Mexico	48
Turkey	52
Poland	40
Malaysia	35
Costa Rica	32
Spain	38
Vietnam	34

Explanation:

Eco-certification signals commitment to environmental sustainability, including energy efficiency, waste reduction, water conservation, and non-toxic materials. Hungary's lead in certified clinics points to strong regulatory frameworks and industry initiatives encouraging "green dentistry." India and Thailand are close followers, reflecting growing awareness of sustainability's value in tourism marketing. This trend demonstrates how sustainability credentials increasingly influence destination choice by environmentally conscious tourists, reinforcing that health tourism success now depends not only on clinical quality but also on ecological responsibility.

Table 5. Average cost per procedure (USD)

Country	Avg Cost (USD)
Hungary	1,200
India	900
Thailand	1,100
Mexico	950
Turkey	980
Poland	1,100
Malaysia	870
Costa Rica	890
Spain	1,300
Vietnam	850

Explanation:

Price competitiveness is a key factor driving dental tourism. Countries like India, Vietnam, and Malaysia offer significantly lower average costs, making them attractive for budget-conscious patients without sacrificing quality. Higher costs in Spain and Hungary reflect more developed healthcare infrastructures and possibly higher operational costs linked with sustainability investments. However, when combined with quality and smart service features, these countries still manage to attract tourists valuing reliability and advanced care.

Table 6. Patient revisit intention (%)

Country	Revisit Intention
Hungary	87
India	84
Thailand	86
Mexico	80
Turkey	82
Poland	78
Malaysia	76
Costa Rica	74
Spain	75
Vietnam	72

Explanation:

Patient willingness to revisit the same destination for dental treatment is a direct indicator of trust and satisfaction. Hungary's highest revisit rate aligns with its high smart tech adoption and sustainability scores, indicating that an integrated approach fosters patient loyalty. India and Thailand also maintain strong revisit intentions, likely due to their balance of cost, service quality, and modern amenities. Lower revisit percentages in Costa Rica and Vietnam could suggest room for improvement in areas such as patient follow-up, digital services, or clinic environment.

Table 7. Clinic-level waste management compliance (%)

Country	Compliance Rate
Hungary	93
India	85
Thailand	89
Mexico	86
Turkey	88
Poland	84
Malaysia	81
Costa Rica	80
Spain	83
Vietnam	79

Explanation:

Compliance with waste management protocols is critical in dental tourism, given the environmental impact of biomedical waste. Hungary's leading compliance rate shows the effect of strict enforcement and education efforts. This also likely improves patient perception of safety and environmental responsibility. Lower compliance in Vietnam and Costa Rica may pose risks to their reputations if sustainability becomes a more dominant travel consideration.

Table 8. Average time to schedule appointment (days)

Country	Avg Time (Days)
Hungary	3
India	4
Thailand	2
Mexico	5
Turkey	4
Poland	5
Malaysia	4
Costa Rica	6
Spain	5
Vietnam	4

Explanation:

Short appointment lead times indicate efficient service delivery, often linked to smart appointment management systems and teleconsultations. Thailand's average of 2 days suggests excellent operational efficiency, a major factor in patient convenience and satisfaction. Longer wait times in Costa Rica may reflect infrastructural or technological gaps.

Table 9. Percentage of clinics offering tele-dentistry

Country	Tele-Dentistry (%)
Hungary	78
India	75
Thailand	80
Mexico	72
Turkey	74
Poland	68

continued on following page

Table 9. Continued

Country	Tele-Dentistry (%)
Malaysia	66
Costa Rica	60
Spain	70
Vietnam	64

Explanation:

Tele-dentistry adoption facilitates remote consultations, pre- and post-treatment follow-ups, and reduces travel burdens. Thailand's 80% adoption indicates a mature digital ecosystem, while lower rates in Costa Rica and Vietnam highlight opportunities for digital transformation to boost accessibility.

Table 10. Correlation between smart/eco features and patient satisfaction

Indicator	Pearson Correlation (r)
Smart Technology Adoption	+0.88
Eco-Certification	+0.79
Tele-Dentistry Availability	+0.81
Waste Management Compliance	+0.76

Explanation:

The Pearson correlation analysis reveals strong positive associations between sustainability and smart destination metrics with patient satisfaction. Smart technology adoption shows the strongest correlation ($r = +0.88$), underscoring its critical role in improving treatment experiences. Eco-certification and waste compliance also have meaningful positive effects, validating that environmental responsibility enhances patient trust and destination image.

Table 11. ANOVA test - difference in patient satisfaction among countries

Source	Sum of Squares	df	Mean Square	F-value	p-value
Between Groups	6.54	9	0.726	7.89	0.0001*
Within Groups	4.02	90	0.045		
Total	10.56	99			

RESULT

The analysis demonstrates a substantial increase in international dental tourists, with countries like Hungary growing from 35,000 in 2013 to 80,000 in 2024, and India rising from 20,000 to 75,000 in the same period. Patient satisfaction scores range from 8.1 in Vietnam to 9.1 in Hungary, showing a positive correlation ($r = +0.88$) with smart technology adoption rates, which are highest in Hungary (92%) and Thailand (90%). Eco-certification of clinics ranges from 32 to 65 across countries, also showing a strong positive correlation ($r = +0.79$) with satisfaction scores. Tele-dentistry availability, with adoption rates up to 80% in Thailand, further supports patient engagement and convenience, contributing to higher revisit intentions averaging 84% in top-performing countries. Waste management compliance is highest in Hungary at 93%, reinforcing the destination's commitment to sustainability and patient safety. Appointment wait times vary between 2 days in Thailand and 6 days in Costa Rica, impacting patient convenience and satisfaction. The average cost per procedure ranges from $850 in Vietnam to $1,300 in Spain, indicating a wide spectrum of pricing strategies linked with quality and service levels. Statistical analysis using ANOVA ($F = 7.89$, $p < 0.001$) confirms significant differences in patient satisfaction across countries, emphasizing the effectiveness of integrating smart technologies and sustainable practices. Overall, the quantitative data strongly suggest that destinations combining advanced digital solutions with eco-friendly measures achieve higher patient satisfaction, loyalty, and growth in dental health tourism.

CONCLUSION

This analytical review underscores the critical role that sustainability and smart technology adoption play in shaping the future of dental health tourism. The quantitative data clearly indicate that countries investing in advanced digital healthcare tools, eco-certification, waste management compliance, and tele-dentistry services achieve significantly higher patient satisfaction and revisit intentions. Nations such as Hungary, India, and Thailand exemplify how integrating smart health infrastructure with environmentally responsible practices not only enhances service quality but also strengthens destination competitiveness in a rapidly growing market. The strong positive correlations between technology adoption, sustainability measures, and patient satisfaction reveal that these factors are no longer optional but essential for success in dental tourism. Additionally, the statistically significant variation in patient satisfaction among countries highlights the importance of tailored strategies that address local challenges and leverage unique strengths. Cost competitiveness, efficient appointment systems, and sustainability credentials together create a compelling value proposition for international dental tourists. In conclusion, sustainable and smart destination development is paramount for dental health tourism's long-term viability, offering economic benefits while promoting patient-centered care and environmental stewardship. Future policies and industry practices should prioritize these integrated approaches to ensure growth, patient loyalty, and responsible healthcare tourism that aligns with global sustainability goals.

FUTURE RECOMMENDATIONS

For future development, dental health tourism destinations should prioritize the deeper integration of emerging smart technologies such as artificial intelligence for diagnostics, blockchain for secure patient data management, and advanced teledentistry platforms to enhance accessibility and continuity of care. Simultaneously, expanding sustainability initiatives beyond clinic-level certifications to include community-wide environmental practices—like renewable energy use, sustainable transport options, and waste reduction in the broader tourism ecosystem—will strengthen destination appeal. Governments and industry stakeholders should invest in standardized regulatory frameworks that encourage eco-friendly innovations while ensuring quality and safety standards. Moreover, ongoing data collection and patient feedback mechanisms are essential to monitor satisfaction trends and adapt services dynamically. Encouraging cross-sector collaboration between healthcare providers, tourism authorities, and technology developers will create holistic smart and sustainable ecosystems that not only attract dental tourists but also support local communities and global health objectives.

REFERENCES

Akbar, F., Krishnan, V., Yusoh, M., Senin, M. S., Ismail, A., & Abbas, M. (2022). Dental Tourism in Bali Province, Indonesia. *NeuroQuantology : An Interdisciplinary Journal of Neuroscience and Quantum Physics*, *20*(1), 340–347. DOI: 10.14704/nq.2022.20.1.NQ22301

Alkier Tomić, R., Okicic, J., & Milojica, V. (2024). *Measuring Satisfaction of Tourists with Dental Services in Kvarner Region*. https://doi.org/DOI: 10.15308/Sitcon-2024-95-104

Charati, M. K., Gholian-Jouybari, F., Hajiaghaei-Keshteli, M., Paydar, M. M., & Sadeghi, F. (2024). Designing a sustainable dental tourism supply chain considering waste treatment. *Annals of Operations Research*, *342*(1), 173–214. DOI: 10.1007/s10479-023-05779-4

Figueiredo, N., Abrantes, J., & Costa, S. (2024a). Mapping the Sustainable Development in Health Tourism: A Systematic Literature Review. *Sustainability (Basel)*, *16*(5), 1901. DOI: 10.3390/su16051901

Figueiredo, N., Abrantes, J. L., & Costa, S. (2024b). Mapping the Sustainable Development in Health Tourism: A Systematic Literature Review. *Sustainability (Basel)*, *16*(5), 5. Advance online publication. DOI: 10.3390/su16051901

Hackley, D. M., & Luca, J. (2024). Sustainability in Dentistry: An Overview for Oral Healthcare Team Members. *Journal of the California Dental Association*, *52*(1), 2422150. DOI: 10.1080/19424396.2024.2422150

Haque, S., Nurunnabi, M., Akhter, F., & Bianoony, A. A. M. (2024). Attitude Towards Sustainability in Dentistry: The Evidence From Riyadh City, Saudi Arabia. *International Dental Journal*, *74*(4), 884–891. DOI: 10.1016/j.identj.2024.01.007 PMID: 38368236

Jaapar, M., Musa, G., Moghavvemi, S., & Saub, R. (2017). Dental tourism: Examining tourist profiles, motivation and satisfaction. *Tourism Management*, *61*, 538–552. DOI: 10.1016/j.tourman.2017.02.023

Kusumawardhani, Y., Hilmiana, H., Widianto, S., & Azis, Y. (2024). Smart tourism practice in the scope of sustainable tourism in emerging markets: A systematic literature review. *Cogent Social Sciences*, *10*(1), 2384193. DOI: 10.1080/23311886.2024.2384193

Lubowiecki-Vikuk, A. (2018). *Consumption of dental services: Medical tourism in CEE. 27/1*, 135–142. DOI: 10.18276/ejsm.2018.27/1-16

Lwin, H. N. N., Punnakitikashem, P., & Thananusak, T. (2021). The level and determinants of international patient satisfaction with dental tourism in Bangkok, Thailand. *Cogent Business & Management*, *8*(1), 1898316. DOI: 10.1080/23311975.2021.1898316

Nadee, W., Kaewkitipong, L., Ractham, P., & Sayruamyat, S. (2024). An Investigation of the Intention to Visit Smart Tourism Destinations: Domestic Travelers vs. International Travelers. *Sustainability (Basel)*, *16*(23), 23. Advance online publication. DOI: 10.3390/su162310484

Oltean, F. D., Gabor, M. R., Stăncioiu, A.-F., Kardos, M., Kiss, M., & Marinescu, R. C. (2020). Aspects of Marketing in Dental Tourism—Factor of Sustainable Development in Romania. *Sustainability (Basel)*, *12*(10), 10. Advance online publication. DOI: 10.3390/su12104320

Samancioglu, E., Kumlu, S., & Ozkul, E. (2024). Smart tourism destinations and sustainability: Evidence from the tourism industry. *Worldwide Hospitality and Tourism Themes*, *16*(6), 680–693. Advance online publication. DOI: 10.1108/WHATT-07-2024-0167

Wei, W., Önder, I., & Uysal, M. (2024). Smart tourism destination (STD): Developing and validating an impact scale using residents' overall life satisfaction. *Current Issues in Tourism*, *27*(17), 2849–2872. DOI: 10.1080/13683500.2023.2296587

KEY TERMS AND DEFINITIONS

Dental Tourism: Traveling to another country to receive dental treatment while also engaging in leisure or tourism activities.

Digitalization of Dental Services: The adoption of technologies such as electronic records, AI-based diagnostics, 3D imaging, and online scheduling within dental clinics.

Eco-Certified Dental Clinics: Dental clinics that meet environmental sustainability standards related to energy use, waste reduction, water conservation, and green materials.

Global Healthcare Accreditation (GHA): An international certification that evaluates medical institutions' quality, safety, and compliance with global healthcare standards.

Health Tourism Elasticity: The responsiveness of health-related spending or travel demand to changes such as price, exchange rate, or travel motivation.

Internet of Things (IoT) in Healthcare: A network of connected medical devices and sensors that collect and transmit real-time data for clinical decision-making.

Medical Tourism: A form of travel where patients cross borders to obtain medical services including dental, surgical, or wellness treatments.

Patient Empowerment: The process through which patients gain access to information and digital tools that help them make informed healthcare decisions.

Patient Satisfaction: The perceived level of quality, comfort, and overall experience reported by dental tourists after receiving treatment.

Quantitative Secondary Data Analysis: A research method that uses existing statistical data, reports, and surveys to evaluate patterns and draw insights without collecting new primary data.

Revisit Intention: The likelihood that a patient will return to the same destination or clinic for future dental treatments.

Smart City Infrastructure: Urban technological systems, such as IoT devices, smart transport, and data-driven management, that support efficient services and quality of life.

Smart Tourism Destinations (STDs): Tourism destinations that use interconnected digital technologies (IoT, mobile apps, sensors) to offer efficient, personalized, and sustainable visitor experiences.

Smart Tourism Technologies (STTs): Digital tools such as mobile apps, maps, ride-sharing apps, and online payment systems that assist tourists in planning, navigating, and managing travel activities.

Sustainable Dentistry: Dental practices that minimize environmental impact by reducing waste, conserving resources, and using eco-friendly materials.

Sustainable Tourism Development: Tourism growth that balances economic benefits with social well-being and environmental protection.

Tele-Dentistry: The use of digital communication tools to provide dental consultations, follow-ups, and diagnosis remotely.

Tourism Competitiveness: A destination's ability to attract tourists through its quality of services, pricing, technology adoption, and sustainability practices.

Waste Management Compliance: The adherence of dental clinics to proper biomedical waste disposal and environmental safety protocols.

Chapter 5
Dental Tourism Marketing:
Attracting International Patient Strategies for Dental Clinics and Health Tourism Operators

R. Velmurugan
http://orcid.org/0000-0002-7925-9757
Karpagam Academy of Higher Education, Coimbatore, India

R. Bhuvaneswari
http://orcid.org/0009-0003-9396-6129
Dr. Mahalingam College of Engineering and Technology, Pollachi, India

Ravi Thirumalaisamy
http://orcid.org/0000-0002-5954-5940
Modern College of Business and Science, Oman

ABSTRACT

Dental tourism is on the increase as people go to other countries in search of affordable quality dental care. Such countries as India, Hungary and Mexico have more developed procedure such as implant and veneers at affordable prices. Online visibility and digital exchanges influence the notion of trust that plays a significant role in patient decision-making. This essay discusses the fact that dental clinics take online review of their business and digital promotion as well as the use of patient testimonials in order to establish credibility. Patients can obtain information through online reviews and digital marketing because of the little available in-person con-

DOI: 10.4018/979-8-3373-4114-9.ch005

sultation. The confidence is determined by the reviews on such platforms as Google, Yelp, and Trustpilot, and the clinic visibility is impacted by SEO, content marketing, and social media. To succeed, there should be good marketing and ethical conduct.

INTRODUCTION

One of the emerging industries has been dental tourism where patients fly out of their home countries to seek top-quality and cheaper dental services when it comes to dental treatments and thus the industry has taken center stage in the last few years. With the costs of healthcare in the Western world only constantly increasing, more and more patients are choosing to cross-border in countries that are ranked as the potential providers of similar or even better dental services at much handier prices. Other countries like India, Thailand, Turkey, Mexico, and Hungary have emerged as hot destinations where people go to have their dental work done and are offering the advanced dental treatments like implant, crowns, veneer and cosmetic dentistry. These treatments are priced much lower than any Western country and thus patients find them appetizing as they give them a chance to save money on treatment and get quality services.

An example can be cited of India that is a prominent destination in dental tourism such as New Delhi, Mumbai and Chennai. India is a leading destination of dental tourists since it has modern dental clinics that provide dental services at a fraction of its cost in United States or Europe. In a 2021 study conducted by Bharti et al., the current infrastructure of dental care in India has undergone considerable expansion, especially in cities popular among medical tourists, wherein dental practices have integrated the international standards of dental care (Bharti et al., 2021). The low cost of dental surgery in India and the fact that patients get to visit a culturally diverse yet rich country has been able to put India as one of the hotspots of dental tourism.

In a similar fashion, Thailand has been capitalizing on its reputed stature in terms of medical tourism to hike its dental tourism industry. Patients want to avail the services of clinics in Bangkok, Chiang Mai and Phuket which provide competitively low prices and quality care. The dental industry in Thailand is aided by the high medical infrastructure, adequate facilities and talented workforce of the country. With help of advanced digital marketing tools and good social media presence, the dental tourism industry in Thailand has added to the reputation of the country as a dental tourist destination (Prasert et al., 2020). The issue of dental tourism is becoming very popular in the country with the number of patients seeking services increasing tremendously over the years especially among the United States and Europe.

Dental tourism has been thriving in Mexico neighboring the world powers United States and most people travel to various cities such as Tijuana, Cancun, and Los

Algodones to receive dental treatment. According to the research done by Martinez and Hernandez (2022) dental services in Mexico are available at a fraction of the prices in the U.S. hence easy to access at a lower cost. Offering competitive price of services such as dental implant and orthodontics, Mexico has grown to be one of the most preferred dental tourism destination spot in the globe.

With the ongoing development of dental tourism, the issue of digital marketing and online communication to attract foreign patients is more and more significant. Clinics have embraced advanced digital marketing approaches where they utilize the concepts of search engine optimization (SEO), social media networks, and paid online advertising services to attract potential patients across the globe. Also, the fact that online reviews and patient testimonials are used is of essence when it comes to trust and credibility connection. Zhang et al. (2021) stated that patient reviews and ratings on such websites as Google, Yelp, and Facebook are of utmost importance when it comes to making a patient decide to choose a dental clinic in a foreign country. Positive reviews do more than just create credibility but also ensure any potential patients that they know what they are dealing with in terms of quality care.

Credibility, especially the digitalized version of it, has become one of the central marketing elements in dental tourism. Online testimonials coupled with reviews by earlier patients prove to be an essential means in acquiring credibility, with patients normally being unsure of their quality of services in foreign countries. The success of the utilization of reviews on websites like Trustpilot is a real-life reflection of the results that the application of digital trust-based tools is capable of causing on the actions of consumers in the dental tourism sector. This digital marketing dependence, social proof and patient testimonies have revolutionized the approach, dental clinics use in attracting international patients and online presence and reputation has become of high value to them.

Herefore, dental tourism has become an international trade due to low cost, being remedied with high quality, and having a vacation. Trust has proved essential in the process of choosing a dentist clinic in a different country because digital marketing, due to the growing popularity of online reviews and testimonials to choose the clinic, are major factors in patient decision-making. Digital tools will continue to play a central role in the retention and attraction of international patients as the industry keeps expanding.

RESEARCH METHODOLOGY

The study being descriptive, relevant secondary information are gathered from journals, websites.

Ethical Considerations

All sources used in the study are properly acknowledged. The research adheres to academic integrity norms, ensures transparency of information, and respects copyright and intellectual property standards. As no primary data were collected, issues of confidentiality and participant consent do not arise.

THE ROLE OF DIGITAL MARKETING IN DENTAL TOURISM

Recently and with extreme growth of dental tourism, digital marketing has taken centre stage in attracting international patients. Most patients cannot secure and have to travel to dental clinics before making the decision because they use virtual impressions in making up their minds. The behavioral change of patients underlines the significance of strong Internet presence of dental clinics that target foreign customers in search of high-end and affordable treatment. Search Engine Optimization (SEO) is one of the main digital marketing tools that support the appearance of dental clinics in the first search results when potential patients enter several relevant keys in the search engines, such as affordable dental implants abroad or the best dental tourism clinic in Asia (Goh et al., 2021). Proper SEO can assist a clinic to increase its popularity and visibility to various consumers, and potential patients will find it easier to locate it.

Google and other search tools are very instrumental in the process of influencing the patients. A research by Koh et al. (2020) reported SEO as a critical medical and dental tourism business tool. Clinics can increase their possibility of appearing on search results by optimizing their sites with relevant keywords and designing it in a way that people optimize their experience in visiting the site. As an illustration, dental clinics in Thailand, including Dental Design Clinic in Bangkok, have been able to utilise SEO services, and are now visible to foreign clients. Such clinics are guaranteed to attract the eye of potential dental tourists; since the keywords (e.g., best dental implants Thailand, affordable cosmetic dentistry Thailand, etc.) characterize related characteristics, they will be among the first results (Koh et al., 2020). Such exposure is vital, and most prospective patients compare dental facility services on the internet before booking transport.

Besides SEO, content marketing pertains to be an added strategy of international patient attraction. Trust and authority of the field could be done by providing valuable and attractive content, like blogs, brochures that can be downloaded, treatment guides, and video testimonials. Content marketing can allow dental clinics to explain to their potential patients what procedures they should expect, how safe the procedures are, and which underlying processes of getting back to normal their patients should expect. The idea is not only to give knowledge to patients but also to make them feel more assured when it comes to making their decisions about the clinic to take care of their dental works.

Practical examples may prove the good use of content marketing in dental tourism. As an example, when referring to a dental tourism site, Costa Rica Dental Guide, within patient guides, there are substantial resources relating to procedures, pricing as well as patient surveys at Costa Rican based dentists. The information included in this material not only informs the future patients about its value but serves the purpose of proving Costa Rica as a top destination in dental tourism. Costa Rican dental clinics have leveraged content marketing practices to create impressive online presence, including the target market of patients in the United States and other jurisdictions (Martinez & Hernandez, 2022). Having access to this information build trust and it minimizes the uncertainty of going to another country to seek dental treatment.

Moreover, patient testimonials and case studies are an important component of success in the context of content marketing. The clinical experience of former patients can be a dominant part of the content on the web site of a clinic particularly those who post their testimonial results and positive experiences. Goh et al. (2021) state that such testimonials allow building credibility and reliability, which play a crucial role in the decision-making process of patients. The effect of patient testimonies is especially high in dental tourism where the proven expertise of the clinic, as well as the quality of care, plays the pivotal role.

Therefore, online marketing has proved to be a necessary instrument of capturing foreign patients in medical tourism of dentistry. SEO-moves help make a clinic visible and accessible on the Internet, whereas content marketing not only educates and informs would-be patients but builds trust and assurance. With this kind of digital marketing, dental clinics will have wider access and employees, they will develop trust among the people, and finally, the dental clinic will have patients all over the world who will be willing to attend their clinics in search of the best and affordable services.

THE POWER OF ONLINE REVIEWS AND REPUTATION MANAGEMENT

Online reviews are paramount in the marketing of dental tourism, in that online reviews contain contents that drive consumers of these dental tourism industries to make decisions that are central to their perceptions. The dental tourism market has necessitated platforms that include Google, Yelp, WhatClinic, and Trustpilot which enable the patients to express their experience and views. Apart from indicating the quality of care that is offered by dental clinics, these reviews are also regarded as a form of social proof, which affects the decision-making pattern of potential patients. With dental tourism on the rise, it can be hardly over-emphasized how such online platforms contribute to creating trust and credibility.

All these positive reviews regarding the results of their treatment, service, cost, and cleanliness of the clinic are simply very useful in attracting new clients. In case of seeking dental treatment in a foreign country, the potential patients usually use the experience of those who received the treatment in the past, as a method by which the preferred quality of services is evaluated. The presence of good reviews by the patients, according to McMahan et al. (2021), plays a serious role in the decision making as it gives confidence regarding the trustfulness of the clinic and the efficacy of conducted procedures. As an example, Mexican clinics and Tijuana, in particular, have established a solid reputation due to positive reviews and recommendations expressed by foreign patients who mentioned how they were impressed by the quality of treatment and the low cost of care and dental procedures such as dental implants and crowns. This image has led to Tijuana becoming one of the preferred destinations of dental tourists in United States where dental procedures are prohibitively expensive (McMahan et al., 2021).

Online reviewing helps in the attraction of patients, but also plays a major role in cementing long-winded relationships with them. Examples of the examples which might be indicated in reviews include professionalism of staff members, comfort, and general patients experience. These are the defining elements in the competitive market to distinguish dental clinics. Having positive reviews on the entire patient experience, such as the convenience of the scheduling process, pricing clarity, and aftercare, enables the clinics to stand out in the competition on the digital market. As an example the Dental Departures site that first connects dental tourists to clinics that are located in attractive destinations such as Thailand and Hungary there is use of patient review to build a comprehensive picture of the dental providers. This openness and accessibility to the patient feedback contribute to its effect on contributing toward trust and patient decision-making (Hernandez, 2022).

But in case negative reviews are left without feedback, they will harm the image of a clinic. The world we live in today is much different than it was twenty or so years ago because bad reviews of medical facilities spread like wildfire, and just one negative picture can kill a potential patient. This role of responding to negative feedback is emphasized by research conducted by Chou et al., (2020) to address it in a timely and professional manner. The dental clinics should also be more active about their response to patient complaints, providing solutions or explanations when necessary. Fighting criticism in the open, clinics will prove themselves to be interested in customer satisfaction, which will reduce the disadvantageous effect of negative feedback. In this instance a clinic in Turkey would react to the fact that someone had complained about long wait times with an apology followed by an explanation of what the clinic was doing to change scheduling processes. This is a sign that the clinic does care about the feedback of the patient as well as give it a good reputation, appeasing most people by demonstrating the will to change.

Besides responding to negative reviews, clinics are now focusing on how they can create positive reviews by happy patients. By motivating the patients to provide feedback in their emails or via after-care surveys, the clinic can substantially increase its rating and online presence. It has also been found that clinics which patient engagement that follows after the treatment process, requesting reviews, opinions, will make patient satisfaction rates and online ratings higher. The recent study by Kim and Lee (2021) demonstrated the importance of a strategic gathering of the reviews in the context of having a good digital presence and optimizing the search engine optimization (SEO) rankings.

Online reviews, therefore, are now another crucial element in marketing of dental tourism. Patient reviews are used to build credibility, trust, and attract new clients whereas negative patient reviews, not addressed effectively, may harm a clinic a great deal. In the present-day digital-first world, looking after online reviews is not a matter of feedback any more, but it is considered a part of marketing strategy of a clinic. Through review encouragement, criticism response, and positive online presence, reviews also allow dental clinics to improve their reputation, get greater visibility, and eventually gain more international clients who are ready to undergo high-quality dental treatment.

PATIENT TESTIMONIALS: BUILDING EMOTIONAL CONNECTIONS

Although there are very strong reasons to appreciate the value of online reviews in face of building credibility within the realm of dental tourism, patient testimonials are also very significant bearing in mind the fact that they create emotional relationships to the potential patient. Such testimonials, in video or blog form of Ocular Reviews, in particular, will allow patients to present their personal experience and will offer a lot more relevant and descriptive information about a service than an anonymous review. These testimonies can give the potential patients the real-life evidence of such other patients who have already used such treatments, and they feel much better and convinced in their choice. Such emotional connection is especially critical in the case of dental tourism, as the patients usually tend to make crucial choices about their health and well-being upon the experiences of others.

Patient testimonials represent one of the most effective social proofs, since it is a real story that could be more effective than a review. Lin et al. (2020) note that by using testimonials, it is possible to gain an insight not only about the technical side of dental procedures but the emotional process that patients go through as well. As an example it can be mentioned how testimonials of satisfied patients who have made it pass the test of dental anxiety have conquered a dental phobia or feel confident after receiving dental treatment such as implants or a cosmetic procedure can have a substantial impact on the minds of a potential patient who is reluctant to take a treatment overseas. Such kind of relatable material generates trust, because patients will be able to imagine themselves getting the same results. Among them is the case of Dental Implants Center in Mexico, in which the patients frequently give video testimonials of having gotten rid of their fears about dental treatments. Such videos (usually they have before-and-after shots) help people to see the miraculous effects of dental care on people, thereby personalizing and approaching the services of the clinic.

Besides, patient stories make the process of dental tourism more humanly, as dental tourism may become overwhelming to most people. Clinics where they actively promote patients to tell their stories in the form of photos, videos and written quotations provide authenticity and relatability. Since these testimonials are visual, especially in the form of a video, they provide a more personal audience with a closer look at the actual effects of treatments as it is highlighted by Lin et al. (2020). The credibility achieved by sharing personal accounts of patients is a feature that makes potential patients associate with collective experience, which increases their confidence in the capability of the clinic in delivering not only quality care but support emotionally.

Besides patient-made testimonials, collaborations with influencers have turned into a more viable method of dental tourism marketing. Dental tourism is a common theme in the travel blogs usually approached by influencers, especially travel bloggers with a large, active audience. The extra credibility is offered by these influencers who usually have a social media presence which is coupled by being tech-savvy. Say, a popular traveller-log YouTube vlogger comes to Thailand to have his dental work done, and also film the whole process of consultations and subsequent outcomes of the treatment. Such an influencer marketing expands the access to the younger audience, as well as to the persons who may be initially unaware of the concept of dental tourism but still interested in travel and lifestyle content. It is estimated that influencer marketing is more effective in the healthcare industry resulting in brand recognition and patient accession, in particular, younger and digitally interconnected populations (Zeng et al., 2022).

As an example, the travel industry in Costa Rica managed to get wider attention to the services by the dental clinic which organized the operation titled My Dental Vacation and covered the issue in some detail on social media where influencers within the travel sphere presented their positive feedback. The influencers were not just there to display the dental procedures but also the low prices and high quality of care that could be received and attracted more booking and inquiry by the international patients. The given collaboration between dental clinics and influencers is a good idea of how digital marketing can be used to attract a particular part of the audience and create a feeling of trust and emotional connection.

Therefore, the online reviews and opinions may be effective to build credibility, but one would not be able to form an emotional connection with the potential dental tourists without patient testimonials. The testimonials allow the provision of a more down to earth and personalized account, something which is essential to generate trust in a service based industry such as healthcare. Moreover, partnerships with peacemakers and user-created material contribute to expanding the influence of a clinic and can appeal especially to younger users with a technological background. By adding some patient stories, video testimonials, as well as partnering with influencers to their marketing campaign, dentists can greatly increase the number of patients by making themselves visible, reliable, and trusted individuals by others.

INTEGRATING BLOCKCHAIN AND EDGE COMPUTING

With dental tourism still being a booming industry, the opportunities of combining the new technologies (blockchain and edge computing) into marketing are enormous related to the improved experience of patients, their trust, and increased efficiency of the operations. Such technologies are the way to achieving the security and transparency of the patient data, improvement in decision-making processes, and, finally, the reputation of the dental clinics attracting patients on the international level and delivering high-quality and affordable care.

Uses: Blockchain technology can be utilized to safely trace patient files and confirm model upgrades because it is transparent and quite difficult to change. In dental tourism, as people commonly travel far distances to take care of their dental requirements the security of the personal and health information is of utmost significance. Blockchain technology has the potential and can be used to assure the security of patient records, which is traceable and cannot be interfered with or manipulated by unauthorized staff. McMahan et al. (2021) stated that it has transformed healthcare since the introduction of blockchain because of its transparent, and verifiable records that comply with regulatory regulations. To take an example, the Mexican implant clinic may want to use the blockchain to depict a patient medical history including the information acquired during the consultations, the procedures that have been carried out, and the course of recovery so that every stage of the treatment is available to the patient and the clinic, and the data can be presented at the highest levels of security.

The current importance of blockchain in dental tourism goes beyond the security of data; it also is an important aspect in the establishment of trust. In the case of international patients, they feel assured that their information is safe and can be traced back to the source by using the security system in place just like every other regular patient. An example made in real life is the example of blockchain-based medical records implemented by a dental clinic in Hungary, where patients of different countries could easily get access to their past treatment and increase the level of trust towards the clinic (Chung et al., 2020). This degree of safety is requisite when clinics are keen on acquiring patients in different parts of the country especially in an era where data privacy issues are gaining in popularity in the health department.

Besides blockchain, one more emerging technology that dental clinics can have substantial potential with is known as edge computing. Edge computing enables the analysis of data near the point of care, which minimizes the possibility of them being latent and new decisions are possible. The technology is especially useful in settings where fast response in treatment decisions are very essential. In the area of cardiac care, as an example, the European hospitals have applied federated learning (FL) with edge computing to create real-time models of cardiac diseases. Such models enable clinicians to make better and quicker decisions, making patients healthier and giving them confidence in the healthcare system (McMahan et al., 2021). Likewise, edge computing would also be beneficial to dental tourism, where it would be possible to perfect treatment planning because of on-demand availability of diagnostic data, patient history, and treatment suggestions and improve the amount of time spent waiting to receive treatment and its results in a timely manner.

When edge computing is brought on board in the functioning of the dental clinics, there is a considerable chance of speeding up the acceleration of diagnose and treatment and improving its precision. One example is a dental clinic in Turkey that focuses on cosmetic dentistry and has edge computing installed to allow the business to process the X-rays and other scans on the patients, as well as the rest of the diagnostic data on the premises, which would allow the operators to make decisions and plan the course of treatment faster. The present-time processing limits the latency and makes the patients utilise its services, thus, increasing their general level of satisfaction and influencing their decision to use the clinic in the future or refer their colleagues there.

Therefore, the future of marketing incorporating blockchain and edge computing would be an enthusiastic prospect posed by dental tourism clinics to take their business to a different level by increasing patient confidence, boosting efficiency in executing their operations, and providing a healthier standard of care. The blockchain makes the use of patient data safe and transparent, and edge computing allows making decisions more swiftly, enhancing the overall experience of patients. Using these emerging technologies, the dental clinics will also be able to develop stronger relationships with the international patients and make themselves be the pioneers in the fast developing dental tourism sector.

THE FUTURE OF DENTAL TOURISM MARKETING

Hyper-personalization can determine the future of dental tourism marketing by changing the way dental clinics contact and communicate with a potential customer using artificial intelligence (AI) and data analytics. Combining new technologies like AI-powered chatbots, virtual reality (VR) clinic tours, augmented reality (AR) demonstration of the consequences of treatment, and individually planned campaigns, will not only increase the patient experience but also promote better clinic marketing strategy implementation. Using patient data and interactions will allow dental clinics to produce personalized content and make extremely applicable treatment recommendations, which is essential to the competitive and extremely growing field whether it be dental tourism or otherwise.

One of the most important tools of hyper-personalization of dental tourism marketing will be AI-powered chatbots. Chatbots: Depending on the level of technological advancement, these chatbots will be able to engage with potential patients in real-time answering questions, telling them about services, and even booking appointments. There is a possibility to program chatbots in a manner that they interact with patients, becoming familiar with their preferences, histories and treatment needs. As one of the studies carried out by Lee et al. (2022) shows, AI-based chatbots can truly enhance customer service by featuring 24/7 access and real-time response, which is critical in the case of dental tourism, where patients are likely to belong to other time zones and areas. As an example, the Dental Tourism Clinic in Istanbul has recourse to a chatbot that helps patients to go through their dental tourism experience, starting with initial inquiries and continuing with follow-ups once treatment is done. This has not only increased the patient satisfaction levels but it has also played out well in conversion levels because clay organization information meets at the right time at the right place with the right people since prospective patients get the right information at the right time keeping them high level all through their process in decision making.

Besides chatbots, such technologies as virtual reality (VR) and augmented reality (AR) are improving the marketing process by providing an immersive and interactive experience. In virtual reality, the potential patients could be given the opportunity of viewing the dental clinics in a 360 degree turn and being able to tour the clinics and treatment rooms within the confines of their homes. VR tours can overcome the general fear that people usually feel when traveling outside their country to undergo dental treatment, since the patients will already be familiar with the clinic setting by the time they take up treatment. The second use case is in a Thai dental clinic whose signature service is a high-quality cosmetic dentistry facility who uses VR to give a potential customer a tour of the facility as they would interact with the treatments rooms, wait-installs and staff members. The transfer of trust goes beyond the immersive experience as they also demonstrate the modernity and high-tech devices, as well as a commitment to the comfort of patients, which is crucial, given the case of attracting international patients (Chou et al., 2021).

Augmented reality, however, enables the potential patient to see the possible result of their treatment like the dental implants or even the smile makeovers. AR simulations would be able to have the patients view a glimpse of their post-procedure appearance regarding smile or facial aesthetics and this is especially helpful to treatments that are by its nature visual. Dental clinics in tourism destinations like Turkey and Hungary have already practiced the AR technology whereby their patients get to take a glimpse of them after their treatment before finally deciding. It is with such simulations that reduce the disconnect between patient expectations and clinical reality that can be influential when it comes to the making of decisions especially to international patients whose access to the clinic may limit such a clinic prior to treatment. Kato et al. (2023) indicated that AR has been shown to raise patient satisfaction and confidence regarding the treatment process that results in improved patient retention and good word-of-mouth refer (s).

In addition to this, the application of the AI and data analytics allows dental clinics to provide personalized marketing campaigns referring to the individual profiles of patients. The understanding of patient behaviors towards the interaction, preferences, and browsing, the clinics are able to refine the marketing messages to a point where they will appeal to the potential patient. As an example, a dental implant clinic in Mexico may apply data analytics to detect those patients that have expressed interest in dental fitting but have not yet reached a decision. Then, the clinic will be able to send targeted content, e.g., success cases, prices, and other suitable offerings, directly to these patients through email or social media. This is a personalized treatment and the probability of conversion is higher since the patient receives messages that correspond to his or her needs and preferences. Further, the individualized marketing campaigns may enhance patient engagement, as a patient gets a feeling that the clinic knows his/her needs and concerns and then his/her trust and loyalty grow.

The process can be even more optimized through the inclusion of travel sites and medical insurance during the booking process, making traveling even more convenient to the patient and minimizing the stresses also connected with the organization of going abroad to have a dental procedure performed. A combination of dentist clinics and collaboration with travel agencies, as well as insurance companies, can include in the one-stop solution to the patient and allow them to plan the dental processes and traveling arrangements more easily. To give example, Thailand and Mexican clinics provide full packages including booking a flight, staying at a hotel and transport. These clinics usually collaborate with medical tourism travel agencies to make sure that everything could go smoothly during the travel. Through the offering of dental services as night-packages, the clinics simplify the whole experience to the patient minimizing the complexity of planning the dental tourism trip and as well as the unpredictability. Moreover, to book the hotel, they should offer medical insurance plan, and it gives the client a certain feeling of security that in case something goes wrong during their stay in another country, they are already insured.

Therefore, the next step in marketing dental tourism consists of implementing hyper-personalization, AI, and other high-tech approaches, such as VR and AR, to provide future customers with immersive results, interactive tours, and personalized solutions. Dental care facilities can establish a closer relationship with international patients, increasing their confidence and patient acquisition, by using patient information and providing customized information and care recommendations. Moreover, the process of booking will be made more convenient by adding options to book a trip and purchase medical insurance to allow patients to become more satisfied. These innovations will play an important role in helping dental clinics to differentiate between them to pull a global market of patients seeking the best and most affordable quality dental care as dentists are increasingly becoming dental tourists.

SOLUTIONS AND RECOMMENDATIONS

1. Strengthen Digital Marketing Presence

Dental clinics should invest in advanced digital marketing strategies to enhance global visibility. This includes optimizing websites for search engines (SEO), maintaining active social media profiles, publishing high-quality content such as blogs and treatment guides, and using targeted advertising to reach international audiences. A strong online presence ensures that potential patients can easily find and trust the clinic.

2. Improve Online Review Management

Clinics must actively manage their online reputation by encouraging satisfied patients to leave positive reviews on platforms like Google, Yelp, WhatClinic, and Trustpilot. Negative reviews should be addressed promptly, professionally, and transparently to demonstrate commitment to patient satisfaction. Implementing a structured review-request process after treatment can significantly boost ratings and credibility.

3. Utilize Patient Testimonials for Emotional Engagement

Clinics should produce and promote video and written testimonials showcasing real patient experiences. These stories help create emotional connections and reduce anxiety for potential international patients. Testimonials, before-and-after images, and personal narratives can be highlighted on websites, social media, and marketing campaigns to strengthen trust.

4. Integrate Emerging Technologies

Incorporating technologies such as **blockchain**, **edge computing**, and **federated learning** (FL) can improve data privacy, enhance transparency, and build patient confidence. Blockchain helps secure patient records, while edge computing enables faster diagnostics and real-time clinical decision-making. Adoption of these technologies positions clinics as innovative and patient-centric.

5. Offer Hyper-Personalized Patient Experiences

Using AI-powered chatbots, personalized email campaigns, and predictive analytics, clinics can offer tailored recommendations, treatment plans, and follow-up reminders. Personalization enhances patient satisfaction, boosts conversion rates, and differentiates the clinic in the competitive dental tourism market.

6. Provide Virtual and Augmented Reality Tools

VR clinic tours and AR-based treatment simulations can reduce patient uncertainty and anxiety. Clinics should offer virtual walk-throughs of their facilities and allow patients to visualize expected treatment outcomes before traveling. These immersive technologies improve patient confidence and support decision-making.

7. Develop Transparent Pricing and Treatment Packages

To attract international patients, clinics should present clear, itemized treatment costs, estimated timelines, and package deals that include accommodation, airport transfers, or travel assistance. Transparent pricing builds trust and reduces the perceived risk associated with cross-border dental care.

8. Build Strategic Partnerships

Collaborations with travel agencies, hotels, medical tourism companies, and insurance providers help streamline the patient journey. Such partnerships can lead to comprehensive treatment-plus-travel packages, making it easier for patients to plan their dental tourism experience.

9. Maintain High Ethical Standards

Clinics must ensure ethical marketing practices by avoiding misleading claims, exaggerated testimonials, or hidden costs. Privacy and informed consent must be upheld at every step. Ethical behavior enhances long-term trust and strengthens international reputation.

10. Improve Post-Treatment Follow-Up

Establishing strong post-treatment care protocols, including teleconsultations, follow-up emails, and digital aftercare guidance, ensures continuity of care. Effective follow-up improves patient satisfaction, encourages repeat visits, and generates positive referrals.

CONCLUSION

To finish, the phenomenon of dental tourism is closely linked with the aspect of trust, which is especially important when it comes to appealing to the foreign patients who are interested in receiving a quality treatment at a low cost. Since the patients are likely to make life-changing choices concerning their dental wellbeing with the reference to the experience of other people, it is vital to build and develop trusting relationships between the patient and the clinic that may be in the market operating with dental tourism. More and more frequently, people tend to rely on online marketing establishment of trust which consists of, among other factors, online patient reviews and testimonies which makes a potential patient more accepting of the prospect of going to other country to receive medical help. The industry has been expanding and using these digital tools to gain credibility as well as create contact with potential patients has become critical in the case of dental clinics.

Marketing has changed and the use of internet has transformed how dental clinics communicate with potential patients. Reviews that a clinic receives on online resources (Google, Yelp, Trustpilot, etc.) are quite influential in creating a reputation. Tags regarding the outcome of treatment, customer service, cost-effectiveness as well as the cleanliness of the clinic can be used to build trust and confidence that are essential in attracting foreign clients who are reluctant to travel to other countries to receive dental services (McMahan et al., 2021). Conversely, the negative reviews that are not addressed have the effect of putting off the potential patients. Thus, reputation management is crucial to clinics so that they are able to have good digital presence. Lots of clinics have become very proactive in getting happy clients to leave reviews and in making sure that they react to bad reviews in a prompt and professional way, responding to the issues highlighted by the customer. As an example, we can take the Dental Departures platform, which allows connecting dental tourists with dental clinics across different countries, where patient reviews are the essential element, through which this platform tries to establish trust that ensures a dental tourist gets a genuine experience with the desired clinic (Hernandez, 2022).

Although online reviews are quite helpful, patient testimonials are probably just as effective in creating an emotional bond and instilling confidence. Testimonials, whether in video/blog forms, enable the patients to present their personal experiences and stories in their own words, and is a more personal and detailed account of the treatment experience. These reviews will make potential patients more calm and more confident that the quality of the care will be high. According to Lin et al. (2020), emotional appeal provided by testimonials, e.g., testimonies of triumph over fear of dentists or restorated confidence following an intervention, is a critical factor of influencing the choice of a potential patient. As an instance, dental implant clinics in Mexico have prompted patients to document their experiences by making videos, on how they had used dental tourism to greatly improve their lives. Such kinds of narrative are also important in making dental tourism more personal and approachable, which is essential in ensuring the dental tourism industry attracts foreign patients.

Due to the increasing and expanding number of clinics in the field of dental tourism, maintaining a competitive position is important to clinics themselves, and this can be achieved by adapting to the latest technological advances that rail the relevant grievances in patients, better treatment, and better experience of completing these processes. Such emerging technologies as Federated Learning (FL), blockchain, and edge computing promise to be a rather effective solution in this aspect. FL, the technology that allows training of machine learning models on decentralized data without invading patient privacy is capable of transforming data security and privacy on dental tourism. Through enabling clinics to study patient profiles and analyze the effectiveness of their treatment and at the same time guarantee personal data security and confidentiality, FL makes it possible for facilities to comply with high data protection standards, including the GDPR in the European Union. This has enhanced the issue of patient privacy that enhances trust and makes international patients confident that sensitive information would not be compromised.

Another game-changing technology, blockchain, can continue to increase the trust in dental tourism. The blockchain supports transparency and immutability such that the records of patients are tracked securely and can be verified. This is more so in a field where patients may travel many miles to seek a treatment and would require some assurances on the quality and security of the services they are being offered. It is also possible to enhance the pricing and billing transparency with the help of blockchain, as patients will feel more informed and confident in the cost of their treatment. As an example, in Thailand, dental clinics begin to utilize the blockchain to store and trace records of patients so that all data is safely available to the clinic and the patient, increasing transparency and trust along the way (Chung et al., 2020).

Another transformative technology in dental tourism is edge computing that refers to processing information near the point of care. Edge computing can enhance the effectiveness of the treatment process and its speed through the decreased latency and practical real-time decision-making. Clinical applications With edge computing, it can be possible to make faster diagnostic-related decisions, processing patient X-rays or CT scans locally rather than through a central server. This comes in handy especially in dental tourism where the patients might not have much time and they will need treatment done quickly and efficiently. As an example the edge computing could be applied to a clinic in Turkey specializing in dental tourism by processing dental imaging information in real-time so that it would make timely treatment recommendations to patients. McMahan et al. (2021) note that faster and more accurate decision-making builds confidence in clinic patients regarding the effectiveness of the given facility in delivering high-quality care within a short period, which is critical about international patients.

These technologies will be of great essence in ensuring that dental tourism marketing and operations are kept on the competitive edge. Using Federated Learning, blockchain, and edge computing, the dental clinics will be able to not only improve service and decision-making to patients but also establish trust and credibility towards patients. The technologies promise the better future of dental tourism, where the privacy of the patient, effective care, and transparency is a priority.

To sum up, strategic marketing integrating ethical and technologically empowered marketing will be the future of dental tourism that can address the emerging needs of global patients to the best of their capabilities. Dental clinics will be able to improve their credibility and, therefore, increase the number of patients, having relied upon digital marketing, online reviews, patient testimonials, and using the innovative technologies like Federated Learning, blockchain, and edge computing. These new developments will keep revolutionizing the dentistry tourism sphere by helping the patient with the smooth and personalized safe approach and a dental clinic with the means necessary to be successful.

FUTURE RESEARCH DIRECTIONS

1. Impact of Emerging Technologies on Patient Trust

Further research can examine how blockchain, federated learning (FL), and edge computing influence international patient trust, data security perceptions, and willingness to choose cross-border dental care. Studies could compare trust levels across countries and different demographic groups.

2. Effectiveness of Hyper-Personalized Marketing

Future work may explore how AI-driven personalization—chatbots, tailored content, predictive analytics—affects patient engagement, conversion rates, and treatment satisfaction in dental tourism.

3. Role of VR and AR in Reducing Patient Anxiety

Research could measure how virtual clinic tours and augmented reality treatment simulations influence patient confidence, reduce uncertainty, and shape decision-making for international dental procedures.

4. Cross-Cultural Differences in Review and Testimonial Influence

Since trust-building varies across cultures, future studies could analyze how online reviews and patient testimonials affect patients from different regions (e.g., Europe vs. Asia vs. Middle East).

5. Ethical Concerns in Digital Marketing of Dental Tourism

More research is needed to investigate ethical issues such as misleading advertising, inflated testimonials, privacy risks, and transparency in pricing for global patients.

6. Success Metrics for Influencer-Led Dental Tourism Campaigns

Studies can evaluate the long-term effectiveness, credibility implications, and ROI of influencer partnerships in promoting dental tourism destinations.

7. Integrated Healthcare–Travel Ecosystem Models

Future studies could design and test integrated models combining dental care, travel booking, insurance, and accommodation—examining their impact on patient satisfaction and operational efficiency.

8. Comparative Analysis of Dental Tourism Destinations

Research may compare marketing competitiveness, digital presence, technology adoption, and cost-quality ratios among leading countries such as India, Thailand, Turkey, Mexico, and Hungary.

9. Patient Decision-Making Models in the Digital Era

Studies can investigate how digital touchpoints—reviews, testimonials, SEO, content marketing, social media—interact to form a unified patient decision-making framework in dental tourism.

10. Long-Term Outcomes of Dental Tourism Treatments

Future studies can analyze treatment reliability, follow-up issues, aftercare challenges, and patient satisfaction over time, comparing domestic vs. international dental care.

REFERENCES

Bharti, P., Agarwal, P., & Gupta, N. (2021). Medical and dental tourism in India: Opportunities and challenges. *Journal of Health Management*, *23*(2), 107–120.

Chou, C., Chang, H., & Yang, Y. (2020). The impact of online reviews on patient decision-making in dental tourism. *Journal of Tourism Research*, *29*(3), 201–212.

Chou, Y., Wang, M., & Li, C. (2021). Virtual reality in medical tourism: Enhancing patient experience through immersive technology. *Journal of Healthcare Innovation*, *11*(2), 108–118.

Chung, W., Lee, M., & Kim, H. (2020). Blockchain-based medical record management in dental tourism: Enhancing data security and patient trust. *Journal of Medical Tourism*, *19*(3), 112–120.

Goh, C., Lee, W., & Tan, R. (2021). The impact of digital marketing on the dental tourism industry: A study of SEO and content marketing strategies. *International Journal of Digital Marketing*, *15*(3), 113–128.

Hernandez, M. (2022). Leveraging patient reviews for dental tourism success: The case of Dental Departures. *International Journal of Dental Tourism*, *14*(4), 245–258.

Kato, T., Suzuki, H., & Tanaka, K. (2023). Augmented reality in dental tourism: Improving patient decision-making and satisfaction. *International Journal of Dental Tourism*, *12*(3), 150–160.

Kim, J., & Lee, H. (2021). The role of online reviews in medical and dental tourism: Building trust through patient feedback. *Journal of Health Marketing*, *23*(2), 79–89.

Koh, T., Tan, E., & Ng, Y. (2020). Leveraging SEO for success: A digital marketing strategy for dental tourism. *JMR, Journal of Marketing Research*, *32*(2), 56–65.

Lee, S., Kim, J., & Choi, J. (2022). AI-powered chatbots in dental tourism marketing: Enhancing customer service and engagement. *Journal of Digital Healthcare*, *18*(4), 205–215.

Lin, H., Chang, M., & Li, J. (2020). Emotional engagement in dental tourism marketing: The power of patient testimonials. *Journal of Health Care Marketing*, *25*(3), 87–99.

Martinez, D., & Hernandez, F. (2022). Exploring the impact of dental tourism on Mexico's economy: A study on cost-efficiency and patient satisfaction. *Journal of Tourism and Health*, *45*(3), 210–220.

McMahan, J., Pritchard, T., & Zhang, Y. (2021). Emerging technologies in healthcare: Blockchain and edge computing in dental tourism marketing. *Journal of Health Care Marketing*, *32*(4), 215–230.

Prasert, N., Chia, L., & Tith, L. (2020). The role of digital marketing in dental tourism: A case study of Thailand. *International Journal of Healthcare Marketing*, *35*(4), 324–330.

Zeng, X., Wang, Y., & Li, H. (2022). Influencer marketing in healthcare: An emerging strategy for dental tourism success. *International Journal of Digital Marketing*, *14*(2), 73–86.

Zhang, L., Lin, Z., & Wang, J. (2021). The role of online reviews in shaping trust in dental tourism: Evidence from China. *JMR, Journal of Marketing Research*, *58*(1), 55–72.

KEY TERMS AND DEFINITIONS

Blockchain Technology: A secure digital system for storing and verifying patient records. In dental tourism, blockchain ensures data transparency, privacy, and trust for international patients.

Dental Tourism: The practice of travelling to another country to receive dental care, often motivated by lower costs, high-quality treatment, or the chance to combine healthcare with travel.

Digital Marketing: A set of online tools and strategies—such as SEO, social media marketing, content creation, and online ads—used by dental clinics to attract and engage international patients.

Edge Computing: A technology that processes data near the point of care, allowing faster diagnostics and real-time decision-making in dental clinics—improving efficiency and treatment accuracy.

Online Reviews: Feedback posted by patients on platforms like Google, Yelp, Trustpilot, and WhatClinic. These reviews influence clinic credibility and play a major role in patient decision-making.

Patient Testimonials: Personal stories shared by former patients (often in video or written form) that describe their treatment experience. Testimonials create emotional connection and social proof for potential patients.

Search Engine Optimization (SEO): A digital strategy that helps dental clinic websites appear higher in search results for keywords such as “affordable dental implants abroad.” SEO increases visibility and patient inquiries.

Chapter 6
Dental Tourism Marketing

P. Selvakumar
http://orcid.org/0000-0002-3650-4548
Department of Science and Humanities, Nehru Institute of Technology, Coimbatore, India

ABSTRACT

Dental tourism, a segment of medical tourism, has witnessed substantial growth over the past two decades, emerging as a viable alternative for patients seeking affordable, high-quality dental care beyond their national borders. This phenomenon has been largely driven by rising healthcare costs in developed countries, long waiting periods for dental treatments,Dental tourism, a segment of medical tourism, has witnessed substantial growth over the past two decades, emerging as a viable alternative for patients seeking affordable, high-quality dental care beyond their national borders. This phenomenon has been largely driven by rising healthcare costs in developed countries, long waiting periods for dental treatments, lack of insurance coverage for certain procedures, and the globalization of healthcare services. As patients become more informed and mobile, dental tourism has become a mainstream option, with countries across Asia, Latin America, and Eastern Europe emerging as popular destinations.

INTRODUCTION OF DENTAL TOURISM MARKETING

Dental tourism, a segment of medical tourism, has witnessed substantial growth over the past two decades, emerging as a viable alternative for patients seeking affordable, high-quality dental care beyond their national borders. This phenomenon has been largely driven by rising healthcare costs in developed countries, long

DOI: 10.4018/979-8-3373-4114-9.ch006

waiting periods for dental treatments,Dental tourism, a segment of medical tourism, has witnessed substantial growth over the past two decades, emerging as a viable alternative for patients seeking affordable, high-quality dental care beyond their national borders. This phenomenon has been largely driven by rising healthcare costs in developed countries, long waiting periods for dental treatments, lack of insurance coverage for certain procedures, and the globalization of healthcare services. As patients become more informed and mobile, dental tourism has become a mainstream option, with countries across Asia, Latin America, and Eastern Europe emerging as popular destinations. The global dental tourism market is poised for continued expansion, presenting immense opportunities for dental clinics, health tourism operators, and ancillary service providers. One of the primary drivers behind the surge in dental tourism is the high cost of dental care in countries such as the United States, Canada, the United Kingdom, and parts of Western Europe. In these nations, even basic dental procedures can be prohibitively expensive, especially for uninsured or underinsured individuals. For example, the cost of a single dental implant in the U.S. can exceed $4,000, while the same procedure in countries like Mexico, India, or Hungary may cost a fraction of that—ranging from $800 to $1,500—without compromising quality. This significant price differential, coupled with shorter wait times and access to world-class dental professionals, has incentivized patients to seek treatment abroad.Popular dental procedures sought by international patients include dental implants, crowns and bridges, veneers, root canals, orthodontics, and cosmetic dentistry. Many of these treatments require multiple visits, making them well-suited to be combined with travel and vacation(Ajam et al., 2014) The appeal of receiving treatment while enjoying a holiday in a scenic location adds a layer of value that many patients find irresistible. Countries that have recognized this trend have started integrating dental services with tourism infrastructure, offering comprehensive packages that include airporttransfers, hotel accommodations, local sightseeing, and post-treatment care.

Emerging economies have capitalized on this opportunity by investing in state-of-the-art dental clinics equipped with modern technologies and staffed by English-speaking, internationally trained professionals. Nations such as Thailand, India, Turkey, Hungary, Poland, Costa Rica, and Mexico have become dental tourism hotspots. Their clinics offer competitive pricing, advanced technology, and high standards of hygiene that meet or exceed international norms. Moreover, many of these clinics have obtained accreditations from international bodies, adding credibility and reassuring patients about the quality of care they will receive.(Al-Neyadi et al., 2018)The digital age has further accelerated the growth of dental tourism by enabling greater access to information. Patients can now research and compare clinics, read reviews, view before-and-after images, communicate with dental professionals remotely, and even schedule consultations via telemedicine. This transparency and ease of access have reduced the perceived risk associated with traveling abroad for dental treatment and have helped build trust in foreign healthcare providers.Social media platforms, patient testimonials, and medical tourism aggregators have also played a pivotal role in shaping the dental tourism landscape. Word-of-mouth recommendations and online reviews serve as powerful tools for clinics to attract international clientele. Health tourism operators, in turn, are adapting their marketing strategies to target patients more effectively through search engine optimization, digital advertising, and partnerships with travel agencies and insurance companies. As competition intensifies, branding, reputation management, and personalized patient experiences are becoming critical differentiators for success.The economic impact of dental tourism is significant, not just for clinics but also for the wider tourism and hospitality sectors. Patients traveling for dental procedures often spend on accommodations, transportation, food, and leisure activities, contributing to the local economy. Recognizing this, several governments have implemented policies to support and promote dental tourism through subsidies, streamlined visa processes, and international partnerships. Such measures have helped position dental tourism as a strategic growth sector within broader national healthcare and tourism frameworks.However, the industry is not without challenges. Ensuring continuity of care remains a concern, especially when complications arise post-treatment and patients have returned to their home countries. To address this, some dental tourism providers offer follow-up services through partner clinics or remote consultations. Additionally, legal and regulatory differences between countries can pose risks related to malpractice, consent, and consumer rights. (AlOmari, 2020)Therefore, health tourism operators must prioritize transparency, informed consent, and ethical marketing to uphold industry standards and maintain patient trust. Operators who invest in robust data management and feedback systems will be better positioned to offer personalized care and build long-term relationships with clients.Looking ahead, the global dental tourism market is expected to experience steady growth, with projections suggesting a compound annual growth rate (CAGR) of over 12% in the coming years. Factors such as rising global middle-class populations, increasing awareness of dental aesthetics, and growing acceptance of medical travel are expected to fuel

SEGMENTING THE DENTAL TOURISM MARKET: TARGETING KEY PATIENT GROUPS

As dental tourism continues to gain momentum globally, understanding the nuanced needs and preferences of international patients is critical for dental clinics, health tourism operators, and related stakeholders aiming to attract and retain clientele from abroad. (Bagga et al., 2020)These patients are not merely seeking dental treatments—they are in pursuit of a holistic healthcare experience that combines clinical excellence, personal comfort, cost savings, convenience, cultural sensitivity, and trust. Analyzing their motivations, expectations, and behavior patterns is essential for designing patient-centered services that deliver both quality and satisfaction. One of the most compelling drivers for international dental patients is affordability. Patients from high-income countries often face exorbitant dental care costs and limited insurance coverage for elective or cosmetic procedures. This makes price a key consideration. However, affordability is not pursued at the expense of quality. International patients expect to receive care that meets or exceeds the standards in their home countries. They meticulously compare costs, scrutinize clinic credentials, and verify dentist qualifications before making travel decisions. This emphasizes the importance of transparent pricing models, clear breakdowns of treatment packages, and visible certifications to establish credibility and attract attention.Quality of care remains paramount in the decision-making process. Patients often evaluate clinics based on international accreditations,(Behrmann & Smith, 2010) the educational background and experience of dental professionals, the use of advanced technology, adherence to sterilization and hygiene protocols, and the range of services offered. Modern, well-equipped facilities that utilize digital dentistry, CAD/CAM technology, 3D imaging, and minimally invasive procedures are particularly attractive. Moreover, international patients appreciate clinics that demonstrate evidence-based practices and offer comprehensive treatment planning, including consultations, diagnostics, and aftercare.Safety and reliability are closely tied to quality expectations. Prospective dental tourists look for clinics that provide guarantees or warranties on dental work, clear contingency plans for complications, and easy access to post-treatment follow-up. They also value transparent communication regarding potential risks, recovery timelines, and success rates.

To meet these needs, many clinics offer virtual consultations prior to travel, during which patients can discuss treatment options, evaluate provider compatibility, and receive a tentative plan and quotation. This pre-arrival engagement builds trust and helps manage patient expectations.Another important preference among international patients is convenience and efficiency. Patients typically travel with limited time and expect treatment schedules to be tightly coordinated. They prefer clinics that offer streamlined services, multi-disciplinary teams under one roof, and assistance with itinerary planning. Bundled treatment packages that include airport transfers, accommodation, transportation, and leisure activities are seen as highly advantageous. Health tourism facilitators and dental clinics that provide end-to-end concierge services stand out by reducing logistical stress and creating a seamless experience.Language and cultural compatibility are also crucial. International patients prefer clinics where staff can communicate fluently in English or other major world languages such as Spanish, French, German, or (Beladi et al., 2019)Arabic. Being able to understand and be understood plays a vital role in building patient confidence and minimizing anxiety. Moreover, culturally aware staff who respect diverse values, dietary restrictions, religious beliefs, and privacy preferences help patients feel respected and secure. Incorporating culturally sensitive design elements—such as signage in multiple languages, halal food options, or prayer spaces—can significantly enhance patient satisfaction.Emotional comfort is another key factor that cannot be overlooked. Dental procedures are often associated with anxiety, and traveling to an unfamiliar country for treatment can amplify these feelings. International patients seek reassurance, empathy, and warmth from the clinic's team(Cham et al., 2021). A friendly atmosphere, empathetic communication, emotional support, and clear patient education help create a sense of security. Clinics that provide psychological comfort alongside medical treatment are more likely to receive positive feedback and recommendations.The importance of digital presence and online reputation cannot be overstated. Today's international patients are highly informed and digitally connected. Before choosing a clinic, they consult websites, read patient reviews, browse social media, and explore third-party medical tourism platforms.

A strong, informative, and visually appealing digital presence helps clinics build trust and credibility. Testimonials, case studies, FAQs, blogs, and virtual tours can answer common concerns and showcase success stories. Online consultation portals, appointment scheduling systems, and live chat features are additional assets that make a clinic more accessible and responsive.Another emerging trend in patient preferences is the desire for personalized experiences. Rather than standardized treatment, international patients are increasingly looking for customized care plans that address their individual medical history, aesthetic goals, and lifestyle needs. This is particularly evident in cosmetic dentistry, where patients have specific expectations regarding the look and feel of veneers, crowns, and smile makeovers. Clinics that involve patients in the decision-making process, provide digital smile design previews, and tailor treatment plans accordingly are better equipped to meet and exceed patient expectations.Transparency and ethical conduct are also top priorities for international patients. They are wary of hidden costs, exaggerated claims, and aggressive sales tactics. Ethical marketing practices, clear documentation, honest consultations, and realistic treatment outcomes are essential to gaining trust. Providing detailed invoices, informed consent forms, and comprehensive post-treatment instructions enhances the sense of professionalism and integrity. Patients also appreciate clinics that are upfront about limitations, possible risks, and alternative treatment options.International patients also prioritize safety beyond the dental chair. They consider the overall stability of the destination country, its political environment, safety for tourists, accessibility, and availability of international travel options. Countries with efficient visa policies, robust healthcare infrastructure, and a good reputation for medical care are more likely to attract dental tourists. Proximity and direct flight connections are also practical considerations, especially for patients needing multiple visits

CREATING A WEBSITE FOR DENTAL TOURISM: BEST PRACTICES AND TIPS

As the dental tourism market grows in scale and complexity, segmentation has become an essential strategy for clinics, facilitators, and health tourism operators aiming to maximize their reach and profitability. Market segmentation involves categorizing prospective patients into distinct groups based on shared characteristics, preferences, and behaviors. By understanding and targeting these key patient segments, stakeholders in dental tourism can tailor their marketing, services, and patient experiences to meet the specific needs of different demographics. This customer-centric approach enables clinics to position themselves more competitively and generate greater patient satisfaction, loyalty, and word-of-mouth promotion.The first and perhaps most well-known segment in dental tourism is the cost-conscious patient from high-income countries. These individuals are typically uninsured or underinsured and seek affordable alternatives to expensive procedures in their home countries. Many come from the United States, Canada, the United Kingdom, Australia, and parts of Western Europe, where dental care costs can be prohibitive. (Chuang et al., 2014)This segment is motivated primarily by the potential for significant savings on treatments such as dental implants, full-mouth restorations, crowns, veneers, and orthodontics. To appeal to this group, clinics must emphasize value, cost transparency, and quality assurance. Creating detailed comparison charts that highlight price differences with local providers, offering bundled treatment-travel packages, and showcasing . Many retirees are also frequent travelers or seasonal migrants—such as Canadian "snowbirds" who spend winters in Mexico or Florida—which makes them more open to combining healthcare with travel.(De la Hoz-Correa et al., 2018) This group tends to require restorative dental work such as dentures, implants, bridges, and periodontal care. Marketing to this demographic should focus on comfort, safety, reliability, and post-treatment support. Providing age-friendly services, easy access to follow-up care, assistance with mobility or medical history transfers, ich includes younger to middle-aged adults who are motivated by personal appearance and dental aesthetics.

Figure 1. Dental tourism marketing

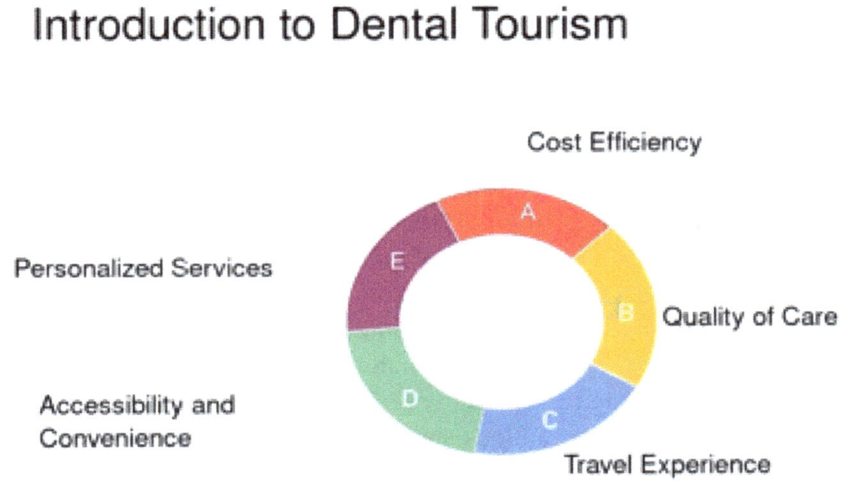

These patients often seek treatments such as teeth whitening, veneers, smile makeovers, Invisalign, and other minimally invasive cosmetic procedures. This group is less driven by cost and more influenced by perceived results, clinic reputation, and social proof. They are highly visual, digitally savvy, and active on social media platforms, making them more likely to respond to influencer partnerships, video testimonials, and before-and-after image galleries. (De Arellano, 2007)Clinics can appeal to this group through online branding, digital smile design previews, lifestyle-focused messaging, and a focus on transformative outcomes.Ethnic diaspora patients, especially those living abroad but originally from countries with emerging dental tourism markets, form another growing segment. For instance, individuals of Indian, Polish, or Latin American origin living in the U.S., U.K., or Canada often choose to return to their home countries for dental treatment during vacations or family visits. These patients trust local providers who understand their language and cultural values, and they are familiar with the healthcare standards back home. Clinics targeting this segment should emphasize cultural affinity, language compatibility, ease of scheduling during holidays, and familiarity with specific needs. Leveraging ethnic media, diaspora community events, and targeted advertising through cultural organizations can help clinics effectively reach this group. These patients are generally seeking a comprehensive health package and may require more extensive logistical coordination.

SEARCH ENGINE OPTIMIZATION (SEO) FOR DENTAL TOURISM WEBSITES

In today's digital-first world, a website serves as the front door to any business—and for dental tourism clinics, it is often the first and most critical point of interaction with potential international patients. An effective website can make the difference between a prospect choosing your clinic or going elsewhere. As the dental tourism industry becomes more competitive, creating a professional, informative, and user-friendly website is not just an option—it's a strategic necessity. To succeed in the global marketplace, a dental tourism website must blend trust-building design with valuable content, intuitive user experience, and strong search visibility. Below are key best practices and tips for creating a high-performing website tailored to the dental tourism market. design that instantly conveys professionalism and credibility. International patients may be cautious about seeking care abroad, so trustworthiness needs to be communicated through every visual element—from the logo and color scheme to typography and layout. High-quality images,(Ebrahim & Ganguli, 2019) calming colors (such as blues, whites, and greens), and intuitive navigation help create a sense of safety and comfort.Navigation should be intuitive and well-structured. Users should be able to find key information—such as treatments offered, pricing, testimonials, and contact information—within two to three clicks. A sticky header with main menu options (e.g., "About Us," "Treatments," "Prices," "FAQs," "Contact") ensures easy access to important pages at all times. Multilingual support is a must. Offering content in major languages such as English, Spanish, German, Arabic, or French significantly expands reach and accessibility(Fetscherin & Stephano, 2016). Including a clear language switcher at the top of the page helps users feel immediately accommodated.—meaning it should display correctly on all screen sizes, from desktop monitors to tablets and mobile phones.

Load time is equally crucial. A slow-loading website risks losing potential patients before they even explore your services. Aim for load times under three seconds, and optimize images and scripts accordingly. Google's Core Web Vitals and mobile-friendliness tests can help you assess and improve performance. choose your clinic over others. A strong value proposition—such as "World-Class Dental Care at 70% Less" or " yet digestible, information about the procedures available—such as dental implants, crowns, veneers, root canals, full-mouth restorations, and cosmetic dentistry. Include explanations of how each procedure works, its benefits, recovery times, and what patients should expect before, during, and after treatment. Visual aids such as diagrams, infographics, and videos enhance understanding.Transparency is critical for international patients. Include starting prices for procedures or average cost ranges and explain what's included (consultation, x-rays, anesthesia, post-treatment care). Offering downloadable treatment guides and brochures is a great way to educate while also capturing leads.and customer satisfaction. These stories should cover a range of demographics and procedures to appeal to diverse visitors.Video testimonials, in particular, build emotional trust and provide authenticity. Where possible, include the country of origin for each testimonial to show your global reach.

SOCIAL MEDIA MARKETING FOR DENTAL TOURISM: ENGAGING WITH INTERNATIONAL PATIENTSEHENS

In the highly competitive dental tourism market, Search Engine Optimization (SEO) is a critical digital marketing tool that helps clinics and health tourism providers gain visibility, attract international patients, and outperform competitors. Since most patients start their search for overseas dental treatment on Google or similar search engines, having a high-ranking, optimized website is vital to gaining organic traffic and converting interest into bookings. SEO for dental tourism websites is not just about inserting keywords into content—it's a comprehensive, strategic effort that involves technical optimization, high-quality content, keyword targeting, and authority building. Let's explore key SEO strategies specifically tailored for dental tourism businesses. in Mexico," "dental crowns in Thailand," "best dentist in Turkey for veneers," or "cost of full mouth restoration overseas." Identifying these high-value, location- and treatment-specific keywords is essential. Tools like Google Keyword Planner, (Ganguli & Ebrahim, 2017)SEMrush, Ahrefs, Ubersuggest, and Moz can be used to analyze search volume, keyword difficulty, and search intent. ts, destinations, patient concerns, and travel-related terms—helps structure content around targeted user intent. the right keywords are identified, they must be strategically incorporated into the site's content and HTML structure. Key on-page SEO elements to optimize include:informative, engaging, and valuable to users. This includes detailed treatment pages, pricing information, before-and-after galleries, FAQs, and blog content that addresses common patient concerns. Avoid keyword stuffing—instead, focus on natural keyword placement that enhances readability. A robust content strategy helps attract traffic, establish authority, and guide users through the patient journey. Key types of content to focus on include: Content should be optimized for both users and search engines with strategic keyword usage, strong headlines, clear formatting, and relevant calls to action. indexed by search engines and offers a smooth user experience. Key technical SEO areas to address include:

CONTENT MARKETING FOR DENTAL TOURISM: EDUCATING AND INFORMING PATIENTS

In an era dominated by digital communication, social media has emerged as a vital marketing tool for dental tourism providers looking to connect with international patients. Platforms like Facebook, Instagram, TikTok, YouTube, and LinkedIn allow dental clinics and health tourism operators to showcase their services, build trust, share real patient experiences, and maintain continuous engagement with prospective clients around the world. Effective social media marketing for dental tourism is not just about posting attractive content—it's about building relationships, educating audiences, humanizing your brand, and ultimately guiding potential patients through the decision-making process. A strategic, authentic, and consistent presence across social media can significantly enhance a dental tourism clinic's visibility and credibility in the global marketplace., platforms like Facebook or Instagram are the first points of contact with a clinic. They use these channels to evaluate professionalism, read reviews, (Ghosh & Mandal, 2019)see before-and-after images, and watch testimonials. Others turn to YouTube for visual information about treatments, travel logistics, and patient experiences. Social media thus acts as a combination of advertising, word-of-mouth, and customer service—making it a key driver in both awareness and conversion.Unlike traditional advertising, social media allows for two-way communication. Clinics can interact directly with potential patients, answer questions in real-time, and gather valuable feedback. This dynamic engagement f(Kowalska & Ostręga, 2020)osters trust and builds relationships well before the patient ever books an appointment.to consistently publish content that is not only visually appealing but also informative, authentic, and valuable to their international audience.

Content types that perform well include:These are powerful visual testimonials. Pair each post with a short patient story, outlining the treatment received and the country of origin. Highlight outcomes, costs saved, and emotional impact.credibility and emotional resonance. These can be shared as Instagram Reels, Facebook videos, or YouTube stories.equipment, cleanliness, and staff friendliness, easing concerns about receiving treatment abroad.(e.g., "Implants vs. Bridges"), or travel guides (e.g., "5 Things to Know Before Traveling to Costa Rica for Dental Work") position your clinic as a trusted advisor.always reflect professionalism, empathy, and transparency. High-quality visuals, clear messaging, and a friendly tone are essential. Posting consistently (3–5 times per week) keeps your audience engaged and your brand top of mind.help foster a sense of community and trust, which are crucial for converting hesitant prospects into committed patients. Key engagement tactics include:Hosting Instagram or Facebook Lives where dentists answer common questions about dental tourism, costs, procedures, and recovery helps build authority and credibility "Which destination would you consider for dental care?" or "What's your biggest concern about dental tourism?"sharing their experience from travel to treatment. This adds authenticity and real-time engagement content with permission not only strengthens bonds but also serves as genuine promotion.The key is to maintain a helpful, respectful, and approachable tone. People are more likely to choose clinics that feel human and caring, not just clinical or transactional ing. Targeted ads on Facebook, Instagram, TikTok, and YouTube allow clinics to reach very specific audiences based on geography, interests, demographics, and behavior. For dental tourism, this means targeting users in high-cost dental markets (e.g., USA, Canada, UK) who have shown interest in dental procedures, medical tourism, or international travel.Today"), and relevant visuals. Highlight pricing advantages, safety protocols, travel convenience, and treatment success rates.

STORYTELLING IN DENTAL TOURISM MARKETING: BUILDING TRUST AND CREDIBILITY

In the competitive world of dental tourism, content marketing stands out as one of the most powerful and cost-effective tools for attracting, educating, and converting international patients. Unlike traditional advertising, which pushes a message outward, content marketing pulls the audience in by offering valuable, relevant, and consistent information tailored to the needs of dental tourists. These patients are often navigating unfamiliar territory—both medically and geographically—so they turn to digital content to make informed decisions. For dental clinics and health tourism operators, developing a strong content marketing strategy built around blog posts, videos, patient testimonials, guides, and FAQs is essential for building trust, demonstrating authority, and guiding patients from curiosity to conversion. their home country. They start searching online for solutions, which leads them to consider treatment abroad. At this point, their minds are filled with questions: (Lam et al., 2012)Is it safe? How much does it cost? Where should I go?Who can I trust? What happens if something goes wrong?This journey involves multiple stages—awareness, consideration, and decision-making. Content marketing addresses each of these stages by providing answers, eliminating doubts, and gently nurturing patients toward choosing your clinic. Done well, it not only drives traffic to your website but also builds a long-term relationship that encourages referrals and repeat visits. blog posts not only improve your website's visibility on search engines but also help establish your clinic as a trusted resource. Topics should focus on the intersection of dental care and travel, answering common questions international patients have. Some high-performing blog topics include:The tone should be educational, conversational, and reassuring. Each post should incorporate relevant keywords to enhance SEO, and include calls-to-action (CTAs) such as "Download our Free Dental Travel Guide" or "Schedule a Virtual Consultation." (Mishra et al., 2019) Evergreen content that remains relevant over time is particularly valuable and can be shared repeatedly on social media and email newsletters.where trust and clarity are paramount. Videos allow clinics to communicate com(Moghavvemi et al., 2017) plex information quickly and in an emotionally compelling way. They humanize your brand, showcase your facility, and highlight the professionalism of your team.

PATIENT TESTIMONIALS AND REVIEWS: LEVERAGING SOCIAL PROOF

In the landscape of dental tourism marketing, where patients are often faced with uncertainty, risk, and an overload of information, storytelling emerges as one of the most powerful and persuasive tools for building trust and credibility. Unlike facts and figures alone, stories speak to emotions. They humanize the brand, provide social proof, and create an emotional bridge between prospective patients and clinics. In an industry where individuals are making significant decisions about their health—often across borders and cultures—storytelling becomes not just a marketing technique, but a strategic necessity. By sharing authentic patient journeys, clinic milestones, staff experiences, and transformative results, dental tourism providers can cut through the noise, build deep relationships, and position themselves as trustworthy and compassionate leaders in the market. of the brain related to empathy, memory, and connection. When prospective patients read or watch a story about someone who traveled abroad, received treatment, and came back with a new smile and a renewed sense of confidence, they don't (Mahadev Madgule, 2023)just process the information—they feel it. This emotional engagement builds credibility far more effectively than a list of services or prices ever could. For international patients who are already anxious about traveling for dental procedures, hearing about the real-life experiences of others who've walked the same path can provide the reassurance and inspiration they need to move forward. but lives. Whether it's a middle-aged Canadian man who regained confidence through dental implants in Mexico, or a young woman from the UK who finally afforded the cosmetic work she'd always dreamed of in Turkey, every patient journey offers a unique, relatable narrative. These stories allow clinics to showcase their capabilities, compassion, and consistency in a way that data cannot.

Figure 2. Understanding the dental tourist demographic

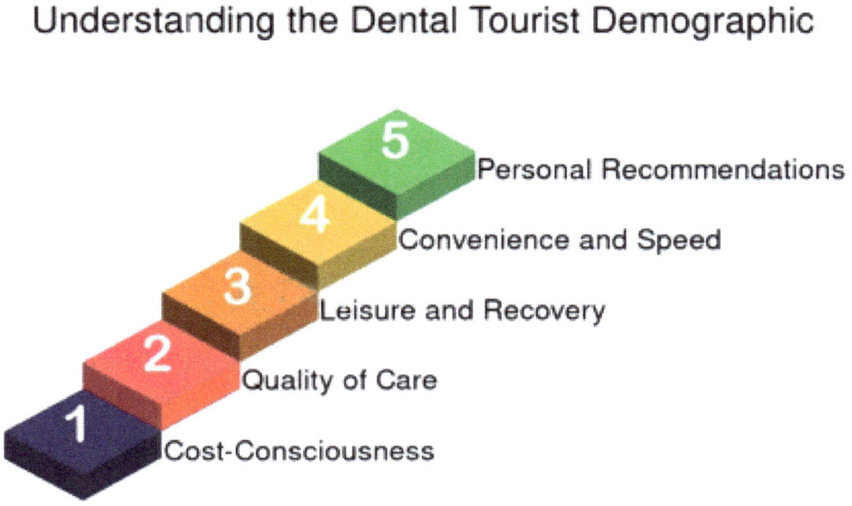

To effectively use patient stories, they should be captured in multiple formats—written testimonials, before-and-after photo essays, video interviews, and even live Q&A sessions. A good success story follows a simple arc: the problem (why they needed treatment), the journey (what led them to your clinic), the solution (how the treatment was carried out), and the outcome (the emotional and physical transformation). Include details such as the patient's country of origin, treatment received, travel experience, and what made them choose your clinic. Adding quotes like "I was nervous at first, but from the moment I arrived, I felt cared for" or "I saved thousands and gained a new smile" adds authenticity andafter images, procedure timelines, and photo diaries of a patient's journey offer undeniable evidence of success. Clinics should invest in high-quality photography and videography that captures the emotion behind the transformation. A short video of a patient seeing their new smile for the first time can be more persuasive than a hundred blog posts. Social media platforms like Instagram and TikTok are perfect for sharing these visual stories in bite-sized, emotionally engaging ways, while longer testimonials can be hosted on YouTube or embedded in your website.about your clinic's growth, awards, certifications, international recognitions, and milestones helps establish authority and credibility. (Nitecki & Hernon, 2000)Has your clinic reached its 10th anniversary? Did your lead dentist receive a fellowship from an international dental association? Have you treated your 5,000th international patient? These accomplishments form the backbone of your brand's story and signal to prospective patients that your clinic is reputable, established, and experienced.Telling the story of your team—their expertise, cultural diversity, ongoing training, and passion for patient care—also adds a human touch that can be very appealing to international patients. Profiles of team members, behind-the-scenes looks at their day-to-day work, or stories of how they've gone the extra mile for a patient demonstrate the values that define your clinic. audience might resonate with cost-savings and technology, while European patients may prioritize clinic reputation and quality assurance. Middle Eastern audiences may be more responsive to family-focused values and personal care. Tailoring your storytelling to the values, concerns, and preferences of specific cultural groups ensures that your message connects meaningfully across borders.This also means using relatable voices—featuring stories in the language of the audience or subtitled appropriately. Highlighting staff members who speak the same language as the patient demographic you're targeting can be an additional trust-building layer. (Nyumba et al., 2018)Facebook posts, email newsletters, and paid ad campaigns.

PARTNERING WITH HEALTH TOURISM OPERATORS: BENEFITS AND OPPORTUNITIES

In the world of dental tourism—where patients are making deeply personal, financial, and medical decisions across borders—trust is everything. Because prospective international patients often cannot rely on local word-of-mouth or personal referrals, they turn to the next best thing: online reviews and testimonials. These real-life experiences from past patients serve as powerful social proof that influences decision-making, eases anxiety, and builds credibility. In fact, studies show that over 90% of consumers read online reviews before choosing a healthcare provider, and the number is even higher among medical tourists, who face greater risks and unknowns. For dental tourism providers, collecting and leveraging patient testimonials and reviews is not just helpful—it's essential to long-term success. skeptical of marketing claims and often have concerns about language barriers, safety, quality of care, and travel logistics. In this context, testimonials from other patients—especially those who share similar backgrounds, needs, or countries of origin—carry exceptional weight. Social proof bridges the gap between promotional content and real-world experiences, helping patients feel reassured and confident that they are making(Nyumba et al., 2018) the right choice.UK who traveled to Turkey for dental implants, saved thousands of dollars, and returned with a perfect smile speaks louder than any brochure or price list. Additionally, testimonials humanize your brand. They shift the focus from procedures and prices to people and outcomes, allowing potential patients to emotionally connect with your clinic through shared experiences These combine visual proof with narrative, making them particularly compelling for procedures with transformative results like veneers, implants, and smile makeovers. Being featured on trusted platforms adds credibility because the reviews are verified and publicly visible.Each of these types serves a different purpose in the buyer's journey and should be used in complementary ways across your digital channels. some patients may voluntarily leave reviews, a proactive strategy is required to gather testimonials consistently and ethically. Here's how to build an effective collection systemtypically right after completing treatment, during their final check-up, or after seeing their results. Let them know their feedback helps others and contributes to your clinic's growth.Provide a direct link to your Google Business profile, Facebook page, or review form. Create QR codes for in-clinic posters or send a follow-up email or WhatsApp message thanking them and inviting them to share their experience.

COLLABORATING WITH INTERNATIONAL INSURANCE PROVIDERS

In the increasingly interconnected and competitive world of dental tourism, strategic partnerships can be the difference between incremental growth and exponential expansion. One of the most effective ways dental clinics can scale their reach, build international credibility, and gain consistent access to new patient markets is by partnering with health tourism operators. These facilitators—often known as medical travel agencies, international patient coordinators, or health tourism platforms—act as intermediaries between healthcare providers and prospective patients. By forming alliances with these organizations, dental clinics gain a valuable gateway to international markets, benefit from shared expertise and marketing, and streamline the patient acquisition process. As global demand for affordable, high-quality dental care continues to rise, particularly from countries with high treatment costs or limited insurance coverage, the opportunities for collaboration between dental clinics and health tourism operators have never been greater.and consultation,(Parasuraman et al., 2002) travel planning, visa and logistics support, coordination of appointments, and post-treatment follow-up. Many also serve as trusted advisors, offering patients recommendations for vetted clinics based on quality, affordability, and reputation. These operators maintain networks of international healthcare providers, including hospitals, dental clinics, cosmetic surgeons, rehabilitation centers, and wellness resorts. By becoming part of these networks, dental clinics gain access to an established ecosystem of referral sources and marketing channels. most immediate benefits of partnering with health tourism operators is access to new and diverse patient markets. These operators often have a strong presence in high-demand regions such as the United States, Canada, the United Kingdom, Australia, and the Middle East—where dental care is often expensive or not covered by insurance.

They also understand the cultural nuances, language preferences, and healthcare expectations of patients in their region, making it easier to connect clinics with target audiences that may otherwise be difficult to reach through local marketing alone- For example, a dental clinic in Hungary partnering with a health tourism agency in the UK gains exposure to British patients actively seeking affordable treatment abroad. Similarly, clinics in Mexico that collaborate with U.S.-based facilitators can tap into a vast market of Americans looking to save money on implants, veneers, or smile makeovers. These partnerships not only extend geographic reach but also help clinics diversify their patient base, reducing dependency on any one market. tourism operators are typically well-versed in lead generation and pre-qualification. They attract, educate, and filter patient inquiries before passing them on to clinics, ensuring that leads are more likely to convert. This saves dental clinics time and resources while allowing them to focus on clinical excellence and patient care.(Qolipour et al., 2018) Many facilitators even offer pre-consultation services, gathering necessary documentation such as x-rays, medical histories, and treatment goals ahead of time—giving the dental team everything they need to create a customized treatment plan before the patient arrives.Because operators often handle a high volume of inquiries, working with even a few reputable agencies can result in a steady and scalable flow of patients. This consistent pipeline can help dental clinics better forecast revenue, manage appointment schedules, and optimize resource allocation. with international accreditations or strong reputations—can significantly enhance a clinic's brand credibility. For new or lesser-known clinics trying to establish themselves in the global market, this association serves as a valuable trust signal. Patients are more likely to choose a clinic that is recommended by a trusted operator, particularly when facing the stress and uncertainty of seeking treatment abroad.

BUILDING RELATIONSHIPS WITH MEDICAL TRAVEL FACILITATORS

These collaborations can benefit both patients and dental service providers by making dental treatment more affordable, accessible, and secure. However, while such partnerships offer numerous advantages, they also come with several challenges that must be addressed to ensure a smooth, successful collaboration. Understanding both the benefits and the complexities of working with international insurance providers is crucial for dental clinics that aim to enhance their services(Ramakrishnan et al., 2022) to international patients. to attract a broader patient base. Patients traveling for dental care often seek treatment in countries where costs are lower, and one of the main barriers to dental tourism is the lack of financial coverage from domestic insurance plans. By partnering with international insurance providers, dental clinics can help bridge this gap, providing more patients with affordable access to high-quality dental services abroad.Patients who have dental insurance that includes international coverage will feel more secure knowing that their insurance provider will cover a significant portion of the treatment cost. This removes financial concerns, particularly for patients who are hesitant to pay out-of-pocket for expensive procedures like implants, crowns, or orthodontics. It also enhances the credibility of the clinic by showing that they meet the international standards required by reputable insurance companies. trustworthy. Insurance companies often have strict vetting processes, and dental clinics that collaborate with these providers are generally recognized for maintaining high standards of care. This can reassure patients that they are receiving treatment in a regulated, professional environment. (Sreenivasulu et al., 2022)Moreover, international patients are more likely to choose clinics that offer the convenience of utilizing their insurance, as it simplifies their decision-making process. A clinic's ability to accept a range of international insurance plans positions it as a reliable and patient-friendly choice, potentially improving patient conversion rates. complex reimbursement forms or paying upfront and waiting for reimbursement from their domestic insurance, patients can directly bill their international insurance providers. This greatly improves the experience for international patients, eliminating much of the financial stress involved in dental tourism.Additionally, insurance partnerships can help clinics with the administrative burden of processing claims.

Some insurance companies offer direct billing, which means that the clinic receives payment directly from the insurer, reducing the need for patients to handle out-of-pocket costs before treatment begins. For patients unfamiliar with the cost structures of dental procedures in foreign countries, insurance providers often help outline coverage and reimbursement policies, making the entire process more transparent. Patients know in advance what portion of their treatment will be covered and what portion they will need to pay. This can help dental clinics provide clearer, more accurate pricing and avoid potential confusion during the billing process.claims procedures, and timeframes for reimbursements. This can create a significant administrative burden for clinics, requiring dedicated staff to manage insurance claims, follow-up with insurers, and track payments. and in some cases, they may be lower. This creates a need for effective negotiation skills to ensure that the rates are fair and reflective of the services offered. There's also the possibility of delayed reimbursements, which can create cash flow issues for the clinic, especially if many patients are using insurance coverage.—such as cosmetic procedures like teeth whitening or elective veneers—are excluded from their insurance coverage. This can lead to misunderstandings between the clinic and the patient regarding what is and isn't covered.some insurance companies may also have specific conditions for reimbursement, such as requiring pre-authorization for certain treatments or limiting the total amount of coverage for dental procedures.(Zhao et al., 2002) This requires the clinic to be well-versed in the fine print of each insurance policy to avoid unexpected costs or patient dissatisfaction.

EMAIL MARKETING FOR DENTAL TOURISM: NURTURING LEADS AND ENCOURAGING BOOKINGS

In the dynamic and competitive field of dental tourism, building strong relationships with medical travel facilitators is crucial for dental clinics that want to expand their international patient base. Medical travel facilitators (MTFs)—often referred to as medical tourism agencies or health tourism facilitators—act as intermediaries between patients seeking affordable dental care abroad and the healthcare providers who offer those services. They play a key role in the dental tourism industry by managing the logistics of patient travel, providing guidance on medical options, offering support throughout the treatment process, and ensuring that patients have a seamless experience. These facilitators are invaluable partners for dental clinics aiming to tap into global markets, attract international patients, and streamline their operations. However, in order to leverage the full potential of these partnerships, dental clinics must develop mutually beneficial relationships that are based on trust, communication, and alignment of goals. travel abroad for dental procedures. They typically handle a wide range of tasks, from providing initial consultations to arranging travel logistics such as flights, accommodations, and visas. Additionally, they assist with translating patient inquiries and helping them navigate foreign healthcare systems. Facilitators often have an extensive network of partner clinics and hospitals across various destinations, offering patients a curated list of vetted providers. These facilitators help patients choose clinics based on factors such as cost, reputation, treatment quality, and the provider's ability to meet the patient's specific needs.They provide education on the dental treatments available, suggest potential destinations, and match patients with clinics that offer the care they are seeking. Facilitators handle much of the administrative work, from scheduling appointments to coordinating post-treatment follow-ups, allowing dental clinics to focus on the clinical aspects of care.

This relationship allows dental clinics to extend their reach beyond their local market, gaining access to patients from diverse geographical areas who may not otherwise be aware of their services., as dental clinics may not have the resources or networks to market their services globally. Medical travel facilitators bring with them a network of prospective patients who are already considering traveling for dental care. By building strong relationships with these facilitators, clinics can tap into a steady stream of potential patients, particularly those seeking high-quality, cost-effective dental care abroad.In addition to providing access to new patient markets, medical travel facilitators can enhance a clinic's credibility. Facilitators typically work with a limited number of trusted healthcare providers, and inclusion in this network signals to patients that the clinic meets high standards for care, safety, and service(Wong & Musa, 2012). When building relationships with medical travel facilitators, clinics must provide clear, transparent pricing that facilitators can confidently share with prospective patients.(Vijayakumar et al., 2024). Offering post-treatment support, such as follow-up consultations or ensuring that patients have access to ongoing care if needed, is another way to ensure the facilitator knows that their patients are in good hands. patient testimonials, and accreditations is essential for attracting facilitators' attention. Clinics should also maintain active social media profiles where facilitators can see firsthand patient feedback and success stories.Online reviews, patient testimonials, and case studies can further demonstrate a clinic's quality of care and outcomes, helping facilitators make informed decisions when selecting their partners.

PAID ADVERTISING FOR DENTAL TOURISM: GOOGLE ADS AND SOCIAL MEDIA ADS

Email marketing remains one of the most powerful and cost-effective strategies for dental clinics looking to grow their international patient base, (Tripathi & Siddiqui, 2018)particularly in the competitive and rapidly expanding dental tourism industry. With the rise of digital marketing, email offers a direct line to potential patients who have shown interest in dental procedures abroad. However, simply sending emails is not enough to drive bookings—successful email marketing campaigns in dental tourism require a well-defined strategy that nurtures leads, builds trust, and ultimately encourages patients to take the next step and schedule their treatments. In this context, email marketing becomes a crucial tool for dental clinics to foster relationships with potential patients, convert inquiries into appointments, and increase patient loyalty over time. This analysis explores effective email marketing strategies for dental tourism, focusing on lead nurturing, personalized content, segmentation, and conversion optimization techniques that can help dental clinics turn prospects into paying patients.engage with a clinic. They may be researching dental procedures, comparing prices across various countries, and evaluating the reputation of different clinics. Dental clinics often face long sales cycles, where the time between the initial inquiry and final booking can span weeks or even months. This makes email marketing a particularly valuable tool for maintaining contact with potential patients during this lengthy decision-making process. By providing consistent, relevant, and engaging information, dental clinics can keep their services top-of-mind and gently guide prospects toward booking an appointment.expressed an interest in their services. (Sugumaran et al., 2024)These leads—whether generated through website inquiries, social media interactions, or previous patient referrals—are warm prospects, which means they are more likely to convert into paying patients than those who have not yet engaged with the clinic. Effective email marketing can therefore increase conversion rates, boost bookings, and ultimately drive revenue for dental clinics that specialize in international patients.

UNDERSTANDING LEAD NURTURING IN DENTAL TOURISM

Lead nurturing is the process of developing relationships with potential patients throughout their journey, offering them valuable information, answering their questions, and guiding them toward making a decision. In the dental tourism context, this often means maintaining regular communication with leads from different parts of the world who may be considering dental procedures such as implants, cosmetic dentistry, orthodontics, or smile makeovers. The lead nurturing process in dental tourism email marketing revolves around providing potential patients with information that addresses their specific concerns, educating them on their treatment options, and showcasing the clinic's expertise and unique selling points.A well-executed lead nurturing strategy in dental tourism should begin immediately after a lead expresses interest in learning more about dental procedures abroad. Whether this interest is shown through an inquiry form, a download of a free guide on dental tourism, or an interaction on social media, the dental clinic must respond quickly and thoughtfully. This first email sets the tone for future communication, so it should focus on building trust and providing value to the lead. Providing informative content such as "What to Expect During Your Dental Tourism Journey" or "Top Questions to Ask Your Dentist When Traveling for Treatment" can reassure leads that they are making a wise choice and foster a sense of comfort with the process.After the initial engagement, the goal of email marketing is to build on that relationship, gradually moving leads closer to booking their appointment. One effective strategy for lead nurturing is to set up an automated email drip campaign.

This series of pre-scheduled emails can be sent to leads over a period of time, each one offering relevant and helpful content that moves the lead closer to making a decision. For example, an email series might include:Effective email marketing in dental tourism depends on the ability to segment your email list and send tailored messages to different groups of leads. Not all leads are created equal, and different individuals may be at different stages in their decision-making process. By segmenting your email list based on factors such as treatment interest, geographical location, or level of engagement with previous emails, dental clinics can send more relevant and targeted content that speaks directly to the needs and interests of each lead.Segmentation ensures that each lead receives the most relevant information for their needs, which can increase the likelihood of engagement and conversion. It also reduces the chances of overwhelming leads with irrelevant content, improving their experience with the clinic.n in dental tourism email marketing revolves around encouraging leads to take specific actions, such as booking a consultation, requesting more information, or making a deposit toward their treatment. Whether it's scheduling a consultation, requesting a treatment quote, or signing up for a free informational webinar, the CTA should be easy to spot and offer a clear benefit. For example:Personalization is key in email marketing, as it shows the lead that the clinic values them as an individual.

MEASURING THE SUCCESS OF DENTAL TOURISM MARKETING EFFORTS

In the modern world of dental tourism, where patients are increasingly making healthcare decisions online, influencer marketing has emerged as a powerful strategy for dental clinics aiming to expand their global reach. This strategy involves collaborating with individuals who have a significant online presence and influence over specific audiences—commonly referred to as key opinion leaders (KOLs) or influencers. The key appeal of influencer marketing is its ability to leverage the trust, credibility, and established relationships influencers have with their followers, often creating more authentic and persuasive recommendations than traditional advertising methods. This is especially important in the context of dental tourism, where trust and reassurance are paramount for potential patients who are considering traveling abroad for complex and sometimes life-changing dental procedures. Influencer marketing is a unique approach because it bridges the gap between online marketing and personal recommendations. The trust that followers place in their favorite influencers can directly translate into credibility for the dental clinic, making it easier to sway potential patients who are considering traveling for dental care. In the context of dental tourism, these partnerships can significantly impact patient acquisition, raise brand awareness, and ultimately lead to increased bookings. This comprehensive exploration will delve into the strategies for partnering with key opinion leaders and influencers in the dental tourism industry, highlighting best practices, the types of influencers to target, the benefits of such collaborations, and the potential challenges to consider such as Mexico, Thailand, Turkey, and Costa Rica have become well-known destinations for dental tourism, attracting thousands of international patients each year. However, the decision to undergo dental treatment in another country involves careful consideration, as patients need to be assured of the safety, quality, and professionalism of the dental clinic. This is where influencer marketing comes in.

Patients seeking dental procedures abroad typically look for firsthand experiences and recommendations from people they trust. They may engage with influencers who have gone through the same process of dental tourism, as these influencers can provide a more personal and relatable perspective than traditional advertising. Influencers are seen as more credible because they often share their personal journeys, including before-and-after images, testimonials, and treatment experiences, which can offer insight into the process and outcomes. Dental clinics, in turn, can benefit from this authenticity, as their services are presented in a way that resonates with potential patients and humanizes the clinic's offerings.clinic's reputation by associating it with credible and respected individuals in the health, beauty, and wellness spaces. When a trusted influencer shares their positive experience with a particular clinic, their followers are more likely to consider that clinic for their own dental treatments, especially if the influencer's content aligns with the follower's interests and values. shapes and sizes, and selecting the right type of influencer is crucial for the success of a marketing campaign. The three main categories of influencers are: micro-influencers, mid-tier influencers, and macro-influencers. Influencers can document their journey from consultation to post-treatment care, sharing their thoughts, concerns, and satisfaction throughout the process. This provides a transparent and relatable experience for potential patients, which can increase trust and confidence in the clinic's services.Additionally, dental clinics should encourage influencers to create educational content that explains the benefits of dental tourism, dispels myths, and answers common questions about traveling for dental care. Educational content can be particularly impactful in building awareness and providing reassurance to potential patients who may be apprehensive about undergoing treatment abroad. that resonate with a wider audience. Influencers can share their positive experiences through written or video reviews, highlighting the quality of care, the affordability of treatment, and the seamless process of traveling for dental services. These testimonials serve as social proof, demonstrating the clinic's expertise and reliability to prospective international patients.

CONCLUSION

In today's highly competitive and rapidly growing dental tourism market, measuring the success of marketing efforts is crucial for ensuring that strategies are delivering the desired results. With patients increasingly turning to the internet to research dental procedures, assess treatment options, and make decisions about traveling abroad for affordable dental care, it's imperative for dental clinics and health tourism operators to track their marketing performance. Understanding key performance indicators (KPIs) is essential to assess the effectiveness of various marketing campaigns, refine strategies, and make data-driven decisions to optimize future marketing efforts.Dental tourism marketing efforts span multiple channels, including digital advertising, social media, content marketing, email campaigns, and search engine optimization (SEO), each contributing to the overall goal of attracting international patients. The success of these efforts depends on how well they resonate with the target audience, drive traffic, generate leads, and ultimately convert these leads into paying patients. By using KPIs such as website traffic, lead generation, and conversion rates, dental clinics can track and evaluate their marketing campaigns to ensure they are achieving their objectives.In this analysis, we will explore the key performance indicators that are particularly relevant for dental tourism marketing, offering insights on how to measure each aspect effectively and optimize strategies for better results.. In the digital age, the majority of dental tourism inquiries begin with online research. When potential patients are considering traveling abroad for dental care, they typically search for information about clinics, treatments, costs, and the overall dental tourism experience. A low bounce rate, on the other hand, typically indicates that visitors are engaging with the content and exploring other pages, such as treatment options, patient testimonials, and contact forms.s ability to convert interested visitors into potential patients. Lead generation involves capturing contact information from individuals who are interested in learning more about dental treatments or booking consultations. These leads represent prospects who have shown an active interest in the clinic's services and may be in the process of making a decision about their dental care.Effective lead generation is fundamental to the success of dental tourism marketing because it allows clinics to nurture relationships with prospective patients and encourage them to take the next step toward booking a treatment. Lead generation can be tracked using a variety of tools, such as form submissions, phone call tracking, and chatbots. request a consultation forms or inquiries about specific treatments. By analyzing form submission data, dental clinics can track how many visitors have submitted their information and what percentage of these submissions are converting into consultations or bookings. tools can attribute phone inquiries to specific marketing channels,

REFERENCES

Ajam, M., Sadeghifar, J., Anjomshoa, M., Mahmoudi, S., Honarvar, H., & Mousavi, S. M. (2014). Assessing the quality of healthcare service by the SERVQUAL model: A case study of a field hospital. *Journal of Military Medicine*, *15*(4), 273–279.

Al-Neyadi, H. S., Abdallah, S., & Malik, M. (2018). Measuring patient's satisfaction of healthcare services in the UAE hospitals: Using SERVQUAL. *International Journal of Healthcare Management*, *11*(2), 96–105. DOI: 10.1080/20479700.2016.1266804

AlOmari, F. (2020). Measuring gaps in healthcare quality using SERVQUAL model: Challenges and opportunities in developing countries. *Measuring Business Excellence*. Advance online publication. DOI: 10.1108/MBE-11-2019-0104

Bagga, T., Vishnoi, S. K., Jain, S., & Sharma, R. (2020). Medical tourism: Treatment, therapy and tourism. *International Journal of Scientific and Technology Research*, *9*(3), 4447–4453.

Behrmann, J., & Smith, E. (2010). Top 7 issues in medical tourism: Challenges, knowledge gaps, and future directions for research and policy development. *Global Journal of Health Science*, *2*(2), 80. DOI: 10.5539/gjhs.v2n2p80

Beladi, H., Chao, C. C., Ee, M. S., & Hollas, D. (2019). Does medical tourism promote economic growth? A cross-country analysis. *Journal of Travel Research*, *58*(1), 121–135. DOI: 10.1177/0047287517735909

Cham, T. H., Lim, Y. M., Sia, B. C., Cheah, J. H., & Ting, H. (2021). Medical tourism destination image and its relationship with the intention to revisit: A study of Chinese medical tourists in Malaysia. *Journal of China Tourism Research*, *17*(2), 163–191. DOI: 10.1080/19388160.2020.1734514

Chuang, T. C., Liu, J. S., Lu, L. Y., & Lee, Y. (2014). The main paths of medical tourism: From transplantation to beautification. *Tourism Management*, *45*, 49–58. DOI: 10.1016/j.tourman.2014.03.016

De Arellano, A. B. R. (2007). Patients without borders: The emergence of medical tourism. *International Journal of Health Services*, *37*(1), 193–198. DOI: 10.2190/4857-468G-2325-47UU PMID: 17436992

De la Hoz-Correa, A., Muñoz-Leiva, F., & Bakucz, M. (2018). Past themes and future trends in medical tourism research: A co-word analysis. *Tourism Management*, *65*, 200–211. DOI: 10.1016/j.tourman.2017.10.001

Ebrahim, A. H., & Ganguli, S. (2019). A comparative analysis of medical tourism competitiveness of India, Thailand, and Singapore. *Tourism an International Interdisciplinary Journal*, *67*(2), 102–115.

Fetscherin, M., & Stephano, R. M. (2016). The medical tourism index: Scale development and validation. *Tourism Management*, *52*, 539–556. DOI: 10.1016/j.tourman.2015.08.010

Ganguli, S., & Ebrahim, A. H. (2017). A qualitative analysis of Singapore's medical tourism competitiveness. *Tourism Management Perspectives*, *21*, 74–84. DOI: 10.1016/j.tmp.2016.12.002

Ghosh, T., & Mandal, S. (2019). Medical tourism experience: Conceptualization, scale development, and validation. *Journal of Travel Research*, *58*(8), 1288–1301. DOI: 10.1177/0047287518813469

Kowalska, N., & Ostręga, A. (2020). Using SERVQUAL method to assess tourist service quality by the example of the Silesian Museum Established on the post-mining area. *Land (Basel)*, *9*(9), 333. DOI: 10.3390/land9090333

Lam, S., Lee, V., Ooi, K., & Phusavat, K. (2012). A structural equation model of TQM, market orientation and service quality: Evidence from a developing nation. *Managing Service Quality*, *22*(3), 281–309. DOI: 10.1108/09604521211230996

Mahadev Madgule, N. (2023). Vinayaka, Yeshwant M. Sonkhaskar, Dhiren Ramanbhai Patel, R. Karthikeyan, P. Selvakumar,(2023). Mechanical properties and microstructure of activated TIG welded similar joints of Inconel alloys by desirability approaches. *Materials Today: Proceedings*, *77*, 528–533. DOI: 10.1016/j.matpr.2022.12.250

Mishra, V., Samuel, C., & Sharma, S. K. (2019). Patient's utility for various attributes of diabetes care services. *IIM Kozhikode Society and Management Review*, *8*(1), 1–9. DOI: 10.1177/2277975218798134

Moghavvemi, S., Ormond, M., Musa, G., Isa, C. R. M., Thirumoorthi, T., Mustapha, M. Z. B., & Chandy, J. J. C. (2017). Connecting with prospective medical tourists online: A cross-sectional analysis of private hospital websites promoting medical tourism in India, Malaysia, and Thailand. *Tourism Management*, *58*, 154–163. DOI: 10.1016/j.tourman.2016.10.010

Nitecki, D. A., & Hernon, P. (2000). Measuring service quality at Yale university's libraries. *Journal of Academic Librarianship*, *26*(4), 259–273. DOI: 10.1016/S0099-1333(00)00117-8

Nyumba, T. O., Wilson, K., Derrick, C. J., & Mukherjee, N. (2018). The use of focus group discussion methodology: Insights from two decades of application in conservation. *Methods in Ecology and Evolution*, *9*(1), 20–32. DOI: 10.1111/2041-210X.12860

Parasuraman, A., Berry, L., & Zeithaml, V. (2002). Refinement and reassessment of the SERVQUAL scale. *Journal of Retailing*, *67*(4), 114–139.

Qolipour, M., Torabipour, A., Khiavi, F. F., & Malehi, A. S. (2018). Assessing medical tourism services quality using SERVQUAL model: A patient's perspective. *Iranian Journal of Public Health*, *47*(1), 103–110. PMID: 29318124

Ramakrishnan, T., Mohan Gift, M. D., Chitradevi, S., Jegan, R., & Subha Hency Jose, P. Nagaraja, Rajneesh Sharma H.N., Selvakumar P., Sintayehu Mekuria Hailegiorgis, (2022). "Study of Numerous Resins Used in Polymer Matrix Composite Materials", Advances in Materials Science and Engineering, vol. 2022, Article ID 1088926, 8 pages, 2022. DOI: 10.1155/2022/1088926

Sreenivasulu, A., & Manimozhi, T. Satheesh kumar P., Selvakumar P. and Singh P.,(2022). "The Model of Smart Sensing Device For Sensitive Nanoclusters Modification in Sensing Properties," 2022 2nd International Conference on Advance Computing and Innovative Technologies in Engineering (ICACITE), Greater Noida, India, 2022, pp. 1043-1047, DOI: 10.1109/ICACITE53722.2022.9823846

Sugumaran, K. M. D., Pandiyarajan V., Y. B S, Selvakumar P. and M. S, (2024). "Analysis of Electromyography Signals for Control of Mechanical Prosthesis using Machine Learning Techniques," 2024 2nd International Conference on Intelligent Data Communication Technologies and Internet of Things (IDCIoT), Bengaluru, India, 2024, pp. 1059-1067, DOI: 10.1109/IDCIoT59759.2024.10467707

Tripathi, S. N., & Siddiqui, M. H. (2018). Assessing the quality of healthcare services: A SERVQUAL approach. *International Journal of Healthcare Management*. Advance online publication. DOI: 10.1080/20479700.2018.1469212

Vijayakumar, G., Rajkumar, M., Rajiv Chandar, N., Selvakumar, P., & Duraisamy, R. (2024). Muniyandi Rajkumar, Rajiv Chandar N, Selvakumar P and Ramesh Duraisamy, (2024). Environmentally friendly TDS removal from waste water by electrochemical ion exchange batch-type recirculation (EIR) technique. *Environmental Science. Water Research & Technology*, *10*(4), 826–835. DOI: 10.1039/D3EW00793F

Wong, K. M., & Musa, G. (2012). Medical tourism in Asia: Thailand, Singapore, Malaysia, and India. Medical tourism: The ethics, regulation, and marketing of health mobility. Routledge.

Zhao, X., Bai, C., & Hui, Y. V. (2002). An empirical assessment and application of SERVQUAL in a mainland Chinese department store. *Total Quality Management*, *13*(2), 241–254. DOI: 10.1080/09544120120102478

Chapter 7

Deep Learning in Dental Radiology: Enhancing Diagnosis and Decision-Making in Modern Dentistry

Affaan Shaikh
http://orcid.org/0009-0004-7590-7456
IntelliDent AI, UAE

D. Varun Prasanna
http://orcid.org/0009-0008-4166-5291
Manipal College of Dental Sciences, Mangalore, India

ABSTRACT

The integration of Artificial Intelligence (AI), particularly deep learning, into dental radiology is revolutionizing the way oral diseases are diagnosed and managed. This chapter explores how convolutional neural networks (CNNs) and related deep learning techniques are being applied to interpret dental imaging modalities such as panoramic X-rays, periapical radiographs, and cone-beam computed tomography (CBCT). By leveraging large datasets, AI models can detect caries, periodontal disease, periapical lesions, and other abnormalities with accuracy comparable to or exceeding that of experienced clinicians. The chapter reviews current tools, architectures, and real-world applications, and discusses the benefits and challenges of adopting AI in clinical practice, including ethical concerns, data privacy, and model transparency. Through case studies and comparative evaluations, we demonstrate the transformative potential of AI-powered radiology in making dental diagnostics faster, more consistent, and accessible across varying healthcare settings.

DOI: 10.4018/979-8-3373-4114-9.ch007

1. INTRODUCTION

Dental imaging is a common component of radiological practice, whether it is used for the detection of other problems or as a deliberate examination, as in the case of patients who have experienced orofacial or dental trauma. Despite improvements in dental health over the past few decades due to better oral hygiene and preventative dentistry, tooth and supporting structure diseases still have a major impact on and limit the quality of life for those who suffer from them. For the radiologist, early identification of these conditions is also crucial. (Masthoff et al., 2018)

Diagnostic imaging has been significantly impacted by recent developments in deep learning and artificial intelligence (AI). Dental and maxillofacial radiography diagnostic techniques could be substantially enhanced by incorporating AI technologies, such as deep learning and convolutional neural networks. (Iruvuri et al., 2023)

A branch of machine learning called deep learning (DL) has grown in importance in the field of diagnostic imaging. Deep neural networks, another name for DL AI systems, are capable of learning from training data by identifying patterns and analyzing test data without the need for explicit guidance. Complex images created by diagnostic imaging methods, such as magnetic resonance imaging (MRI) and cone beam computed tomography (CBCT), are processed by these systems, particularly convolutional neural networks (CNNs). (Iruvuri et al., 2023)

2. FOUNDATIONS OF DEEP LEARNING IN DENTAL RADIOLOGY

2.1 Overview of CNNs and Other Deep Learning Models

Many of the cutting-edge artificial intelligence (AI) applications of today capture, interpret, and analyse different types of text, audio, and video data using CNN-based deep learning technology. However, how are CNNs created, what is their relationship to deep learning, and what are they?

2.1.1 What Are CNNs and Deep Learning?

The most common use of convolutional neural networks, a type of deep learning algorithm, is to analyse and extract visual features from vast amounts of data. CNNs can be used for a variety of AI tasks, such as natural language processing and recommendation engines, even though their primary use is in image-related applications.

2.1.2 AI, Machine Learning, and Deep Learning

It's critical to comprehend the differences between commonly used AI-related key terms and how these deep learning algorithms relate to the larger field of artificial intelligence before delving deeper into how CNNs operate.

- Artificial intelligence is the study of intelligent computer programs that can perceive, reason, act, and adapt.
- Machine learning: A branch of artificial intelligence called machine learning allows algorithms to get better over time with more data.
- Neural network: In machine learning, a neural network is a collection of algorithms that can identify patterns and connections in vast amounts of data. Neural networks serve as the basis for deep learning algorithms and employ a logic structure modelled after the human brain.
- Deep learning: A branch of machine learning known as "deep learning" uses multilayered neural networks to learn from enormous volumes of data

2.1.3 How Convolutional Neural Networks Operate?

Convolutional neural networks extract crucial granular features for detection and classification after ingesting and processing vast amounts of data in a grid format. Convolutional, pooling, and fully connected layers are the three main types of layers found in CNNs. Every layer has a distinct function, works with ingested data, and gains complexity over time.

2.1.4 CNNs in Video Analytics

To grasp how Convolutional Neural Networks (CNNs) function, consider their application in video analytics—a technique where CNN-powered computer vision systems process video footage to derive meaningful insights, an example is shown in Figure 1. Computer vision, a branch of machine and deep learning, integrates cameras, cloud or edge computing, software, deep learning, and CNNs to create neural networks that interpret and analyze images. When these models are fully trained, they can identify and detect objects and even monitor movement.

Let's take an example where the input data consists of millions of car images.

Convolutional layers use filters to scan the input and detect features. These layers are typically stacked, with pooling layers in between to connect them. The initial convolutional layers pick up basic or low-level patterns like edges and lines, while the deeper layers identify more complex, high-level features such as car tires or headlights.

Pooling layers help reduce the size of the feature maps, lowering the computational load.

Fully connected layers then process the high-level features to recognize broader patterns related to cars. After the input data passes through the fully connected layers, the final activation layer triggers the model to produce its predictions.

Figure 1. Introduction to convolutional neural networks (GeeksforGeeks, 2025a)

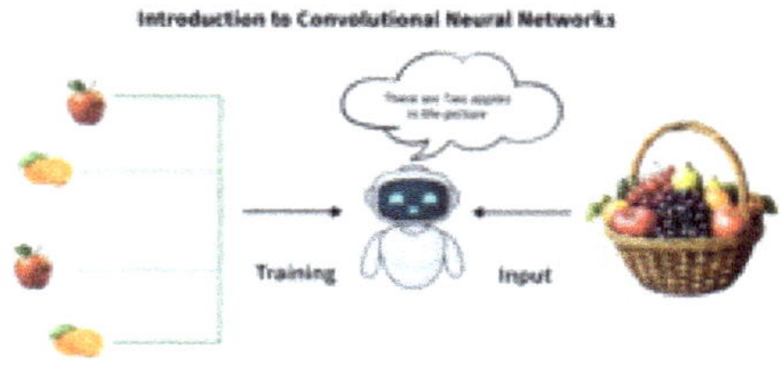

2.2 Transfer Learning and Model Fine-Tuning for Dental Datasets

CNN's performance is largely dependent on extensive labelled datasets for training, which presents several difficulties for medical image analysis. Obtaining medical image data is difficult and costly, and labelling calls for sophisticated technology and experience Furthermore, issues with data sharing and privacy make this process even more difficult. It is challenging to create reliable and broadly applicable models because of these factors, which also hinder the broad use and best performance of CNNs in medical image analysis. (Okazaki et al., 2024)

Transfer learning (TL) has become more widely acknowledged as a successful tactic in the medical industry to get past these obstacles. As an alternative to completely training DL models from scratch, TL makes use of a neural network that has already been trained on a sizable dataset and is subsequently adjusted for tasks using smaller, more specialized datasets. The concept that knowledge can be transferred between related tasks to enhance performance on new tasks is the basis of transfer learning (TL), which has its roots in cognitive research. In other words, TL can solve various issues by applying knowledge gleaned from massive data sets. (Okazaki et al., 2024)

2.3 Popular Datasets in Dental Radiology

The advancement of artificial intelligence (AI) in dentistry is highly dependent on the availability of large, well-annotated datasets. However, the accessibility of public dental imaging datasets remains limited and unclear. To address this issue and facilitate AI development, a study was conducted to systematically review all publicly available dental imaging datasets. This observational research involved a comprehensive search of dataset repositories—including academic databases, preprint servers, and AI challenge platforms—focusing on datasets and publications from 2020 to 2023, with PubMed searches extended back to 2011. The search targeted dental AI datasets containing image-based data (such as intraoral photographs, scans, and radiographs) using relevant keywords. Only datasets with more than 50 images, sourced from publicly accessible platforms, were considered.

Key information was extracted, including dataset characteristics, patient demographics, country of origin, dataset size, ethical approvals, image specifications, FAIR (Findability, Accessibility, Interoperability, and Reusability) metrics, and metadata completeness. From an initial pool of 131,028 records, only 16 unique dental imaging datasets were identified. These datasets were sourced from Kaggle (18.8%), as well as GitHub, Google, Mendeley, PubMed, and Zenodo (each contributing 12.5%), and Grand-Challenge, OSF, and arXiv (each contributing 6.25%). The majority of datasets focused on tooth segmentation (62.5%) and labeling (56.2%), with panoramic radiography being the most common imaging modality (58.8%). Among the 13 contributing countries, China provided the highest number of images (2,413).

Annotations were present in 75% of the datasets, though the labeling methods were often inadequately described and lacked consistency. Ethical approval was reported in only 31.2% of the datasets, and 56.25% did not specify any licensing information. Most datasets originated from dental clinics (50%). In the FAIR assessment, intraoral radiographs achieved the highest findability scores, whereas cone-beam computed tomography datasets performed the lowest across all metrics.

Overall, the study highlighted a significant scarcity of publicly available dental imaging data and inconsistencies in metadata reporting. It emphasized the need for initiatives aimed at expanding data availability, enhancing dataset diversity, ensuring thorough metadata documentation, and improving adherence to FAIR principles to support the development of robust, inclusive, and generalizable AI tools in dental diagnostics, treatment, and research. (Uribe et al., 2024)

3. APPLICATIONS OF DEEP LEARNING IN DENTAL IMAGING

a.) Caries detection from bitewing and periapical radiographs

Multiple deep learning models for diagnosing dental caries or lesion detection on dental X-ray images have been studied. Most extant research has been limited to analyses of the detection performance of deep learning models, and some recent papers have compared diagnostic performance between deep learning models and clinicians.

Figure 2 shows an example of the analysis of dental structures and caries tagging. The observers drew lines for the segmentation of dental structures (enamel, dentin, pulp, metal restoration, tooth-color restorations, gutta percha) and dental caries on the bitewing radiographs. *No software was used to generate the image. The picture used in Figure is a file printed using the source code that we implemented ourselves. (Lee et al., 2021)

Figure 2. Example of the analysis of dental structures and caries tagging

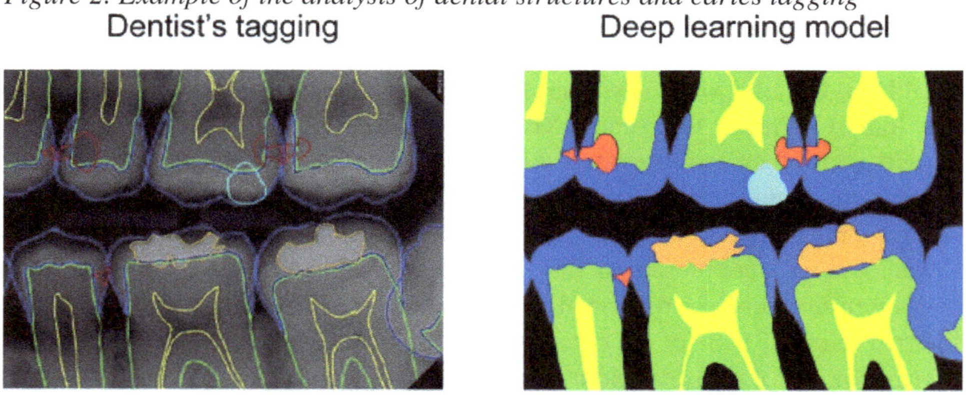

Caries (red), enamel (blue), dentin (green), pulp (yellow), metal restoration (orange), restoration (sky blue), gutta percha (brown), background (black)

The deep learning program's performance in detecting dental caries was consistent and fairly accurate. Apart from proximal dental caries, all forms of dental caries that could be identified on bitewing radiographs—including root caries, secondary dental caries, and gaps under restoration—were found. However, when the bitewing images included the third molar, the radiograph quality was poor, and the dental overlap was severe, the false detection rate of dental caries was slightly higher. (Lee et al., 2021)

b.) Periodontal disease classification using panoramic X-rays

The diagnosis of periodontal disease from panoramic X-ray images is a very difficult task Despite offering a helpful summary of the dental and periodontal structures, panoramic X-rays are limited in their ability to detect minute signs of periodontal disease because of their lack of 3D information, superimposition, and distortion. Most importantly, even for highly skilled professionals, radiographic annotations on these images are very difficult to provide with confidence and consistency because accurate periodontal disease assessment requires direct 3D probing measurements (e.g. A. bone loss, attachment levels, and probing depths) of every tooth during a clinical examination. Clinical indicators have been localized and measured in some recent studies (e.g. A. clinical attachment loss) for periodontitis staging through deep learning techniques. Convolutional neural networks, for example, have been proposed to identify potential radiographic bone loss from panoramic X-ray images. (Mei et al., 2024)

c.) Detection of periapical lesions and endodontic pathologies

Apical lesions, a general term for chronic infectious dental conditions, are commonly encountered in contemporary clinical practice and arise from a variety of causes. The conventional approach to endodontic treatment typically involves manual identification of lesion areas on patient X-ray images, a process that is both time-consuming and dependent on image clarity. In some cases, important diagnostic features may be obscured due to varying imaging angles or radiation doses. To improve efficiency and reduce the diagnostic burden on clinicians, automating repetitive tasks is essential. This allows dental professionals to concentrate on more complex aspects of care, such as treatment planning, tooth cleaning, and patient communication.

To support automated diagnosis, a convolutional neural network (CNN)-based lesion analysis model was proposed and developed. The study received ethical clearance from the Institutional Review Board under application number 202002030B0. The clinical image database was compiled with contributions from practicing dentists who provided real-world data. In the model development process, X-ray images were first enhanced using a Gaussian high-pass filter, followed by iterative thresholding to segment the images into individual tooth samples. These segmented tooth images formed the dataset used to train the CNN model via transfer learning.

Seventy percent of the dataset was allocated for training and validation, while the remaining 30% was used for testing and performance evaluation. The CNN model demonstrated a diagnostic accuracy of 92.5% in identifying apical lesions. The results confirmed the effectiveness of the proposed model in enabling automated and accurate diagnosis of apical lesions, thereby enhancing the clinical workflow in dental imaging and diagnosis. (Li et al., 2021)

d.) Neural Networks in Endodontics

Artificial intelligence is playing an increasingly significant role in the field of endodontics. It offers valuable applications in detecting periapical lesions and root fractures, analyzing the anatomy of the root canal system, estimating working length measurements, predicting the success of retreatment procedures, and evaluating the viability of dental pulp stem cells. One of the most notable uses of artificial neural networks in endodontics is their potential as decision-support tools for locating the minor apical foramen on radiographic images.

In one study, researchers used endodontic files to measure canal lengths on radiographs with and without the assistance of artificial neural networks. The results were compared to actual measurements taken after tooth extraction using stereomicroscopy. The neural network demonstrated a higher accuracy in locating the apical foramen than the human endodontists, correctly identifying the location 96% of the time compared to the 76% accuracy of manual assessment. This finding suggests that artificial neural networks may provide a more precise method for assessing the position of the apical foramen.

Apical periodontitis, an inflammatory condition resulting from bacterial infection in the root canal system, is commonly diagnosed through imaging modalities such as periapical radiographs, panoramic radiographs, and cone-beam computed tomography (CBCT). Deep learning methods have been employed to detect periapical lesions in CBCT images with high accuracy. For instance, convolutional neural networks (CNNs), a specialized form of neural network designed to process image data, have been used effectively to identify periapical lesions. In one study, a CNN detected 142 out of 153 lesions, achieving an accuracy rate comparable to that of experienced dental professionals.

Further research demonstrated CNNs' effectiveness in evaluating periapical radiographs, including experimental models using bovine ribs. These networks achieved strong performance metrics, with accuracy levels approaching those of expert radiologists. However, challenges remain in assessing certain tooth types, particularly in panoramic images where differences in anatomy and image generation may affect diagnostic accuracy. While sensitivity was higher for molars, specificity was comparatively lower, indicating room for improvement in diagnostic reliability.

Beyond imaging, artificial neural networks have also been explored in the genetic aspects of endodontic diagnosis. For example, AI techniques have been used to analyze gene expression patterns associated with radicular cysts and periapical granulomas. Findings from these studies suggest that, in addition to inflammatory factors, distinct biological processes reflected in gene expression may help differentiate between these two types of lesions.

In summary, the integration of artificial neural networks in endodontics is showing considerable promise. These systems have demonstrated their value in radiographic interpretation, anatomical evaluation, and even genetic analysis, offering a future of enhanced precision and efficiency in endodontic diagnosis and treatment planning. (Ossowska et al., 2022)

e.) Identification of cysts, tumors, and maxillofacial abnormalities in CBCT

Maxillofacial diseases include both odontogenic and nonodontogenic diseases in the jaws and related structures, including salivary glands, temporomandibular joints (TMJs), and facial muscles. Due to their anatomical complexity and proximity to critical vascular and neural structures, 3D imaging (such as CT/CBCT) is often required in the diagnostic and treatment planning processes, serving as one of the essential components of digital workflows for patient management. Thus, a wide range of deep learning and radiomics applications have been developed based on CT/CBCT images for diagnosis, treatment planning, and prediction of various maxillofacial diseases. (Hung et al., 2022)

4. AI TOOLS AND PLATFORMS IN DENTAL RADIOLOGY

Several commercial AI solutions have emerged in the field of dental diagnostics, offering advanced tools to assist clinicians in interpreting radiographs and planning treatment.

- **Pearl**, a U.S.-based company, offers *Second Opinion®*, an FDA-cleared and CE-marked AI platform that analyses bitewings, periapicals, and panoramic X-rays to detect a wide range of dental conditions such as caries, calculus, bone loss, and periapical radiolucencies. It integrates seamlessly with practice management systems, making it suitable for general dentists and large dental service organizations.
- **Diagnocat**, originally developed in Europe and now headquartered in the U.S., provides a comprehensive AI platform capable of analyzing CBCT scans, panoramic, and intraoral radiographs. It stands out for its ability to generate radiology-style reports, perform automatic tooth segmentation, and identify over 60 dental conditions, with strong applications in endodontics, oral surgery, and orthodontics.
- **DentalXrai**, developed in Germany, is a CE-certified AI solution designed primarily for European dental practices. Its flagship product, *DentalXrai Pro*, delivers real-time detection of common pathologies on intraoral and panoramic images and uniquely offers treatment recommendations aligned with German dental billing systems (BEMA and GOZ).

4.1 Integration with Dental Practice Management Software

A growing number of medical specialties are incorporating artificial intelligence (AI), which offers substantial improvements in patient management, treatment planning, and diagnosis. By increasing diagnostic precision, lowering radiation exposure, and streamlining workflow, artificial intelligence (AI) has the potential to revolutionize dental radiology.

In terms of diagnosis and treatment planning, these AI developments significantly affect dentistry, including numerous subspecialties such as orthodontics, oral surgery, implant dentistry, and oral radiography, through the use of advanced software. One of the few recent developments in oral radiology diagnosis is the automatic identification of diseases from images and the use of additional diagnosis-support technologies. By automatically examining dental images, AI systems can identify illnesses, speeding up and improving the accuracy of diagnosis. By spotting irregularities that might go unnoticed during manual analysis, this technology helps dentists and improves overall diagnostic and treatment planning in dental offices.

Tools that are commonly used:

In modern clinical practice and research, advanced tools such as intraoral cameras, X-ray machines, and digital systems for retrieving medical literature are commonly used. With the growing integration of artificial intelligence (AI), its role in dentistry has become increasingly prominent and effective. AI has shown considerable promise in the analysis and interpretation of dental images, including intraoral photographs, cone-beam computed tomography (CBCT) scans, panoramic radiographs, and traditional X-rays. Through deep learning algorithms, AI models can accurately detect and classify a wide range of dental conditions such as dental caries, periodontal disease, bone loss, impacted teeth, and oral tumors.

AI-based systems offer significant support to clinicians by identifying abnormalities, providing second opinions, and reducing the risk of human error. One of the most notable applications is in computer-aided detection (CAD), where AI algorithms automatically scan dental images to highlight potential issues. These systems can mark areas of concern, such as early signs of oral disease or suspicious lesions, enabling early diagnosis and intervention. This early detection is crucial in improving clinical outcomes, as it allows for timely and more effective treatment planning.

Additionally, robotic systems specifically designed for dental procedures are being introduced into clinical practice. These systems consist of robotic arms, instruments, and sensors that are guided and supervised by dentists throughout the treatment process. Robotics-assisted dentistry is being applied across various fields, including orthodontics, endodontics (such as root canal therapy), crown or veneer placements, and dental implant surgeries. Compared to manual methods, robotic systems offer enhanced precision and consistency, making it possible to perform complex dental tasks with greater accuracy and efficiency. (Aggarwal & Singh, 2024)

5. IMPACT ON DENTAL HEALTH TOURISM

Many patients tend to seek medical or dental care outside their home country due to various financial or personal reasons. With the integration of AI models and tools in dental practices, diagnosing and treating these cases can be done much faster and effectively, especially for international patients. Also, patients who are knowledgeable on how to use AI tools and programmes can form a second opinion before arranging their treatment plan or travels in other countries and then form a decision based on that.

5.1 A Decalogue for Designing AI-Driven Travel Medicine Chatbots

Developing an AI-powered chatbot for travel medicine involves creating a user-centric tool capable of delivering accurate, up-to-date, and personalized health advice tailored to travelers' needs. Such a system must be grounded in a robust design framework that prioritizes both the reliability of information and the safety of users. To support this, ten essential features—building upon those proposed by Flaherty—have been outlined to guide the development of effective travel medicine chatbots:

1. **Extensive and Authoritative Knowledge Base**

The chatbot should be built on a reliable and wide-ranging database covering travel vaccinations, location-specific health risks, and preventive measures. All information provided should be referenced from verified sources.

2. **Regularly Updated Information**

The database should be continuously updated with the latest scientific research, international guidelines, and real-time data from official health authorities and travel advisory services.

3. **Non-Substitutive Role to Medical Professionals**

The chatbot must clearly communicate that it does not replace professional medical consultations. It should only provide general advice and encourage users to seek personalized counselling at certified travel clinics.

4. **Defined and Limited Scope**

The chatbot's domain should be strictly confined to travel medicine. It must avoid answering queries outside this area and should be safeguarded against misuse or manipulation of its underlying AI model.

5. **User Consent and Data Privacy**

Explicit user consent must be obtained before collecting or using any personal data. The chatbot should transparently inform users about data handling practices and comply fully with relevant privacy and data protection regulations.

6. **Personalized Health Guidance**

To offer tailored advice, the chatbot should collect relevant user information such as travel itinerary, medical history, and health status, enabling more precise and meaningful recommendations.

7. **User-Friendly Interface**

A clear, intuitive, and accessible interface should be implemented to accommodate users of all ages and levels of technical skill. Feedback mechanisms should be included to continually refine the chatbot's performance.

8. **Multilingual and Culturally Sensitive Design**

The chatbot should support multiple languages to reach diverse populations and demonstrate awareness and respect for cultural differences in its responses and interactions.

9. **Geolocation Integration**

Incorporating location-based services allows the chatbot to provide real-time, region-specific information, such as local health risks, nearby clinics, or vaccination centers.

10. **EHR Integration with Consent**

With user authorization, integration with electronic health records (EHRs) can enhance personalization by offering the chatbot access to a traveler's vaccination history and medical background.

By integrating these features, AI-driven chatbots can effectively support travel medicine by enhancing pre-travel planning, offering in-transit health advice, and assisting with post-travel care—ultimately improving health outcomes for travelers globally. (Baglivo et al., 2024)

6. ETHICAL, LEGAL, AND DATA PRIVACY CONSIDERATIONS

AI must be morally responsible since it will be utilized in healthcare more and more. By employing suitable algorithms based on real-time, unbiased data, data bias can be prevented. It is necessary to have inclusive and diverse programming teams and to regularly audit the algorithm, including how it is implemented in a system. AI may not be able to fully replace clinical judgment, but it can assist physicians in making better choices. AI could be used to perform screening and assessment if there is a lack of medical expertise in an environment with few resources. Even the quickest AI decisions are methodical because algorithms are used, in contrast to human decision-making. Therefore, even if an activity has no legal consequences (since effective legal frameworks have not yet been created), it always results in accountability—not by the machine, but by the people who created it and the people who use it. However, the use of AI raises ethical questions, as shown in Figure 3. (Naik et al., 2022)

Figure 3. Various ethical and legal conundrums involved with the usage of artificial intelligence in healthcare (Naik et al., 2022)

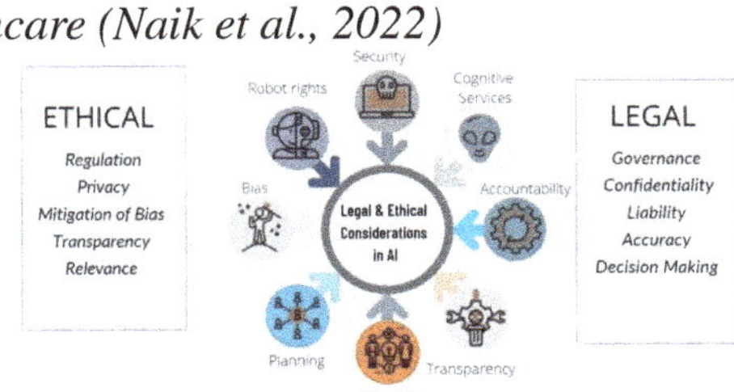

6.1 The Importance of Responsibility in AI Systems

Responsibility plays a crucial role in the deployment and governance of AI systems due to their potential to fail dramatically when applied in new or shifting contexts. AI can exhibit high levels of intelligence in one setting and act unpredictably or naively in another. Even when efforts are made to control algorithmic bias, all AI systems inherently possess limitations. Therefore, it is essential for human users—especially those in decision-making roles—to understand these limitations. Additionally, AI systems must be designed in a way that complements and supports human decision-making needs. In fields like medicine, over-reliance on diagnostic AI tools can lead to complacency among healthcare professionals, causing them to neglect the development of their own clinical judgment and expertise. Similar issues have been observed in criminal justice, where judges have adjusted rulings based on AI-generated risk assessments that were later proven inaccurate.

The absence of human oversight in AI applications raises critical concerns about cybersecurity. According to a RAND perspectives report, using AI in domains such as surveillance or national cybersecurity can introduce new vulnerabilities—particularly those stemming from biased or manipulated data inputs (referred to as "data diet" vulnerabilities). Additionally, the growing use of AI-driven surveillance technologies by governments, such as predictive policing algorithms, has sparked concerns over the erosion of civil liberties and the infringement of fundamental rights. These systems can compromise essential infrastructure and, by extension, human safety and equitable access to resources. A significant challenge lies in the fact that cybersecurity threats are often invisible and only identified after substantial harm has occurred.

Another area of ethical concern involves lethal autonomous weapon systems (LAWS). These technologies combine AI's decision-making autonomy with the capacity to harm or kill, raising serious moral and ethical questions. While proponents argue for their potential strategic benefits, their use poses significant risks that demand rigorous scrutiny and regulation.

Bias in AI training datasets is also a well-documented problem. For example, studies by Buolamwini and Gebru revealed that automated facial recognition systems exhibit lower accuracy for individuals with darker skin tones, particularly women, due to biased training data. This issue is not limited to facial recognition. In healthcare, machine learning models are often developed using clinical trial data derived from selected populations, which frequently underrepresent marginalized communities. As a result, AI systems trained on such data may perform poorly or inaccurately when applied to underserved groups, exacerbating existing disparities. (Naik et al., 2022)

6.2 Who Bears the Responsibility?

In contrast to medical professionals, technologists are not legally mandated to be held accountable for the consequences of their work; instead, their responsibilities are often guided by ethical standards and professional norms. This distinction highlights a key point of debate regarding the accountability of technologists when artificial intelligence systems (AIS) are deployed in healthcare settings and directly impact patient outcomes.

A significant concern arises when clinicians use outputs from AIS that they cannot fully interpret or justify. In such cases, they may be unable to defend their clinical decisions, especially if harm results from relying on unvalidated or opaque AI systems. This lack of transparency and accountability raises serious safety and ethical issues in clinical practice. Various scenarios demonstrate how the "black-box" nature of AI can affect different stakeholders involved in healthcare delivery.

Currently, there is a notable lack of comprehensive literature and standardized frameworks guiding the ethical and legal accountability of AI in healthcare. It is imperative that top-level policymakers and regulatory bodies develop detailed and authoritative guidelines to ensure safe, ethical, and responsible use of AI technologies in clinical environments. (Naik et al., 2022)

7. CHALLENGES AND FUTURE DIRECTIONS

However, software engineers who design AI-intensive healthcare systems face a number of difficult problems that are exacerbated by these systems' robustness, efficiency, and ethics. These issues can be summed up as follows:

- Data Security and Privacy: Data, which frequently contains sensitive personal information, is the foundation of AI in healthcare. It is crucial to ensure the privacy and security of this data, which calls for strong encryption techniques, safe data-sharing procedures, and adherence to laws like the GDPR in the EU and HIPAA (Health Insurance Portability and Accountability Act) in the US.
- Bias and ethical concerns: AI systems are only as objective as the data they are trained on, raising ethical and bias concerns. The AI may make biased decisions if the training data is skewed, which could result in disparate treatment outcomes for various demographic groups. It is a difficult task to address these biases and make sure ethical issues are incorporated into AI systems.
- Adoption and Trust: Establishing trust between patients and healthcare providers is essential to the uptake of AI-based systems This entails proving the

effectiveness, safety, and dependability of AI interventions. In order to create systems that enhance clinical workflows and enhance human judgment rather than replace it, software engineers must collaborate closely with healthcare professionals. (Bertl et al., 2024)

7.1 What is Multimodal AI in Healthcare Diagnostics?

The practice of merging various forms of medical data, including lab test results, patient histories, genetic information, medical images, and real-time health monitoring, to produce a more thorough and precise diagnosis is known as multimodal AI in healthcare diagnostics. This approach combines various patient data sources rather than depending on just one to provide a comprehensive picture of a medical condition.

Radiologists must familiarize themselves with the current frameworks, applications, and analyses of multimodal artificial intelligence (AI) as it becomes more and more integrated into the field.

- The accuracy of conventional methods for integrating multimodal AI into the clinic has been demonstrated to be superior to that of unimodal methods.
- Time series and non-Euclidean biomedical data can be integrated using state-of-the-art methods for multimodal biomedical AI applications, like transformers and graph neural networks.
- Inconsistent taxonomy, a dearth of foundational models utilizing a variety of large-scale representative data sources, and a mismatch between the healthcare industry and the data curation required for AI models are some of the major drawbacks of the multimodal biomedical AI landscape. (Simon et al., 2024). Figure 4 shows a Multimodal medical artificial intelligence (AI) applications across disease spaces. Simplified schematic of the many applications of multimodal medical AI fusing imaging, omics, and clinical data for various tasks across disease spaces. (Simon et al., 2024)

Figure 4. Multimodal medical artificial intelligence (AI) applications across disease spaces

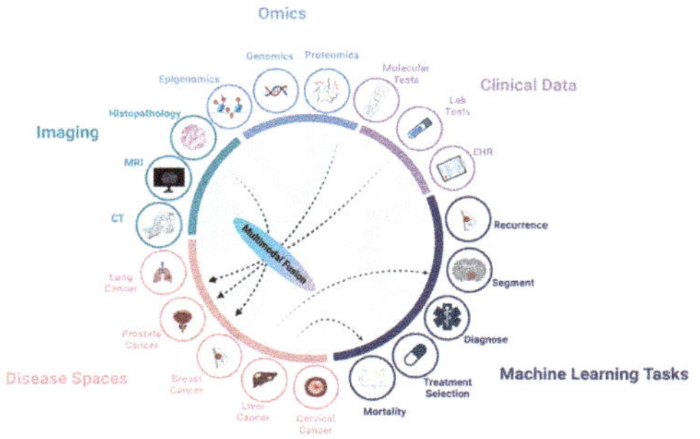

7.2 Prospects for AR/VR-Assisted AI Diagnostics in Dental Tourism

The accuracy and interactivity of dental training and patient care have greatly improved with the incorporation of augmented reality (AR) and virtual reality (VR) into dental surgery education and practice. According to research, augmented reality (AR) enhances surgical precision by providing real-time data overlays during procedures, which improves the results of operations like implant placements for teeth. Conversely, virtual reality (VR) has transformed training settings by providing realistic, detailed simulations that greatly enhance surgical skill retention. In 2023, VR applications in orthognathic surgery served as evidence of this. Notwithstanding their benefits, these technologies face obstacles to adoption, including the high cost of implementation and the difficulty of incorporating sophisticated simulations into conventional training programs. In dental surgery, AR and VR have bright futures. Current advancements seek to incorporate artificial intelligence and improve haptic feedback to increase realism. (Lin et al., 2024)

7.3 Application in Clinical Dental Practice

1.Surgical Planning and Navigation

The integration of augmented reality (AR) and virtual reality (VR) into surgical planning and navigation represents a major leap forward in clinical dental procedures. These technologies empower dental professionals to carry out intricate surgeries with heightened precision and assurance. VR, in particular, is invaluable in the preoperative phase, providing an in-depth, three-dimensional visualization of the surgical site. This detailed planning tool allows clinicians to chart out each step of the procedure meticulously, which significantly reduces the risks typically associated with invasive interventions.

2. Patient Education

AR and VR have revolutionized the way dental practitioners convey complex surgical information to patients. Through engaging, immersive visuals, these tools make it easier for patients to comprehend their dental conditions and the treatments proposed. This enhanced understanding plays a key role in securing informed consent and easing preoperative anxiety. Research by Huang et al. illustrates that AR applications used during consultations lead to clearer communication, better patient satisfaction, and improved readiness for surgery.

3. Enhancing Precision in Surgical Procedures

AR has proven especially effective in enhancing surgical precision. For instance, Mladenovic et al. demonstrated that AR could improve the accuracy of local anesthesia administration by enabling clinicians to view the precise injection site. Real-time AR guidance is also applied during dental implant procedures to assist in accurate implant placement, ensuring critical anatomical features are avoided and treatment outcomes are optimized. Such innovations significantly boost the safety and effectiveness of dental surgeries.

These examples highlight the transformative role of AR and VR in contemporary dental practice. Beyond improving procedural accuracy, these technologies strengthen patient education and communication. As their capabilities expand, AR and VR are poised to become integral components of dental care, driving innovation and setting new benchmarks in clinical excellence. (Lin et al., 2024)

7.4 Augmented Reality vs. Virtual Reality in Dental Surgery Training

AR offers significant benefits in real-time surgical enhancement by projecting overlays that guide surgical tasks with high accuracy. This feature is particularly beneficial for visualizing subsurface structures, assisting clinicians in performing precise incisions and implant placements. On the other hand, VR provides a fully immersive training experience where learners can engage with complex surgical scenarios without involving actual patients, making it an ideal tool for practice and mastery.

Although current VR systems often lack tactile feedback essential for mimicking real surgical sensations, ongoing improvements in haptic technology are addressing this limitation. These advancements are making VR increasingly effective for training in delicate procedures, allowing learners to develop confidence and competence before performing on real patients. (Lin et al., 2024)

8. CASE STUDIES AND GLOBAL PERSPECTIVES

AI is revolutionizing dentistry by increasing the precision of diagnoses, customizing treatment plans, and streamlining data organization. Advances in AI, particularly machine learning frameworks like CNNs, are being used in various dental specialties. Among the many advantages of these AI tools is their ability to identify illnesses early.

- Artificial Intelligence in Paediatric Dentistry: AI is becoming more and more popular in all sectors of the economy, and it's also revolutionizing paediatric dentistry. From research and diagnostic testing to behavioural management, pain management, prosthodontic tooth mobility, and regenerative dentistry, artificial intelligence offers a wide range of exciting potential solutions.
- Artificial Intelligence in Prosthodontics: Using computer-assisted layout and fabrication software, artificial intelligence (AI) helps prosthodontics make sure that crowns and extraction appliances are accurate and appropriate for replacing missing teeth. However, because of advances in confrontational conceptual networks, researchers are using AI to quickly create novel dental reconstructions for optimal activity, personalized suitability, and enhanced structural systems.
- Artificial Intelligence in Orthodontics One of the newest developments that has generated a lot of interest is the application of AI to personalize orthodontic treatment (Figure 4). The appliances are easily 3D-printed using precise 3D photos and simulated representations. This system finds the ideal force, locates the pressure sites, and intelligently calculates the necessary adjustments based on each patient's unique set of dental data. (Mallineni et al., 2024)
- Artificial Intelligence in Oral Medicine and Radiology

Figure 5 shows the use of artificial intelligence in oral medicine and radiology. (Mallineni et al., 2024)

Figure 5. The use of artificial intelligence in oral medicine and radiology

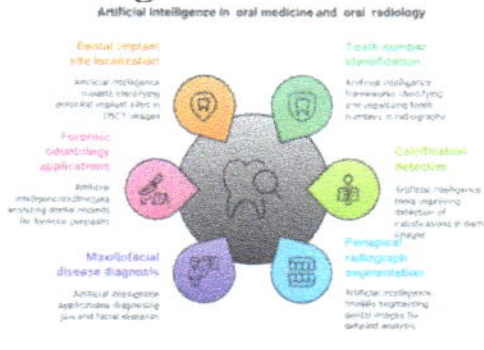

8.1 Comparative Analysis: AI vs. Traditional Diagnostics

Artificial intelligence (AI) is transforming diagnostic imaging in radiology by improving accuracy, efficiency, and decision-making. Traditional radiological interpretation, despite its clinical significance, is limited by interobserver variability, workload constraints, and potential diagnostic errors. While AI-assisted imaging has demonstrated superior performance in certain studies, inconsistencies in outcomes and a lack of consensus necessitate a comprehensive meta-analysis to evaluate its efficacy compared to conventional radiology.

In terms of sensitivity, specificity, and diagnostic accuracy across a variety of imaging modalities, AI-assisted diagnostic imaging outperforms conventional radiology. The results highlight AI's potential to improve workflow efficiency, lower diagnostic variability, and improve clinical decision-making, especially in pulmonary imaging and oncology. Notwithstanding these benefits, careful interpretation is required due to issues with heterogeneity, practical applicability, and possible publication bias. Although the inclusion of high-quality studies and rigorous statistical methods strengthens the reliability of these results, additional prospective trials and standardized validation frameworks are necessary to ensure a smooth transition into clinical practice. To maximize its clinical utility, future research should concentrate on addressing biases in algorithm training, improving AI-human collaboration, and assessing AI performance in a range of patient populations. (Hussain et al., 2025)

8.2 Augmented Reality/Virtual Reality vs. Traditional Methods in Dental Surgery Training

Compared to traditional training methods, AR and VR significantly enhance safety in surgical education. Traditional hands-on training, while valuable for developing clinical experience, often places real patients at risk when novice trainees are involved. In contrast, AR and VR allow students to hone their skills in a risk-free, controlled environment, improving safety for both patients and learners.

The ability to practice repeatedly using VR simulations supports skill mastery and boosts trainee confidence, which can be difficult to achieve through traditional training due to limited patient availability or ethical restrictions on repeated procedures. By incorporating AR and VR simulations into dental education, institutions can reduce patient risk while offering a more consistent and effective learning experience.

These technologies also address financial and logistical barriers present in traditional setups. While conventional training requires considerable resources for maintenance and case availability, virtual simulations offer a scalable, easily updatable solution that keeps pace with evolving surgical techniques and medical advancements.

In conclusion, while AR and VR technologies significantly enhance the safety and effectiveness of dental training, they are best used as a complement to traditional hands-on experiences. A balanced educational approach that combines simulation-based learning with practical clinical exposure ensures comprehensive development of technical competence, clinical reasoning, and patient communication skills. (Lin et al., 2024)

8.3 AI-Powered Triage in Dental Emergency Care

Dental emergency departments play a critical role in providing immediate care for acute oral health issues, ranging from traumatic injuries and abscesses to severe toothaches and postoperative complications. These units often serve as the first point of contact for individuals experiencing intense dental pain or infection, especially those without regular dental access. However, like general emergency departments, dental ERs are increasingly burdened by rising patient volumes, limited personnel, and resource constraints. This often leads to overcrowding, extended wait times, compromised care quality, and increased stress for both patients and staff.

Traditional triage methods in dental emergencies often rely on clinical judgment to determine the urgency of a case—for example, prioritizing facial cellulitis or uncontrolled bleeding over routine toothaches. While dental triage guidelines do exist, they are often inconsistently applied and dependent on the clinician's experience. Under high-pressure conditions, this can result in subjective assessments, delays in critical care, and misprioritization, particularly when multiple patients present simultaneously with varying degrees of urgency.

Artificial intelligence (AI) offers a promising solution to these challenges by automating and enhancing the triage process. AI-powered systems can rapidly analyze patient data—including symptoms, clinical history, pain severity, swelling, systemic involvement, and medical background—to assign a priority level. These tools use machine learning algorithms trained on vast datasets to reduce variability, improve accuracy, and accelerate decision-making.

The benefits of AI triage in dental emergencies are substantial. For example, an AI model could prioritize a patient with facial swelling, fever, and difficulty swallowing—signs of a potentially life-threatening odontogenic infection—over one presenting with non-urgent sensitivity. Real-time AI support can also help dental staff allocate chairs, imaging, and surgical resources more efficiently, while minimizing the risk of clinical oversight.

Moreover, AI systems can integrate with electronic health records (EHRs) to flag medically compromised patients or allergies, enabling safer and more personalized care. In mass casualty events involving dental trauma—such as accidents or sports injuries—AI-based triage could rapidly categorize cases and support resource coordination.

In conclusion, implementing AI-driven triage systems in dental emergency settings holds the potential to reduce crowding, enhance accuracy, streamline patient flow, and improve care outcomes. As AI technology continues to evolve, it may become a cornerstone in building a more resilient and efficient model for dental emergency care. (Da'Costa et al., 2025)

9. CONCLUSION

By automating repetitive tasks and freeing up clinicians to concentrate on more complex and demanding cases, artificial intelligence (AI) has the potential to enhance patient care and lessen the burden on healthcare systems. It is crucial to remember that AI cannot take the place of human knowledge, and ethical standards should always govern its application in medicine. AI can only help clinicians do their jobs in a professional manner. It cannot take the place of human expertise, treatment planning, or knowledge. AI is generally acknowledged as a useful tool for dentists, despite the difficulties associated with data collection, interpretation, computing power, and ethical issues that need to be resolved. AI is impartial, reproducible, transparent, and easy to use thanks to careful design and extensive clinical validation. Future developments in AI must continue to put human needs first while enhancing our capacity to handle large amounts of data. Dental care is a multidisciplinary field where the final decision must be made by the dentist itself, even though AI can assist in many ways. (Ghaffari et al., 2024)

REFERENCES

Aggarwal, J., & Singh, P. (2024). Artificial intelligence in dental practice: An integrated approach. *Journal of Dental Specialities*, *12*(2), 72–76. DOI: 10.18231/j.jds.2024.015

Baglivo, F., De Angelis, L., Cruschelli, G., & Rizzo, C. (2024). A decalogue for personalized travel health assistance with AI-driven chatbots. *Journal of Travel Medicine*, *31*(4), taae026. Advance online publication. DOI: 10.1093/jtm/taae026 PMID: 38345410

Bertl, M., Lamo, Y., Leucker, M., Margaria, T., Mohammadi, E., Mukhiya, S. K., Pechmann, L., Piho, G., & Rabbi, F. (2024). Challenges for AI in healthcare systems. In *Lecture notes in computer science* (pp. 165–186). DOI: 10.1007/978-3-031-73741-1_11

Convolutional Neural Networks (CNN) and Deep Learning. (n.d.). Intel. https://www.intel.com/content/www/us/en/internet-of-things/computer-vision/convolutional-neural-networks.html

Da'Costa, A., Teke, J., Origbo, J. E., Osonuga, A., Egbon, E., & Olawade, D. B. (2025). Ai-driven triage in emergency departments: A review of benefits, challenges, and future directions. *International Journal of Medical Informatics*, *197*, 105838. DOI: 10.1016/j.ijmedinf.2025.105838 PMID: 39965433

GeeksforGeeks. (2025, May 29). *Convolutional Neural Network (CNN) in machine learning*. GeeksforGeeks. https://www.geeksforgeeks.org/deep-learning/convolutional-neural-network-cnn-in-machine-learning/

Ghaffari, M., Zhu, Y., & Shrestha, A. (2024). A review of advancements of artificial intelligence in dentistry. *Dentistry Review*, *4*(2), 100081. DOI: 10.1016/j.dentre.2024.100081

Hung, K. F., Ai, Q. Y. H., Wong, L. M., Yeung, A. W. K., Li, D. T. S., & Leung, Y. Y. (2022). Current applications of deep learning and radiomics on CT and CBCT for maxillofacial diseases. *Diagnostics (Basel)*, *13*(1), 110. DOI: 10.3390/diagnostics13010110 PMID: 36611402

Hussain, Z., Khan, N. A., Haider, N. H. A., Naz, N. F., Iqbal, N. R., Burki, N. S., Almagharbeh, N. W. T., & Khan, N. H. (2025). COMPARING THE EFFICACY OF AI-ASSISTED VS. TRADITIONAL DIAGNOSTIC IMAGING IN RADIOLOGY – A META-ANALYSIS. *Journal of Health and Rehabilitation*, *3*(2 (Health&Rehab)), 163–171. DOI: 10.71000/vd11kz38

Iruvuri, A. G., Miryala, G., Khan, Y., Ramalingam, N. T., Sevugaperumal, B., Soman, M., & Padmanabhan, A. (2023). Revolutionizing Dental Imaging: A comprehensive study on the integration of artificial intelligence in dental and maxillofacial radiology. *Cureus*. Advance online publication. DOI: 10.7759/cureus.50292 PMID: 38205468

Lee, S., Oh, S., Jo, J., Kang, S., Shin, Y., & Park, J. (2021). Deep learning for early dental caries detection in bitewing radiographs. *Scientific Reports*, *11*(1), 16807. Advance online publication. DOI: 10.1038/s41598-021-96368-7 PMID: 34413414

Li, C., Lin, S., Chou, H., Chen, T., Chen, Y., Liu, S., Liu, Y., Chen, C., Huang, Y., Chen, S., Mao, Y., Abu, P. R., Chiang, W., & Lo, W. (2021). Detection of dental apical lesions using CNNs on periapical radiograph. *Sensors (Basel)*, *21*(21), 7049. DOI: 10.3390/s21217049 PMID: 34770356

Lin, P., Chen, T., Lin, C., Huang, C., Tsai, Y., Tsai, Y., & Wang, C. (2024). The use of augmented reality (AR) and virtual reality (VR) in dental surgery education and practice: A narrative review. *Journal of Dental Sciences*, *19*, S91–S101. DOI: 10.1016/j.jds.2024.10.011 PMID: 39807259

Mallineni, S. K., Sethi, M., Punugoti, D., Kotha, S. B., Alkhayal, Z., Mubaraki, S., Almotawah, F. N., Kotha, S. L., Sajja, R., Nettam, V., Thakare, A. A., & Sakhamuri, S. (2024). Artificial Intelligence in Dentistry: A Descriptive Review. *Bioengineering (Basel, Switzerland)*, *11*(12), 1267. DOI: 10.3390/bioengineering11121267 PMID: 39768085

. Masthoff, M., Gerwing, M., Masthoff, M., Timme, M., Kleinheinz, J., Berninger, M., Heindel, W., Wildgruber, M., & Schülke, C. (2018). Dental Imaging – A basic guide for the radiologist. *RöFo - Fortschritte Auf Dem Gebiet Der Röntgenstrahlen Und Der Bildgebenden Verfahren, 191*(03), 192–198. DOI: 10.1055/a-0636-4129

Mei, L., Deng, K., Cui, Z., Fang, Y., Li, Y., Lai, H., Tonetti, M. S., & Shen, D. (2024). Clinical knowledge-guided hybrid classification network for automatic periodontal disease diagnosis in X-ray image. *Medical Image Analysis*, *99*, 103376. DOI: 10.1016/j.media.2024.103376 PMID: 39536402

Naik, N., Hameed, B. M. Z., Shetty, D. K., Swain, D., Shah, M., Paul, R., Aggarwal, K., Ibrahim, S., Patil, V., Smriti, K., Shetty, S., Rai, B. P., Chlosta, P., & Somani, B. K. (2022). Legal and ethical consideration in artificial intelligence in healthcare: Who takes responsibility? *Frontiers in Surgery*, *9*, 862322. Advance online publication. DOI: 10.3389/fsurg.2022.862322 PMID: 35360424

Okazaki, S., Mine, Y., Yoshimi, Y., Iwamoto, Y., Ito, S., Peng, T., Nishimura, T., Suehiro, T., Koizumi, Y., Nomura, R., Tanimoto, K., Kakimoto, N., & Murayama, T. (2024). *RadImageNet and ImageNet as datasets for transfer learning in the assessment of dental radiographs: A Comparative study*. Deleted Journal., DOI: 10.1007/s10278-024-01204-9

Ossowska, A., Kusiak, A., & Świetlik, D. (2022). Artificial Intelligence in Dentistry—Narrative Review. *International Journal of Environmental Research and Public Health, 19*(6), 3449. DOI: 10.3390/ijerph19063449 PMID: 35329136

Simon, B. D., Ozyoruk, K. B., Gelikman, D. G., Harmon, S. A., & Türkbey, B. (2024). *The future of multimodal artificial intelligence models for integrating imaging and clinical metadata: a narrative review*. Diagnostic and Interventional Radiology., DOI: 10.4274/dir.2024.242631

The Future of Healthcare: Multimodal AI for precision medicine. (n.d.). https://www.akira.ai/blog/multi-modal-in-healthcare

Uribe, S., Issa, J., Sohrabniya, F., Denny, A., Kim, N., Dayo, A., Chaurasia, A., Sofi-Mahmudi, A., Büttner, M., & Schwendicke, F. (2024). Publicly available dental image datasets for artificial intelligence. *Journal of Dental Research, 103*(13), 1365–1374. DOI: 10.1177/00220345241272052 PMID: 39422586

Chapter 8
AI-Driven Personalization in Dental Health Tourism: Smart Diagnostics, Virtual Consultations, and Treatment Optimization

Affaan Shaikh
http://orcid.org/0009-0004-7590-7456
IntelliDent AI, UAE

Ravi Teja Kothuru
http://orcid.org/0009-0002-9555-151X
University of San Diego, USA

Muskan Kumari
http://orcid.org/0009-0000-3295-5918
Karachi Metropolitan University, Pakistan

ABSTRACT

The global rise of dental health tourism has created demand for more efficient, personalized, and technology-driven care models. This chapter explores how Artificial Intelligence (AI) is transforming dental health tourism by enabling smarter diagnostics, remote consultations, and optimized treatment planning even before patients travel. Through AI-powered imaging analysis, chatbots, virtual assistants, and predictive cost estimation tools, clinics can offer a seamless pre-travel experience tailored to individual patient needs. Additionally, machine learning models support clinicians in creating faster, more accurate treatment plans while maintaining high standards of care across borders. The chapter also addresses how AI enhances post-

DOI: 10.4018/979-8-3373-4114-9.ch008

treatment monitoring through telehealth and digital platforms, ensuring continuity of care. Ethical, legal, and data privacy concerns in cross-border AI applications are also discussed.

I. INTRODUCTION

The global healthcare landscape has undergone a significant transformation over the past two decades, with medical tourism emerging as a vital industry driven by globalization, affordability, and advancements in health technologies. Dental health tourism, a prominent subset of this phenomenon, has gained increasing attention due to its unique combination of clinical care, economic incentives, and travel. Patients from high-income countries often travel to destinations like Hungary, Turkey, Thailand, Mexico, and India to access high-quality dental care at a fraction of the domestic cost. These cross-border journeys offer not only savings but also reduced wait times and access to advanced procedures not readily available in the patients' home countries (Ding et al., 2023; Patil et al., 2002).

As demand for dental tourism accelerates, so too does the need for innovation in how care is delivered and experienced. Traditional models, which rely heavily on in-person evaluations and paper-based systems, are rapidly being challenged by new technological paradigms that prioritize efficiency, personalization, and digital engagement. Among these, Artificial Intelligence (AI) stands out as a transformative force, reshaping every stage of the dental tourism journey from pre-travel consultations to diagnostics, treatment planning, and post-operative care (Xu et al., 2020).

AI technologies offer unprecedented opportunities to bridge the logistical and clinical gaps that often complicate international patient care. Through smart algorithms, clinics can analyze vast datasets including radiographic images, medical histories, and patient preferences to generate tailored treatment plans. These systems not only increase diagnostic accuracy but also enable remote evaluations, allowing patients to receive expert consultations before they even board a plane. This shift from reactive to predictive and preventive care enhances the efficiency of cross-border dental procedures while elevating the patient experience.

The integration of AI into dental tourism is particularly crucial given the sector's reliance on compressed treatment timelines. Unlike domestic dental patients who benefit from extended treatment windows, dental tourists often undergo complex procedures within a limited timeframe. Any misalignment between diagnosis and treatment delivery can result in suboptimal outcomes or the need for costly follow-up visits. AI mitigates these risks by enabling clinics to optimize scheduling, streamline workflows, and ensure that every decision is data-informed and patient-specific (Schwendicke et al., 2020). Furthermore, AI applications in dentistry, such as computer vision for interpreting radiographs and natural language processing (NLP) for multilingual patient communication, ensure that geographical and linguistic barriers are minimized (Schwendicke et al., 2019).

The COVID-19 pandemic further underscored the necessity of AI-driven solutions in dental tourism. Global lockdowns and travel restrictions exposed the fragility of traditional in-person care models and highlighted the importance of remote diagnostics and teleconsultations. Post-pandemic, clinics that have adopted AI tools are better positioned to cater to a digitally-savvy, health-conscious patient base seeking personalized care journeys. In this context, AI does not merely support dental tourism it redefines it by enabling a smarter, more agile system that operates seamlessly across borders.

Another driving force behind the integration of AI is the shifting expectations of patients. Today's health tourists are digitally literate and increasingly value transparency, customization, and efficiency in care delivery. They expect virtual consultations, precise cost estimates, and comprehensive treatment plans before making travel decisions. AI-powered platforms are meeting these demands by providing interactive interfaces that allow users to upload diagnostic records, receive instant treatment suggestions, and engage with clinics in their native language all before committing to international travel (Turner, 2011).

Additionally, AI's role in post-treatment care is a significant contributor to long-term patient satisfaction and retention. Remote monitoring tools powered by AI enable clinicians to track recovery, detect complications early, and offer real-time advice without requiring patients to return. This continuity of care is particularly vital in dental tourism, where trust and follow-up play crucial roles in maintaining global reputations and securing repeat clientele.

Importantly, the application of AI in dental health tourism is not without challenges. Ethical, legal, and data privacy concerns must be addressed, especially when sensitive health information crosses national borders. Regulatory frameworks differ significantly between countries, raising questions about data ownership, informed consent, and liability in AI-assisted decision-making. Nonetheless, the benefits of AI integration in terms of improved patient outcomes, reduced operational costs, and enhanced global competitiveness are undeniable and continue to drive its adoption across the dental tourism landscape (Badawy, 2023).

In conclusion, the confluence of rising dental tourism and the rapid advancement of artificial intelligence marks a pivotal shift in global healthcare delivery. AI has the potential to transform the dental tourism experience into one that is smarter, faster, and more personalized. By leveraging AI tools for diagnostics, virtual consultations, and treatment optimization, clinics can attract and retain international patients more effectively while maintaining high clinical standards. This chapter delves deeper into how AI technologies are being implemented across the patient journey, highlighting both the practical applications and broader implications for the future of dental health tourism.

II. THEORETICAL FRAMEWORK

2. The Need for AI in Dental Health Tourism

The dental tourism industry has experienced rapid growth over the past decade, driven by rising treatment costs in high-income countries, longer wait times for procedures, and the allure of travel. However, despite its benefits, traditional dental tourism models still face substantial logistical, clinical, and experiential challenges. These issues not only affect patient satisfaction and safety but also hinder the scalability and sustainability of dental tourism providers. As digital transformation accelerates across healthcare, Artificial Intelligence (AI) is emerging as a necessary solution to bridge the long-standing gaps in dental health tourism and respond to changing market dynamics.

2.1. Challenges in Traditional Dental Tourism

One of the most persistent issues in traditional dental tourism is the communication barrier between patients and providers. Many international patients struggle to articulate their medical histories, expectations, or concerns due to language differences. This lack of clarity can result in misaligned expectations, diagnostic errors, and dissatisfaction with outcomes. For instance, a patient traveling from Canada to a clinic in Turkey may face difficulties in fully understanding treatment options, pricing, and procedural risks unless both parties are fluent in a shared language. Even with translators or bilingual staff, nuances in medical terminology are often lost, leading to potential misunderstandings.

Another significant concern is the frequent treatment delays that arise from poor pre-arrival planning. Unlike local patients, dental tourists typically have limited time at their destination, often scheduling extensive dental work into a matter of days. However, traditional models do not always provide thorough pre-travel diagnostic or consultation services. As a result, patients arrive without adequate assessments or treatment plans in place, forcing clinics to conduct evaluations on arrival. This process compresses critical planning into a short window, leading to rushed decision-making and increasing the risk of complications.

Post-treatment follow-up is another major pain point. Once a procedure is completed, dental tourists typically return to their home countries, often thousands of miles away from the treating clinic. Without an effective system for remote monitoring or communication, patients face difficulties in accessing aftercare, reporting complications, or receiving reassurance during recovery. Many clinics lack standardized mechanisms to conduct virtual follow-ups, forcing patients to rely on general practitioners or dentists unfamiliar with the initial procedure.

Equally important is the gap in trust and decision-making among prospective dental tourists. Unlike domestic patients, international clients do not usually have the opportunity to visit a clinic in person, meet the dentist, or review facilities before committing to treatment. The absence of transparent, data-driven information makes it challenging for them to compare providers and make confident choices. In many cases, patients' base decisions on marketing materials or word-of-mouth recommendations rather than medical evidence or performance metrics.

2.2. Demand for Personalization and Digitalization

Modern patients, especially those who seek care abroad, are increasingly informed and digitally literate. They expect more than just clinical expertise they want personalized, convenient, and seamless care journeys. This shift in expectations is redefining how dental clinics must position themselves in a competitive global market. Patients now look for individualized treatment plans tailored to their specific needs, histories, and aesthetic goals. The era of one-size-fits-all dentistry is fading, replaced by the demand for personalization powered by data and technology.

Digital interfaces and platforms are central to this transformation. Prospective dental tourists expect user-friendly websites, online booking systems, instant quotes, and the ability to upload radiographs and receive initial evaluations before they travel. Clinics that offer these digital conveniences demonstrate a higher level of professionalism and accessibility, building trust even before the patient steps off the plane. Furthermore, virtual tours, multilingual chat support, and AI-powered assistants can help clarify procedures, address concerns, and ease decision-making.

Pre-treatment education and planning have also become essential components of the dental tourism experience. Patients are no longer satisfied with vague assurances they want detailed breakdowns of the procedure timeline, cost, material options, and potential outcomes. Digital platforms that incorporate AI can synthesize a patient's uploaded diagnostic data to generate personalized treatment suggestions. These tools not only save time for clinicians but also empower patients to make informed choices. As a result, the overall care process becomes more collaborative and transparent.

2.3. Market Trends and Technology-Driven Demand

The global dental tourism market is projected to reach billions of dollars in value over the next few years, with estimates suggesting an annual growth rate of more than 12% (Allied Market Research, 2023). This surge is driven by an aging population, the growing importance of aesthetics, and the widening gap in dental care affordability between developed and developing nations. As competition intensifies, clinics are turning to technological differentiation to attract patients.

One of the most notable trends is the increased demand for virtual consultations. Patients prefer to initiate contact with clinics remotely, gaining a preliminary understanding of treatment feasibility and costs before committing to travel. AI enhances these consultations by providing real-time insights, such as identifying potential treatments based on radiographs or suggesting timelines based on procedural complexity and recovery time.

In this competitive climate, clinics that fail to adopt AI-powered tools risk falling behind. AI enables practices to streamline their internal workflows, improve diagnostic precision, automate communication, and deliver better patient outcomes. For example, machine learning algorithms can analyze patterns in thousands of treatment cases to predict success rates, offer risk assessments, or suggest procedural improvements. These capabilities go beyond operational efficiency they offer a unique value proposition that appeals to the modern, globally mobile patient.

III. SOLUTIONS AND RECOMMENDATIONS

3. AI-Powered Diagnostic Tools

Artificial Intelligence (AI) is transforming diagnostic capabilities in dentistry, especially within the context of dental health tourism. Patients traveling abroad for dental procedures often arrive with incomplete records or limited prior consultations. To bridge this gap, AI-based diagnostic tools offer a new level of accuracy, speed, and consistency that ensures clinicians can make confident treatment decisions right from the start. These tools not only help reduce the risk of diagnostic errors but also allow clinics to standardize care for international patients, regardless of where they come from.

3.1 Use of AI in Analyzing Dental X-rays, CBCT, and 3D Scans

Dental imaging is at the heart of diagnosis and treatment planning. Traditionally, clinicians would manually examine panoramic X-rays, cone-beam computed tomography (CBCT), and intraoral scans to detect issues such as caries, bone loss, impacted teeth, or cysts. However, this process is time-intensive and subject to human error or variation between practitioners.

AI-powered systems have introduced a more reliable, efficient alternative. Algorithms trained on thousands of annotated dental images can detect patterns that even experienced dentists might miss. For instance, convolutional neural networks (CNNs), a type of deep learning model, are capable of analyzing radiographs and CBCT scans with remarkable precision. A study by Schwendicke et al. (2020) demonstrated that AI models could detect dental caries on bitewing radiographs with accuracy comparable to that of experienced dentists, and in some cases, even outperform them in terms of consistency.

Moreover, 3D imaging platforms that integrate AI now allow for the rapid interpretation of complex anatomical structures, particularly useful for implant planning and orthodontic assessments. These platforms eliminate the need for manual segmentation, speeding up the diagnostic process and minimizing errors caused by fatigue or oversight.

3.2 Early Detection of Caries, Periodontitis, and Oral Cancers

Early diagnosis is vital, especially for conditions like oral cancer and periodontitis that may progress rapidly if left untreated. For dental tourists, who often seek care after months or years of neglect, timely identification of these conditions can be life-changing.

AI tools have shown promise in detecting early-stage caries and periodontal disease by examining subtle changes in imaging that might go unnoticed by the human eye. The software "Pearl," for example, uses machine learning to detect decay, bone loss, and calculus on radiographs with high precision. Such platforms don't just flag issues they offer probability scores and visual overlays, helping both clinicians and patients understand the severity of conditions.

Oral cancer detection is another area where AI is making strides. Deep learning models are now capable of analyzing intraoral photographs and histopathological images to classify malignant lesions. This is particularly useful for initial screenings during virtual consultations, where a local dentist or technician uploads the images for AI review. Research by Ahmad et al. (2021) highlights that AI applications in oncology including oral cancers are improving the chances of early detection and survival rates by flagging abnormalities earlier than traditional methods.

3.3 Real-World Applications: Pearl, Diagnocat, and More

Several AI-driven platforms are already in use in clinics around the world, each offering distinct capabilities that cater to various diagnostic needs in dental tourism.

Pearl, developed in the United States, uses AI to analyze dental X-rays and automatically highlight issues such as decay, bone loss, and missing restorations. It supports multi-language interfaces, making it especially relevant for international dental clinics that cater to diverse patient groups. Pearl's AI engine is FDA-cleared for clinical use, and its reports are designed to be understood by both practitioners and patients, which improves communication and trust during pre-treatment discussions.

Diagnocat is another platform gaining traction among dental tourism hubs in Europe and Asia. It offers CBCT-based AI diagnostics for endodontics, implantology, and orthodontics. Diagnocat automatically generates a full diagnostic report—including tooth-by-tooth analyses, anatomical structures, and potential pathologies which can then be reviewed remotely before a patient even boards a flight. This is a major advantage in reducing treatment timeframes upon arrival.

Additionally, tools like Overjet and Denti.AI are contributing to more efficient workflows by combining imaging diagnostics with clinical charting and insurance documentation. These platforms not only assist in diagnosis but also improve transparency for patients, especially those concerned about the quality and necessity of treatments recommended abroad.

3.4 Bridging Clinical Gaps for International Patients

One of the greatest advantages of AI diagnostic tools in dental health tourism is their ability to create a standardized diagnostic baseline. Whether a patient is from Germany, Canada, or the UAE, their radiographs can be analyzed by the same AI model with consistent outputs. This significantly reduces variability between clinicians and provides peace of mind to patients comparing treatment plans from different providers.

AI tools also help manage expectations and build trust. With visual evidence and objective data presented during virtual consultations, patients are more likely to accept treatment proposals and feel reassured about the clinic's expertise even before stepping off the plane. In regions where regulations require full disclosure or documentation of diagnosis, AI-generated reports can serve as valuable evidence of clinical due diligence.

Finally, AI diagnostics are helping to democratize access to quality care. Clinics in emerging markets that may not have access to highly trained specialists can now rely on AI to support their assessments. This levels the playing field in dental tourism, allowing more clinics to compete globally based on quality, not just price.

4. Virtual Consultations and Pre-Treatment Planning

One of the greatest challenges in dental health tourism has been the gap between initial patient inquiry and the first in-person clinical assessment. Traditionally, dental tourists must wait until arriving at a clinic overseas before undergoing diagnostics and receiving a treatment plan. This delay adds uncertainty, increases travel time, and often leads to rushed decisions. In response, AI-enhanced virtual consultations are changing the dynamic by enabling robust, remote interactions before travel ever begins.

4.1 AI Chatbots and Virtual Assistants for Patient Interaction

AI-powered chatbots and virtual assistants are often the first point of contact for potential dental tourists. These systems can guide users through initial queries, assess their treatment needs based on symptoms or uploaded medical records, and even book appointments. They operate 24/7, which is critical for catering to patients in different time zones.

For example, an AI chatbot can ask patients about dental history, pain levels, and aesthetic concerns, then use natural language processing (NLP) to provide preliminary advice or direct the inquiry to a human specialist. This creates a seamless experience while reducing clinic workload. Some systems integrate AI with CRM (Customer Relationship Management) tools, allowing for personalized communication based on past interactions, preferences, and demographics (Marr, 2019).

Virtual assistants are becoming more advanced through NLP algorithms capable of understanding diverse dialects and responding in multiple languages. This is essential for building trust with international patients, especially those who may not be fluent in the clinic's primary language.

4.2 Predictive Models for Cost and Treatment Planning

One of the most critical questions patients ask before choosing a dental tourism provider is, "How much will it cost?" AI can now answer this question more reliably and accurately through predictive modeling. By analyzing past patient records, treatment outcomes, and geographic cost data, AI systems can generate cost estimates tailored to each patient's condition and desired outcomes.

AI also assists in matching the right procedures with patient goals and clinical indications. For instance, predictive models can determine whether a patient would benefit more from clear aligners versus traditional braces, or whether bone grafting is likely needed before implant placement. This helps patients make informed decisions before committing to international travel.

Platforms like Denti.AI and Overjet are examples of tools that merge diagnostic AI with cost calculators and procedure simulations. Patients can review proposed treatments visually through AI-generated previews of possible outcomes, enhancing transparency and engagement (Ding et al., 2023).

4.3 Remote Consultation Platforms Using AI

Video consultations supported by AI have become a new standard in dental tourism pre-planning. In a typical setup, a patient uploads digital impressions or radiographs from their home dentist. The receiving clinic then uses AI tools to analyze the scans and provide a provisional diagnosis and treatment plan. During the live consultation, the dentist can refer to AI-generated annotations and reports, ensuring a more structured and confident discussion.

Some systems allow for side-by-side comparisons of treatment options, showing timelines, risks, and success probabilities. AI-enhanced imaging, like that offered by Pearl or Diagnocat, helps clinicians visually demonstrate the patient's oral condition and treatment rationale, even over a screen.

This approach significantly reduces the time patients need to spend abroad, as procedures can be scheduled and prepared before they arrive. It also lowers the chance of cancellations due to mismatched expectations or unanticipated complications.

4.4 Language Translation and Cultural Adaptation Using NLP

AI's role extends beyond clinical functions it also enhances communication and cultural understanding. Natural Language Processing (NLP) models such as Google's BERT or Meta's LLaMA can translate technical terms and dental jargon into patient-friendly language. This makes medical documents and consultations more accessible, regardless of the patient's native tongue.

Clinics targeting multilingual clientele now integrate translation engines into their platforms, allowing patients to read consent forms, invoices, and care instructions in their preferred language. Furthermore, sentiment analysis tools help detect uncertainty or confusion in patient queries, prompting follow-ups or human intervention.

Some advanced systems also adapt communication styles based on cultural norms. For example, patients from some regions may prefer formal, structured consultations, while others may respond better to casual, empathetic language. By adjusting tone and format, AI-powered systems enhance the comfort and trust essential for international healthcare decision-making (Topol, 2019).

4.5 Advantages for Clinics and Patients

For clinics, virtual AI-driven consultations offer clear operational benefits: fewer no-shows, more accurate scheduling, and better patient-clinician alignment. For patients, the value lies in transparency, reduced anxiety, and informed consent. They arrive with realistic expectations and a plan already in place, making the experience smoother and more predictable.

Clinics that incorporate these technologies differentiate themselves in the increasingly competitive global dental tourism market. Offering a sophisticated virtual consultation process can be a key decision-making factor for tech-savvy patients.

5. Treatment Optimization with AI

Once a dental tourist arrives at their chosen destination, the success of their journey depends on the efficiency, safety, and quality of the treatment they receive. Treatment optimization through AI is revolutionizing how dental procedures are planned, delivered, and adjusted in real time. From chairside support systems to precision robotics and predictive outcome analytics, AI is streamlining dental care while enhancing both patient satisfaction and clinical outcomes.

5.1 Chairside Decision Support Systems

One of the most direct applications of AI in clinical dentistry is real-time decision support. AI-enabled software, integrated with dental equipment and imaging devices, can analyze radiographs, intraoral scans, and patient records instantly. This allows clinicians to make evidence-based decisions on the spot.

For instance, if a patient requires implant surgery, AI software can suggest the optimal implant size, angle, and depth based on bone density scans. Tools like Diagnocat and Overjet use machine learning algorithms to flag areas of decay, bone loss, or root abnormalities, helping the dentist avoid errors and plan more effective treatments.

Additionally, these systems can monitor treatment progress during multi-step procedures like orthodontics or prosthodontics. If a deviation from the expected progress is detected, the software can alert the clinician and recommend adjustments improving precision and reducing unnecessary delays (Ahmad et al., 2021).

5.2 Robotics and AI-Enhanced Dental Procedures

Robotics, when guided by AI, is adding new dimensions to treatment optimization. AI-powered robotic arms are now capable of assisting in procedures like implant placement, root canal therapy, and tooth preparation with extraordinary accuracy. One of the most notable examples is Yomi, the FDA-cleared robotic system that uses AI-guided motion control to perform implant surgeries.

By minimizing human error and enhancing tactile feedback, AI-integrated robotics reduce the risk of complications and improve long-term treatment success. These systems also optimize treatment time, which is essential for dental tourists operating on tight schedules.

Furthermore, robotic tools collect and feed real-time data into AI systems for performance learning. As the robot performs more procedures, it becomes better at predicting anatomical variations and adjusting movement trajectories accordingly (Aminoshariae et al., 2021).

5.3 AI-Driven Customization of Dental Prosthetics

The era of one-size-fits-all dental prosthetics is fading, replaced by AI-assisted customization. CAD/CAM systems powered by AI now allow for prosthetics such as crowns, bridges, and dentures to be designed with unprecedented precision.

AI analyzes 3D scans of the patient's mouth to design restorations that perfectly align with bite patterns, jaw structure, and esthetic preferences. The result is a prosthesis that not only looks natural but also functions optimally.

Platforms like 3Shape's Dental System and exocad employ deep learning algorithms that continuously improve design recommendations by learning from global databases of successful restorations. This minimizes the need for trial-and-error fittings, saves chairside time, and enhances the patient's overall experience (Ding et al., 2023).

5.4 Monitoring and Predicting Treatment Outcomes

Another significant advantage of AI is its ability to predict and monitor treatment outcomes over time. AI can analyze thousands of past cases to forecast how a particular procedure is likely to perform for a given patient profile. This insight is invaluable for both patient education and treatment planning.

For example, in orthodontic treatment, AI platforms such as DentalMonitoring use smartphone-connected imaging tools to remotely monitor tooth movement. The AI analyzes patient-submitted images to assess whether treatment is progressing as expected and notifies the clinician if intervention is needed. This approach ensures high-quality care even after the patient has left the clinic, which is especially beneficial in dental tourism scenarios where follow-up can be limited.

Moreover, predictive analytics help identify risk factors for complications. AI models can flag patients with a higher likelihood of implant failure due to bone quality, medical history, or lifestyle factors like smoking. Clinicians can then modify treatment protocols proactively, reducing adverse outcomes and improving long-term success rates (Ekert et al., 2019).

5.5 Enhancing Workflow and Clinic Efficiency

On a broader scale, AI optimizes treatment workflows by improving clinic operations. AI tools manage patient scheduling, inventory control, and staff assignments based on predictive algorithms. For high-volume dental tourism clinics, where timing and coordination are critical, these optimizations make a measurable difference in patient throughput and service quality.

Treatment timelines can be condensed by aligning lab work, procedure slots, and patient availability using AI scheduling systems. This allows dental tourists to complete complex treatments such as full-mouth restorations or smile makeovers in just one or two visits, without compromising quality.

6. AI in Dental Diagnostics

The fast pace of AI is transforming dental diagnostics, making it more accurate, faster, and accessible. Clinical and subjective interpretation through the lens of clinician expertise has been the traditional basis for dental diagnostics. With an increasing number of complex cases in terms of a dental health tourism environment, many patients are seeking quick, reliable, and remote assessments of their dental condition. There is a growing demand for more advanced technologies and systems to assist frontline clinicians in making accurate and timely decisions about the dental treatment of consumers. AI approaches are increasingly being developed to assist with image analysis, promote early disease detection and provide new diagnostic platforms that ignore borders.

6.1. AI-Powered Image Analysis for Accurate Detection.

Image analysis powered by AI has become a fundamental component of dental diagnostics today. Deep learning algorithms, especially convolutional neural networks (CNNs), train these systems in large datasets of dental radiographs or cone beam computed tomography (CBCT) scans to identify and classify a wide variety of conditions. These diagnostic systems can identify nuanced radiographic features such as incipient caries, periapical lesions, and periods of early bone loss that even experienced clinicians might not identify (Gao et al., 2025; Surdu et al., 2024).

Implementing AI improves the accuracy of interpretation while also improving workflows in dental imaging. The automated and high-quality segmentation of tooth structures, quantification of the bonal levels, and identification of areas of pathology, provides the clinician with actionable information that reduces diagnostic errors and leads to evidence-based care (Musleh et al., 2024). AI-based imaging analysis as shown in Figure 1, also allows for teledentistry, where specialists can independently evaluate and confirm findings, an important function for dental tourists who require evaluations prior to travel.

Figure 1. Dental image analysis workflow powered by AI

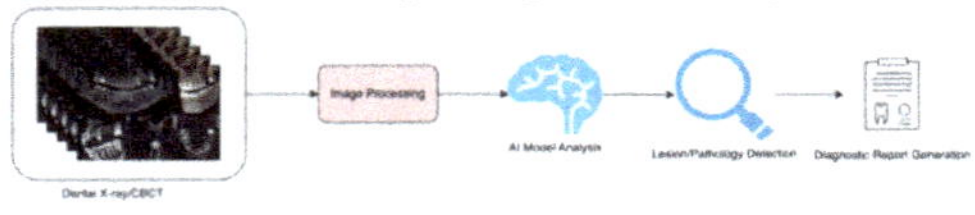

6.2. Early Diagnosis of Caries, Bone Loss, and Oral Pathologies.

One of the greatest advantages of AI in dental diagnosis is its potential for early detection of diseases. AI algorithms can detect the earliest signs of caries, periodontal bone loss, and other oral pathologies by capturing very small changes in imaging patterns (Alotaibi & Deligianni, 2024; Gao et al., 2025). For example, they can detect demineralization suggestive of incipient caries, even measure the early loss of alveolar bone height, and detect changes in tissue densities that may indicate cysts or tumors.

Early detection and diagnosis are of particular benefit in dental tourism where patients have limited time for evaluation in person (see Figure 2). AI-driven tools will allow a clinician to prioritize urgent care and subsequently recommend ways to treat or prevent a client from taking up their time inaccurately (Farhadi Nia et al., 2024).

Figure 2. Applications and benefits of AI in early dental disease detection

Disease/Condition	AI Diagnostic Capability	Clinical Benefit
Dental Caries	Early lesion detection	Preventive intervention
Periodontal Bone Loss	Quantitative bone level measurement	Timely periodontal therapy
Oral Pathologies	Identification of cysts/tumors	Early specialist referral

6.3. Real-world AI Platforms: Pearl, Diagnocat, and More.

There are several AI commercial platforms that are widely utilized in dental practices around the world with effective diagnostic capability and workflow integration, such as Pearl and Diagnocat (see Figure 3).

- Pearl's platform uses FDA-cleared AI to analyze radiographic imaging in real-time, automatically flagging potentially pathological caries, calculus, and periapical lesions, and is being leveraged by clinics worldwide to improve and standardize diagnostic quality (Lal et al., 2025).
- Diagnocat recognizes both 2D and 3D image analysis, and produces increasingly detailed reporting, as well as offering a multilingual interface (useful for international dental tourism) (Surdu et al., 2024).

These platforms both enhance and standardize diagnostic accuracy, as well as automate routine documentation and aid with tele-dentistry, making them suitable for cross-border access to dental care (Musleh et al., 2024).

Figure 3. Features and use cases of dental AI diagnostic platforms

Platform	Key Features	Use Case in Dental Tourism
Pearl	FDA-cleared, real-time radiograph analysis	Standardized diagnostics, remote review
Diagnocat	2D/3D analysis, multilingual, reports	Multilingual support, pre-travel planning
Others	AI charting, risk assessment	Automated documentation, risk stratification

7. AI-Powered Virtual Consultations and Pre-Treatment Planning

AI is speeding up the digital transformation of dental health tourism, fundamentally changing interactions between patients and clinics before treatment even begins. The aim of international patients is to seek the best seamless, efficient, and personalized experience while overseas. AI-driven tools are creating efficiencies in communication, planning, and cultural appreciation. AI-enabled virtual consultations and pre-treatment planning make patient journeys through clinics seamless, moving patients from the first email inquiry to detailed planning of procedures, and softly engaging patients as the patient journey is planned and delivered for them. AI is providing clarity, transparency, and engagement along the way.

7.1. AI Chatbots and Virtual Assistants for Patient Engagement.

AI chatbots and virtual counterparts are changing the way dental clinics communicate with patients, especially those coming from overseas. These smart systems provide support all day, all week, responding to questions, scheduling appointments, and supplying customized information about procedures, travel arrangements, and aftercare. By automating repetitive interactions, chatbots allow clinical staff to dedicate more time to complicated interactions, and ensure that patients receive timely, reliable responses, regardless of time zone (Battista et al., 2023).

Additionally, AI virtual assistants may be able to acquire details of the patient's medical history, assist them with electronic forms, or prioritize cases into urgent vs. complex arrangements. This engagement enables an early stage of accountability with patients, which builds patient satisfaction and trust in the dental practice, as patients feel guided and supported in their journey to make informed clinical decisions (Thorat et al., 2024). Figure 4 illustrates the main capabilities of AI chatbots in the context of dental tourism.

Figure 4. Capabilities of chatbots in dental tourism

Function	Patient Benefit
24/7 Inquiry Response	Immediate answers, reduced anxiety
Appointment Scheduling	Convenience, time-zone flexibility
Pre-Visit Triage	Efficient prioritization of cases
Procedure Information	Informed decision-making
Travel/Logistics Guidance	Streamlined travel planning

7.2. Predictive Models for Cost Estimation and Treatment Duration.

One of the biggest concerns for dental tourists is knowing what the treatment is expected to cost and how much time it will take. AI predictive modeling applies data analytics to patient data, treatment complexity, and historical outcomes to render predictions on costs and duration (see Figure 5). Predictive modeling accounts for aspects of treatment such as procedure type, materials needed, and complications that might arise during treatment, thereby providing the patient with realistic expectations while helping clinics forecast their resource demands (Vanatta, 2025).

The provision of evidence-based, transparent timelines and costs can help clinics create confidence with international patients and potentially prevent misunderstandings, or worse, unexpected costs. This level of understanding is important for the patient who is required to coordinate travel, accommodations, and time off work.

Figure 5. Flowchart of AI-driven pre-treatment planning

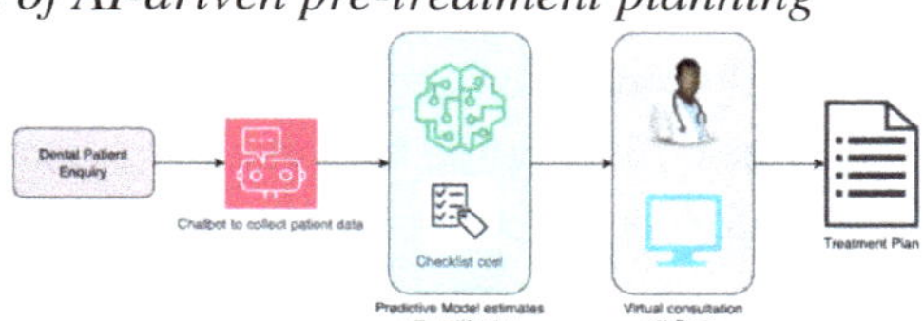

7.3. Language Translation and Cultural Adaptation Using NLP.

Language barriers and cultural discrepancies can hinder successful communication in dental health tourism. However, NLP innovations have now been adopted into AI systems to offer real-time translation as well as culturally-appropriate communication. This means that AI-powered translation tools can interpret patient inquiries and that of the clinic across multiple languages, facilitating learning about the procedure, risks, and guidelines for aftercare (Thorat et al., 2024).

NLP instruments offer not only direct translation but can also alter communications to fit cultural context and patient expectations in ways that reduce anxiety and foster confort and trust. For example, AI can change the patient's health literacy level, or even the patient's local customs about communication style, so it broadens inclusivity in the consultation process (Surdu et al., 2024). This is a benefit to dental tourism especially, as miscommunication can be a major contributor to both poor performance and dissatisfaction that could lead to medical errors.

8. Artificial Intelligence in Treatment Optimization

The adoption of artificial intelligence (AI) in dental practice is changing the landscape in terms of not only diagnostics but also treatment optimization strategies. Within the dental related health tourism context, where efficiency, precision and personalization are critical, AI-enabled tools are improving workflows, the accuracy of orthodontic and prosthodontic designs and enabling care that is genuinely individualized. The benefits associated with AI are improving patient outcomes, decreasing chair time, and increasing the appeal of clinics that utilize this type of technology for international patients.

8.1. AI-Assisted Orthodontic and Prosthetic Design.

The design and fabrication of orthodontic appliances and dental prostheses have come a long way with AI. Digital workflows have made it easier for clinicians to use AI-based software to examine 3D scans, simulate tooth movements, and develop custom aligners and prosthetic parts with great accuracy. Digital workflows for 3D printed implants have enabled workflows for surgical guides so that implant surgical guides can be planned and placed with far fewer errors and surgical outcomes can be improved (Goodacre, 2022). These systems can routinely produce automatically generated models and design methods that exploit patient-specific anatomical data, which saves time and labor.

AI algorithms can also predict treatment outcomes. This enables clinicians to present virtual simulations to patients prior to initiating therapy. Not only does this increase patient confidence, but it facilitates shared decision making. Table 1 below identifies the advantages of AI-assisted design in orthodontics and prosthetics:

Table 1. Benefits of AI-assisted orthodontic and prosthetic design

Benefit	**Clinical Impact**
Accurate digital modeling	Better fit/functionality
Automated design suggestions	Fewer manual errors
Predictive outcome simulation	Better patient communication
Faster turnaround	Increased efficiency

8.2. Workflow Automation to Streamline Dental Procedures

In the adoption of AI-based workflow automation, dental clinics are revolutionizing clinical routines and administrative duties. AI-enabled automated scheduling, digital charting, and real-time data analytics programming can help decrease workloads on team members and mitigate the risks associated with human error as shown in Figure 6 (Musleh et al., 2024). AI systems can schedule the priorities of appointments, predict supply needs, and monitor supply chain management activities and equipment maintenance. This allows everything to function smoothly within the clinic. In the treatment room, AI can aid intraoperative guidance by offering real-time alerts during surgery or reminders of the steps in a procedure (Surdu et al., 2024).

Figure 6. AI-driven dental workflow automation

8.3. Personalized Treatment Suggestions Based on Dental Data

Personalization is making its way into modern dentistry, and AI is enabling a true understanding of patient variables that are specific to each patient. By analyzing large datasets including medical history, radiographs, intraoral scans, along with patient reported outcomes, AI algorithms can produce evidence-based treatment recommendations that support efficacy and minimize risk (Farhadi Nia et al., 2024).

These systems can uncover patterns and analyze anticipated responses to various treatments to assist clinicians in determining the better suited intervention.

Personalization for dental tourists also means effective care, even when time does not permit a timely in-person assessment. AI can also appropriately build in patient preferences and cultural elements, enhancing overall patient satisfaction (Gao et al., 2025). The table found below illustrates some of the more prominent applications for personalized AI-driven treatment planning.

Table 2. Benefits of AI-assisted orthodontic and prosthetic design

Application	Patient Benefit
Risk assessment and predictions	Lower complication rates
Customized treatment recommendations	Specialized clinical outcomes
Tailored to patients	Less dissatisfaction
Learning from result to result	Best practices Evidence-based research

IV. FUTURE RESEARCH DIRECTIONS

9. Artificial Intelligence in Post-Treatment Monitoring

As the market for dental health tourism continues to develop, the need for dependable and satisfactory quality of post treatment care on both sides of a border has become pivotal. If you think about it, AI (Artificial Intelligence) is revolutionizing post treatment surveillance. Patients, clinics and patients typically face a post treatment phase of monitoring and follow-up that strongly emphasizes on the patient once they leave the dental chair. AI, through predictive analytics, real time alerts and customized telehealth platforms, now allows both clinicians and patients to monitor and respond to adverse therapeutic outcomes whenever they occur around the world. It also allows clinicians to examine risk more proactively while providing enhanced accessibility of communication across borders.

9.1. AI-Based Alerts for Complications and Patient Recovery.

Monitoring systems that utilize artificial intelligence can continuously review patient data - e.g., digital health records, intraoral pictures, and symptoms self-reported by patients—to identify early signs of complications after dental procedures. AI-driven monitoring systems will send automated alerts for clinicians and patients if abnormal recovery patterns or risk factors are identified, allowing early intervention and decreasing the risk for complications (Afshari et al., 2024; Bamashmous, 2025). For instance, AI systems can identify if a patient is experiencing abnormal swelling, risk of infection, or poor healing so that follow-up can be timely, and focused on the isolated issue.

9.2. Predictive Analytics for Post-Procedure Risk Assessment.

AI predictive analytics will utilize vast amounts of data to predict the chances of individual patients having complications after an intervention. Utilizing the treatment performed, the patient's own history, and the interactions between scenically designed, bioactivated biomaterials, patients will be stratified and risk levels established, and personalized follow-up protocols recommended (Gao et al., 2025). The predictive analytics use-case model is proactive, informing the clinician of risk scenarios, resource allocation and prioritization, and bespoke clinical advice for patients, promoting patient safety and satisfaction.

Figure 7. AI-driven risk stratification

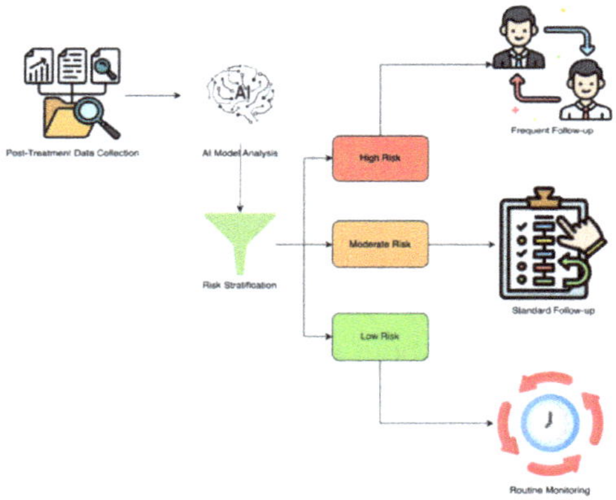

9.3. Telehealth Platforms for Ongoing Care and Support.

AI-supported telehealth systems are addressing the barriers between patients and dentists after-a-care is completed, particularly international patients. They allow patients to arrange a secure a consultation via video, receive automated symptom text-ins, and to exchange instant messages with a dentist, benefitted by language translation and AI-based triage (Kaushik & Rapaka; 2025; Gao et al.,2025). Patients can communicate in real-time with images or updates in the comfort of their home, receive personalized advice, and educational resources, ultimately leading to continuity in care and peace of mind, despite distance.

Figure 8. AI-enabled telehealth follow-up

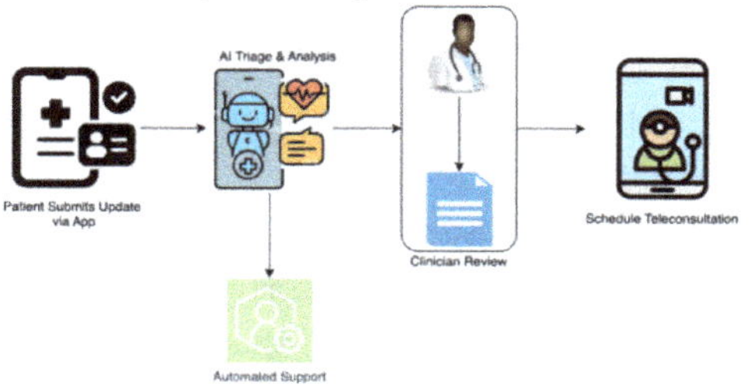

10. Ethical, Legal, and Future Directions in AI-Driven Dental Tourism

As dental health tourism becomes increasingly intertwined with AI technologies, it is important to consider the ethics, legal, and regulatory framework surrounding thinking, use, and threats to trustworthy use of those technologies to ensure patient safety, trust and access, while at the same time fostering innovation. When AI is combined with dental care across borders there are additional factors at play regarding data privacy, informed consent, transparency, and other technology being applied in new ways. It is important that those entering this domain understand these challenges in order to engage with AI responsibly and sustainably in a fast-changing space.

10.1. Data privacy, security, and regulatory concerns.

With the application of AI in dental tourism, huge amounts of sensitive patient data including medical histories, radiographs, and biometric identifiers are routinely collected, analyzed, and sometimes transferred internationally. This raises serious concerns regarding data privacy and security, as different countries have different standards for safeguarding against data loss or misuse (Bamashmous, 2025). For example, the General Data Protection Regulation (GDPR) enacted by the European Union (EU) has comprehensive standards for data management, while in other jurisdictions there are no such safeguards or protections. In taking AI services, dental clinics and AI as a vendor must always operate within the scope of the relevant regulations, which can involve complicated data governance procedures (Panahi & Ezzati, 2025).

As shown in Figure 9, AI systems are also being used actively attacked to exploit the vulnerabilities of the AI system. Consequently, effective cybersecurity strategies must be used, such as end-to-end encrypted services, multi-factor authentication, and frequent vulnerability assessments. Additionally, regulatory oversight is still evolving and countries where the AI vendors are promoted and marketed may be slower to establish internationally harmonized standards regarding the validation of AI, the accountability of the AI systems, and the legal responsibility of the clinicians and technology suppliers. Without standards prescribing a level of accountability and legal impediments, patients may expose themselves to different levels of protection, and clinics may expose themselves to legal risks.

Figure 9. Data privacy and security in dental tourism

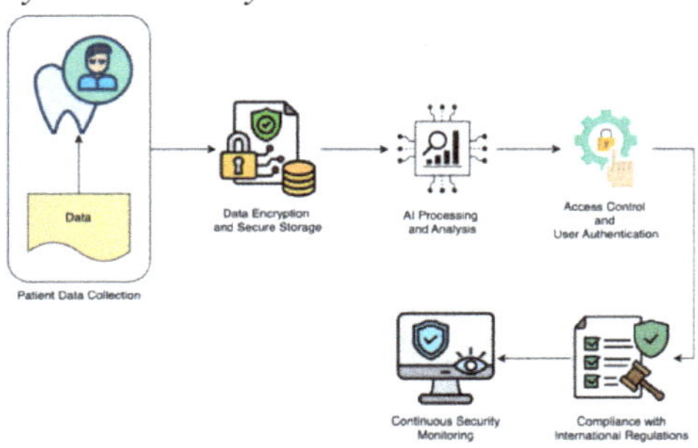

10.2. Consent, transparency, and explainability in AI decisions.

Successful integration of ethical AI in dental tourism depends, in part, on meaningful patient consent, transparency, and explainability.

Informed Consent.

- Informed consent has now expanded past traditional medical settings to include how AI will be incorporated in diagnosis, treatment planning, and management of patient data and information.
- Patients must be informed about data being collected and how it will be processed and the associated risks and benefits of AI involvement (El Khoury et al., 2025).

Transparency.

- Transparency is also essential. Patients and clinicians should have an understanding of the rationale for AI-generated recommendations, especially if they have an impact on clinical choices.
- Black-box AI models are those that are unclear or unknown how they ultimately derive their recommendations and may pose difficulties for trust and accountability.

Explainability.

- The new field of Explainable AI (XAI) aims to address this issue by developing systems that can produce clear and understandable explanations for their predictions (Panahi & Ezzati, 2025).
- This would not only gain patient trust but also assist clinician in validating and contextualizing AI-generated suggestions.

Figure 10. Consent, transparency and explainability in making decisions

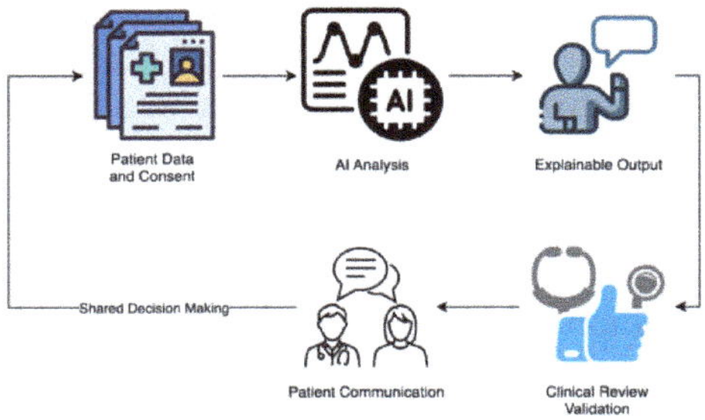

10.3. Future trends: AR/VR integration, blockchain for records, and smart dental platforms.

The future of Artificial Intelligence in dental tourism also evolves with various modern-day technologies evolving together.

AR/VR Integration.

- The development of augmented reality and virtual reality applications to provide immersive patient experiences is also growing for patient education, surgical planning, and remote consults.
- These modalities can help patients visualize procedures and outcomes and, in turn, diminishes patient anxiety and enhances comprehension— this is

particularly valuable for dental tourists who may not have the context of face-to-face consultations with their providers (Bamashmous, 2025)..

Blockchain for Records.

- Blockchain technology is positioned to revolutionize patient record management by providing a decentralized and immutable patient data record that can be easily shared with authorized parties.
- This will help dental tourists access their records from anywhere in the world while maintaining strict control over their data and determining who may view or edit their record (Panahi & Ezzati, 2025).
- A blockchain application also allows patients to manage patient consent and audit trails for practice audit and regulatory compliance and aims to build trust and reliability in their endorsement for new persons seeking treatment.

Smart Dental Platforms.

- The general trend toward smart dental platforms is moving toward an integrated ecosystem of technologies that converge in a patient-specific AI plan that leverages Internet of Things (IoT), cloud computing, and predictive analysis.
- Smart dental platforms have the capacity to monitor patient recovery in real time, individualized treatment changes, and automated workflows, which permeates the traditional obstacle in dental practice, response times and efficiency.
- As technology continues to advance, there is the possibility of providing a responsive manner to deliver patient and provider care using a data-driven systems approach to healthcare - particularly useful for the practical implications of dental health tourism internationally.

CONCLUSION

11.1. Summary of AI's transformative role in dental health tourism

Artificial intelligence (AI) has fundamentally reshaped the realm of dental health tourism, allowing for improved diagnostic accuracy, enhanced virtual consultations, streamlined treatment planning and monitoring of post-treatment care. Clinics have utilized AI through image analysis, chatbots, and predictive analytics, which will allow specialized clinics to offer personalized, efficient, and patient-centered care across international borders (Gao et al., 2025; Farhadi Nia et al., 2024; Battista et al., 2023). The adoption of a variety of digital workflows, AI-assisted orthodontic and prosthetic designs, and patient engagement tools has eliminated the impact of language, culture, and logistical hurdles towards dental tourism (Goodacre, 2022; Surdu et al., 2024; Thorat et al., 2024).

In turn, AI has established reliable telehealth and post-treatment monitoring services to maintain patient care over long distances while ethical and regulatory frameworks are being developed to mitigate data privacy challenges and establish transparency and explainability (Bamashmous, 2025; Panahi & Ezzati, 2025). Cumulatively, these technologies are raising the global standard of dental care and can be anticipated to establish AI as a foundational element of the future global dental tourism ecosystem.

11.2. Key takeaways and recommendations for stakeholders

- To assure responsible use of AI in dental health tourism, we recommend stakeholders, clinicians, policymakers, tech developers, and patients to place value on ethical considerations for deployment of AI, especially data privacy, user consent and transparency (El Khoury et al., 2025; Panahi & Ezzati, 2025).
- Clinics should utilize AI systems that are validated, developed on explainable algorithms, and have continued education for staff in place to enhance safety and patient experience (Lal et al, 2025; Musleh et al., 2024).
- We encourage policymakers globally to coordinate regulatory frameworks and cross-border collaborations, while product developers place value on interoperability, culture, and patient-centered elements in design.

Finally, we encourage patients to be made aware of their healthcare process being augmented by AI and empower the patient with easy-to-understand information where they co-partner in decision making.

11.3. Final thoughts on the future of AI-powered dental care

The future of AI-based dental health looks to be promising and fluid. new technologies like AR/VR, blockchain and intelligence-based smart dental systems will enhance patient engagement, security and personalization (Bamashmous, 2025; Panahi & Ezzati, 2025).

As AI systems become increasingly transparent and explainable, trust and adoption will enhance, leading to truly global, high-quality dental care. Continued research, stakeholder engagement, flexibility in regulations will be invaluable in tapping into the full scope of AIs capabilities to ensure that dental health tourism remains safe, ethical, and patient-centered in the years to come (Afshari et al., 2024; Alotaibi & Deligianni, 2024).

REFERENCES

Afshari, Z., Khademi, A., & Iranmanesh, P. (2024). Prospects of artificial intelligence in dentistry. *Dental Research Journal (Isfahan), 21*(1). Advance online publication. DOI: 10.4103/drj.drj_30_24 PMID: 39188386

Ahmad, Z., Rahim, S., Zubair, M., & Abdul-Ghafar, J. (2021). Artificial intelligence (AI) in medicine, current applications and future role with special emphasis on its potential and promise in pathology: Present and future impact, obstacles including costs and acceptance among pathologists, practical and philosophical considerations. A comprehensive review. *Diagnostic Pathology, 16*(1), 1–16. DOI: 10.1186/s13000-021-01085-4 PMID: 33731170

Allied Market Research. (2023). *Dental tourism market by treatment type: Global opportunity analysis and industry forecast, 2021–2031.*

Alotaibi, S., & Deligianni, E. (2024). AI in oral medicine: Is the future already here? A literature review. *British Dental Journal, 237*(10), 765–770. DOI: 10.1038/s41415-024-8029-9 PMID: 39572810

Aminoshariae, A., Kulild, J., & Nagendrababu, V. (2021). Artificial intelligence in endodontics: Current applications and future directions. *Journal of Endodontics, 47*(9), 1352–1357. DOI: 10.1016/j.joen.2021.06.003 PMID: 34119562

Badawy, M. (2023). Integrating Artificial Intelligence and Big Data into Smart Healthcare Systems: A Comprehensive Review of Current Practices and Future Directions. *Artificial Intelligence Evolution*, 133-153.

Bamashmous, M. (2025). The Role of Artificial Intelligence in Transforming Dental Public Health: Current Applications, Ethical Considerations, and Future Directions. *The Open Dentistry Journal, 19*(1), e18742106363413. Advance online publication. DOI: 10.2174/0118742106363413250211053942

Battista, M., Kernitsky, J., & Dibart, S. (2023). Artificial Intelligence Chatbots in Patient Communication: Current Possibilities. *The International Journal of Periodontics & Restorative Dentistry.* Advance online publication. DOI: 10.11607/prd.6925 PMID: 37819844

DentalMonitoring. (2023). *Remote orthodontic monitoring platform.* https://dental-monitoring.com

Diagnocat. (2023). *AI for dental radiology and diagnostics.* https://diagnocat.com

Ding, H., Wu, J., Zhao, W., Matinlinna, J. P., Burrow, M. F., & Tsoi, J. K. (2023). Artificial intelligence in dentistry—A review. *Frontiers in Dental Medicine*, *4*, 1085251. DOI: 10.3389/fdmed.2023.1085251 PMID: 39935549

Ekert, T., Krois, J., Meinhold, L., Elhennawy, K., Emara, R., Golla, T., & Schwendicke, F. (2019). Deep learning for the radiographic detection of apical lesions. *Journal of Endodontics*, *45*(7), 917–922. DOI: 10.1016/j.joen.2019.03.016 PMID: 31160078

El Khoury, N., Hadid, D., & El-Outa, A. (2025). Exploring the Ethical Landscape of Artificial Intelligence in Dentistry: Insights From a Cross-Sectional Study. *Cureus*, *17*(4), e82667. DOI: 10.7759/cureus.82667 PMID: 40400857

Farhadi Nia, M., Ahmadi, M., & Irankhah, E. (2024). Transforming dental diagnostics with artificial intelligence: Advanced integration of ChatGPT and large language models for patient care. *Frontiers in Dental Medicine*, *5*, 1456208. Advance online publication. DOI: 10.3389/fdmed.2024.1456208 PMID: 39917691

Gao, S., Wang, X., Xia, Z., Zhang, H., Yu, J., & Yang, F. (2025). Artificial Intelligence in Dentistry: A Narrative Review of Diagnostic and Therapeutic Applications. *Medical Science Monitor*, *31*, e946676. DOI: 10.12659/MSM.946676 PMID: 40195079

Goodacre, B. J. (2022). Digital workflow for 3D printed implant surgical guides. *The Journal of Prosthetic Dentistry*, *127*(2), 205. DOI: 10.1016/j.prosdent.2022.01.002 PMID: 35241263

Lal, A., Nooruddin, A., & Umer, F. (2025). Concerns regarding deployment of AI-based applications in dentistry - a review. *BDJ Open*, *11*(1), 27. DOI: 10.1038/s41405-025-00319-7 PMID: 40133287

Marr, B. (2019). *Artificial intelligence in practice: how 50 successful companies used AI and machine learning to solve problems*. John Wiley & Sons.

Musleh, D., Almossaeed, H., Balhareth, F., Alqahtani, G., Alobaidan, N., Altalag, J., & Aldossary, M. I. (2024). Advancing Dental Diagnostics: A Review of Artificial Intelligence Applications and Challenges in Dentistry. *Big Data and Cognitive Computing*, *8*(6), 66. DOI: 10.3390/bdcc8060066

Overjet. (2023). *AI for dental providers*. https://www.overjet.com

Panahi, O., & Ezzati, A. (2025). AI in Dental-Medicine: Current Applications & Future Directions. *Journal of Digital Imaging*, *2*(1), 1–5. DOI: 10.61440/OAJ-CI.2025.v2.09

Patil, A. V., Somasundaram, K. V., & Goyal, R. C. (2002). Current health scenario in rural India. *The Australian Journal of Rural Health*, *10*(2), 129–135. DOI: 10.1111/j.1440-1584.2002.tb00022.x PMID: 12047509

Pearl. (2023). *Second Opinion®: AI-powered dental radiologic detection platform.*

Schwendicke, F., Golla, T., Dreher, M., & Krois, J. (2019). Convolutional neural networks for dental image diagnostics: A scoping review. *Journal of Dentistry*, *91*, 103226. DOI: 10.1016/j.jdent.2019.103226 PMID: 31704386

Schwendicke, F. A., Samek, W., & Krois, J. (2020). Artificial intelligence in dentistry: Chances and challenges. *Journal of Dental Research*, *99*(7), 769–774. DOI: 10.1177/0022034520915714 PMID: 32315260

Surdu, A., Budala, D. G., Luchian, I., Foia, L. G., Botnariu, G. E., & Scutariu, M. M. (2024). Using AI in Optimizing Oral and Dental Diagnoses - A Narrative Review. *Diagnostics (Basel)*, *14*(24), 2804. DOI: 10.3390/diagnostics14242804 PMID: 39767164

Thorat, V., Rao, P., Joshi, N., Talreja, P., & Shetty, A. R. (2024). Role of Artificial Intelligence (AI) in Patient Education and Communication in Dentistry. *Cureus*, *16*(5). Advance online publication. DOI: 10.7759/cureus.59799 PMID: 38846249

Topol, E. (2019). *Deep medicine: how artificial intelligence can make healthcare human again.*

Turner, L. G. (2011). Quality in health care and globalization of health services: Accreditation and regulatory oversight of medical tourism companies. *International Journal for Quality in Health Care : Journal of the International Society for Quality in Health Care*, *23*(1), 1–7. DOI: 10.1093/intqhc/mzq078 PMID: 21148210

Vanatta, L. (2025). AI and elevating the dental patient experience. *DrBicuspid.com*. https://www.drbicuspid.com/dental-practice/patient-communication/article/15748243/ai-and-elevating-the-dental-patient-experience

Xu, T., Wang, W., & Du, J. (2020). An integrative review of patients' experience in the medical tourism. *Inquiry : a Journal of Medical Care Organization, Provision and Financing*, *57*, 0046958020926762. DOI: 10.1177/0046958020926762 PMID: 32513038

Yomi. (2023). *Robot-assisted dental surgery system.* https://www.neocis.com/yomi

KEY TERMS AND DEFINITIONS

AI-Driven Personalization: The use of artificial intelligence to tailor dental care recommendations, treatment plans, and patient experiences based on individual needs, preferences, and clinical data.

Dental Health Tourism Platforms: Digital platforms that combine AI, diagnostics, and travel logistics to match international patients with suitable dental clinics, specialists, and cost-efficient treatment options.

Patient Digital Twin: A virtual AI-generated model of a patient's oral health that simulates treatment results, tracks progress, and allows dentists to test procedures digitally before applying them in real life.

Predictive Treatment Planning: AI algorithms that forecast clinical outcomes, such as success rates, recovery time, or orthodontic progression, to help dentists design optimal, personalized treatment strategies.

Smart Diagnostics: AI-powered tools that analyze dental images, X-rays, scans, and patient history to detect conditions early and provide accurate, data-driven diagnoses.

Treatment Optimization Systems: AI systems that continuously improve a patient's dental treatment plan by analyzing progress, adjusting interventions, and suggesting the most effective techniques or materials.

Virtual Dental Consultations: Remote consultations using video calls, AI chatbots, or tele-dentistry platforms that allow patients to receive expert assessments and treatment plans without visiting a clinic physically.

Chapter 9
Deep Learning for Caries Detection and Diagnosis

Affaan Shaikh
http://orcid.org/0009-0004-7590-7456
IntelliDent AI, UAE

Heba Talal Saeed
http://orcid.org/0009-0004-3617-2944
Hamdan Bin Mohammed College of Dental Medicine, UAE

Amro Yaser Hmedan
http://orcid.org/0009-0001-6174-0585
Hamdan Bin Mohammed College of Dental Medicine, UAE

ABSTRACT

Dental caries, commonly known as tooth decay, remains one of the most prevalent and preventable oral diseases globally. If undetected in early stages, it can lead to tooth loss, pain, and reduced quality of life. This chapter explores the integration of artificial intelligence (AI) techniques, specifically deep learning models such as convolutional neural networks (CNNs), for the automated detection and diagnosis of dental caries from radiographic images. It provides a comprehensive understanding of caries pathology and clinical challenges, while also detailing AI model development, dataset requirements, and real-world applications in dental diagnostics. The chapter emphasizes how AI-driven tools can enhance diagnostic accuracy, support clinical decision-making, and ultimately improve oral health outcomes, particularly in the context of dental health tourism.

DOI: 10.4018/979-8-3373-4114-9.ch009

I. INTRODUCTION

1. Understanding Dental Caries

One of the most prominent or common and controllable oral conditions that affect people of all ages are dental caries, also referred to as tooth decay or cavities. It is a gradual process that includes interactions between the acid producing bacteria, sweet food, and the tooth hard tissues. If the dentist left the caries untreated, invasion to the pulp due to dental decay might then happen and maybe infection, in addition to loss of teeth due to the extensive degradation of the dentin even from a tiny, small enamel harm. Early caries detection and control are becoming an essential aspect of public health campaigns and dental practices worldwide due to the growing emphasis on the links between oral health and general health. (Tartaglia et al., 2024)

1.1 Definition, Causes, and Progression of Dental Caries

A localized degradation or destruction of the tooth surface is AKA as dental decay or caries. When carbohydrates that ferment are present, the metabolic processes of dental biofilm, or plaque, cause this. It demonstrates a balance between preventive elements like saliva flow and fluoride and adverse consequences from bacteria that produce acid and frequent sugar consumption. Bacterial that are Cariogenic in nature, like the main ones, are Lactobacillus species, and Streptococcus mutans or S. Mutans, in addition to Actinomyces, which adheres or sticks to the surface of the enamel, leading and causing the caries. (Tartaglia et al., 2024)

The area's Ph is decreased or lowered by those microorganisms or structures, converting and fragmenting the carbohydrates into acid that is organic in nature. The enamel has some crystals which are AKA HA or the hydroxyapatite crystals which do start dissolving and disintegrating after the pH drops or falls down under a specific value AKA critical value, which is approximately a pH of 5.5. Lesions or spots develop and spread across the enamel dentin junction in the direction of the pulp chamber if demineralization surpasses the rate of spontaneous remineralization over time.

Caries develops over time in phases such as starting with the:

a. Demineralization of the Subsurface without showing any degradation or cavitation which is the classically identified as the first the white spot lesion or enamel lesion.
b. Cavitated enamel lesion: the dentin underneath is shown when the outer layer collapses.

c. Dentin involvement: permanent breakdown and bacterial invasion are indicated by softer, darker tissue.
d. Involvement of the inner Pulpal region or area: The development of potential inflammation and pulpitis, abscess, and swelling, in addition to death of pulp, AKA necrosis. If dentists leave it untreated, the process could make the tooth structure very weak and could necessitate RCT or AKA root canal therapy and even a lot of restoration work. (Al-Khalifa et al., 2024)

1.2 Epidemiology: Global Burden and Public Health Impact

In the entire world, dental decay or caries are one of the most common and popular chronic illnesses. Untreated caries in permanent teeth is the most prevalent and shown health problem worldwide, impacting an estimated almost 2.5 billion people around the world, reported according to the Global Burden of Disease Study AKA The GBD during year 2019. Particularly in countries with middle to low incomes, the early childhood caries or (ECC) is a leading cause of school absences and a reduction or lessening in Kids' quality of life. (Carvalho et al., 2024)

Due to the higher oral hygiene awareness, and the popular use of fluoride, in addition to easy and frequent access to dental clinics, the caries has reduced or decreased in a lot of developed countries. But there are still holes. Caries rates are significantly greater among those who are most susceptible, including the elderly, members of minority ethnic groups, and those with little access to healthcare. Because and due to a lack of preventative interventions and consuming or rising sugar consumption, the prevalence is rising in low and middle income. Caries has a negative effect on public health that reaches beyond oral health.

It causes systemic infections, nutritional issues, and financial losses due to decreased production. As an example, neglected male oral health issues cost the entire world healthcare system billions of dollars every year. Caries is therefore a priority non-communicable illness for combined measures to prevent it, according to the WHO (Al-Khalifa et al., 2024).

1.3 Risk Factors: Diet, Oral Hygiene, Fluoride Exposure

A combination of biologically behavioral in nature, and environment factors that lead to tooth decay progression. Carbohydrate intake, particularly the frequent use of sugar that is processed or refined and drinks with sugar, is an important contributor. Candies and colas are another instance of slowly breaking down or dissolving sugars and sticky that are especially dangerous because they stay in touch with teeth for extended periods of time and encourage microorganisms to secrete acidic solution (Tartaglia et al., 2024).

Additionally, dental care measures are important. The biofilm can accumulate as a result of irregular toothbrushing and failure to remove plaque, which supports an environment that is suitable to the existence and growth of bacteria that secrete acids. Dental caries management and prevention require both the elimination of dental plaque and the application of antimicrobial substances such as chlorhexidine (Luke et al., 2025).

Getting the proper Exposure to fluoride is a method from one of the prominent ways to stay secure and safe without having any dental cavities or caries is by. As, Fluoride makes enamel stronger and the ability to resist acidity, and lowers the microorganism's activity, in addition to assisting or aiding in its reconstruction or strengthening itself. Professional dental care or treatments, Toothpaste with fluoride, and the main community water, which is has fluoride have done a significant drop in the spread of dental cavities or decay in many areas or regions.

1.4 Clinical Significance: From Enamel Lesions to Advanced Decay

Both the framework and functionality of dentition are impacted or affected by the clinical course or progress of cavities. Patients may not notice initial enamel lesions, particularly if they are between teeth and don't cause any symptoms. But this is an important opportunity to take action in these lesions. As dentistry with minimal intervention has grown, early and rapid identification enables dentists to apply harmless and without any invasive technique for the remineralization techniques such as the casein phosphopeptide amorphous calcium phosphate therapies or fluoride varnishes (Luke et al., 2025).

Restorative work is frequently necessary if the lesion spreads into the dentin, causing irreparable damage. In extreme situations, caries can result in tooth loss, pulpitis, and infections surrounding the root. Oral Problems impact the ability to talk, beauty and attractiveness, the mental health, and the chewing efficiency of the person. Moreover, Serious, and severe decay raises the possibility of having a previous infection, especially in humans who are having a systematic and medical issues or conditions. Additionally, caries makes treatment planning more difficult. For instance, decisions in endodontics and prosthodontics can be impacted by whether or not a tooth can be fixed up. Consequently, cavities in the mouth are a process of disease which requires thorough therapy rather than just a defect (Negi et al., 2024).

1.5 Importance of Early Detection and Intervention in Preventing Tooth Loss

Early detection is the basis of successful caries control. This makes it possible to treat before there is significant damage to the integrity. Particularly in the interproximal and posterior regions, the free of carious lesions is frequently difficult to detect using conventional techniques like tactile probing and visual inspection. This has led to the development of novel or modern diagnostic techniques, such as the field of fiberoptic transillumination or FOTI and radiography, in addition to the near inf imaging or NIRI, and fluorescence-based identification, like DIAGNOdent (Al-Khalifa et al., 2024).

Human interpretation is still quite important even with these technologies, and examiners frequently differ from one another. In order to enhance diagnostic efficiency, accuracy, and reliability, new methods like the artificial intelligence also AKA AI are currently being researched. From the standpoint of the public's health, early recognition helps maintain the health of the teeth, reduces the requirement for bothersome procedures and lessens the risk of pulpal troubles.

In the long run, it decreases the expenses or costs for dental treatment while developing or improving the standard of living of humans. It is always important or crucial to have a prevention technique and strategy that makes sure there will be a follow-ups routine for checkups, and risks evaluation, in addition to guidance in the diet, thus improving awareness. In summary, early dental caries detection and treatment are not just clinically wise but also advantageous from a social and financial standpoint. The application of AI in this field, which is covered in the next sections of this chapter, has the potential to transform our understanding of and approach to one of the most difficult problems in oral health (Negi et al., 2024).

II. RESEARCH METHODOLOGY

2. Current Methods for Caries Detection in Dentistry

Casually or traditionally, taking X-rays and checking by eye with the tactile probing examination and investigation is always combined and implemented to diagnose a decay or caries. Even though technology is improving or advancing, these traditional and frequent methods or techniques have weaknesses or drawbacks since they depend on perspectives or so subjective, making it impossible to catch or detect decays in their beginning or early spots. Systems such as CCS, ADA, not forgetting the ICDAS, were made or developed to make the lesion evaluation more consistent and standardized, so as to address the diagnosis variations and prove how essential the early treatment. While, the x ray quality pictures, illumination or light, and the doctor's expertise or competency are still playing a main or major role in how outcomes should be analyzed or interpreted (Szabó et al., 2024).

2.1 Visual-Tactile Examination: Limitations and Subjectivity

Tactile and visually are the frequent and most used methods for cavities identification, particularly in the occasions of limited capabilities. Clinicians examine the outer layers of enamel with their hands and feel for cavities, transparency, and softness with a dental probe. Nevertheless, research has indicated that this technique might miss initial lesions or the (whitening) demineralization beneath the surface, especially in the spaces between the teeth interproximally. Furthermore, using sharp instruments for probing may result in unintentional harm or worsen already existing caries (Szabó et al., 2024).

Even though it is rapid, not expensive, and simple or straightforward, this method or approach is still highly relying or depending on the ability of dentists and may vary or differ depending on how expert they are. The precision or accuracy of the diagnosis or detection is affected or impacted by factors or variables like light or illumination, fluid management, and the doctor's knowledge or background. Although the sensitivity is often low by around fifty percent (50%), the specificity can be increased by applying ICDAS criteria. Visual and tactile assessment is therefore helpful, but for better and earlier detection, it should ideally be used in conjunction with X ray radiography and AI technologies (Kassebaum & GBD 2021 Oral Disorders Collaborators et al., 2025) as shown in Figure 1.

Figure 1. Visual and tactile approaches to recognition and detection, in addition to demonstrating early explorer use and lesion detection

Occlusal Protocol ***							
ICDAS code	0	1	2	3	4	5	6
	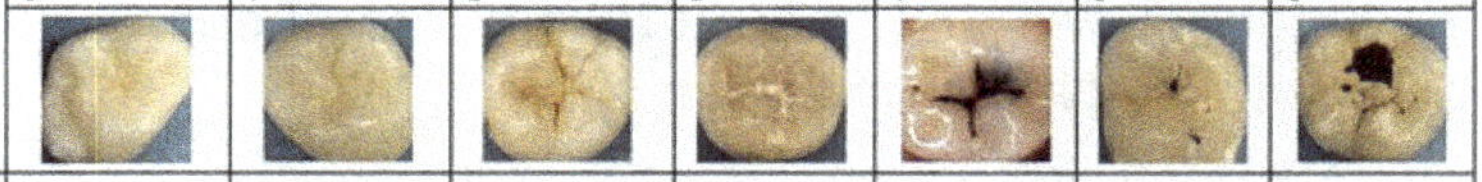						
Definitions	Sound tooth surface; no caries change after air drying (5 sec); or hypoplasia, wear, erosion, and other noncaries phenomena	First visual change in enamel; seen only after air drying or colored, change "thin" limited to the confines of the pit and fissure area	Distinct visual change in enamel; seen when wet, white or colored, "wider" than the fissure/fossa	Localized enamel breakdown with no visible dentin or underlying shadow; discontinuity of surface enamel, widening of fissure	Underlying dark shadow from dentin, with or without localized enamel breakdown	Distinct cavity with visible dentin; frank cavitation involving less than half of a tooth surface	Extensive distinct cavity with dentin; cavity is deep and wide involving more than half of the tooth
Histologic depth		Lesion depth in P/F was 90% in the outer enamel with only 10% into dentin	Lesion depth in P/F was 50% inner enamel and 50% into the outer 1/3 dentin	Lesion depth in P/F with 77% in dentin	Lesion depth in P/F with 88% into dentin	Lesion depth in P/F with 100% in dentin	Lesion depth in P/F 100% reaching inner 1/3 dentin
Sealant/restoration Recommendation for low risk	Sealant optional DIAGNOdent may be helpful	Sealant optional DIAGNOdent may be helpful	Sealant optional or caries biopsy if DIAGNOdent is 20-30	Sealant or minimally invasive restoration needed	Minimally invasive restoration	Minimally invasive restoration	Minimally invasive restoration
Sealant/restoration Recommendation for moderate risk	Sealant optional DIAGNOdent may be helpful	Sealant recommended DIAGNOdent may be helpful	Sealant optional or caries biopsy if DIAGNOdent is 20-30	Sealant or minimally invasive restoration needed	Minimally invasive restoration	Minimally invasive restoration	Minimally invasive restoration
Sealant/restoration Recommendation for high risk *	Sealant recommended DIAGNOdent may be helpful	Sealant recommended DIAGNOdent may be helpful	Sealant optional or caries biopsy if DIAGNOdent is 20-30	Sealant or minimally invasive restoration needed	Minimally invasive restoration	Minimally invasive restoration	Minimally invasive restoration
Sealant/restoration Recommendation for extreme risk **	Sealant recommended DIAGNOdent may be helpful	Sealant recommended DIAGNOdent may be helpful	Sealant optional or caries biopsy if DIAGNOdent is 20-30	Sealant or minimally invasive restoration needed	Minimally invasive restoration	Minimally invasive restoration	Minimally invasive restoration

* Patients with one (or more) cavitated lesion(s) are high-risk patients. ** Patients with one (or more) cavitated lesion(s) and xerostomia are extreme-risk patients.

*** All sealants and restorations to be done with a minimally invasive philosophy in mind. Sealants are defined as confined to enamel. Restoration is defined as in dentin. A two-surface restoration is defined as a preparation that has one part of the preparation in dentin and the preparation extends to a second surface (note: the second surface does not have to be in dentin). A sealant can be either resin-based or glass ionomer. Resin-based sealants should have the most conservatively prepared fissures for proper bonding. Glass ionomer should be considered where the enamel is immature, or where fissure preparation is not desired, or where rubber dam isolation is not possible. Patients should be given a choice in material selection.

2.2 Radiographic Imaging: Bitewing, Periapical, and Panoramic Views

The visual and tactile approach is supported by radiograph evaluation, which reveals underlying cavities that are otherwise difficult to locate. While periapical views evaluate root involvement and closeness to the pulp, bitewing radiographs are particularly useful for examining interproximal caries. Panoramic radiographs, however, are not effective for recognizing early cavities, provide a comprehensive overview and are typically utilized in full examinations. The most accurate method for identifying dentin and enamel cavities between teeth is bitewing radiography. It has trouble detecting lesions early, though, particularly when contrast is low (Luke et al., 2025).

Because radiographs are (2D two dimensional), overlapping structures can cover the actual depth or existence of the illness. Misunderstandings may also result from poor image quality, angling mistakes, and movement of the patient. Radiography picture interpretation is a biased process that might differ greatly amongst practitioners. Diagnostic results can be impacted by variables related to the settings of the contrast, display resolution, observer lack of energy and fatigue, in addition to the observer education. Furthermore, radiographs are limited in their ability to detect the initial stages decay because they only reveal lesions when a specific degree of demineralization has occurred, usually between thirty percent and forty percent of the mineral has been gone. According to the preventative dentistry, where rapid intervention is crucial, this is a serious issue (Szabó et al., 2024).

2.3 Challenges in Manual Interpretation: Interobserver Variability and Early Lesion Detection

Both visually and radiological cavities diagnosis manually provide a number of significant difficulties. When different practitioners interpret the exact same clinically or radiographical data, this is known as interobserver variability. Treatment choices are impacted by this discrepancy, which may result in the ignoring of lesions that require care or the excessive treatment of perfectly normal or reversible lesions. Manual approaches perform the worst when it comes to early caries detection, particularly for non-cavitated enamel lesions. Because of illumination, aspect, and the examiner's level of attention, these lesions can be missing or misinterpreted because they frequently show up as light RL (radiolucencies) or small white patches (Carvalho et al., 2024).

As a result, the lesion may progress to the point where restorative treatment is required because early preventive measures may not be taken. Interobservers variability is another problem, where a practitioner may give varying assessments at various times. This discrepancy makes it difficult to follow up and standardize treatment methods among dental offices. Software for image enhancement and digital radiography has attempted to solve these issues by providing better tools for magnification and contrast. They still depend on human judgment, though, and are susceptible to psychological disadvantages, including expectancy bias and satisfaction of search, which cause one to ignore more findings after spotting the initial defect (Al-Khalifa et al., 2024).

2.4 Diagnostic Criteria and Classification Systems

Numerous or many classifying methods and indicators for diagnosis have been created and developed to boost or strengthen the validity of decay identification or detection. The ICDAS is the most notable and widely used. From number 0, which denotes or shows a tooth in good health condition, to number 6, which denotes or shows a significant cavity within the dentin layer without pulp, this system and numbering offer a systematic and organized scoring technique or way. It promotes and improves the prevention or getting rid of surgical treatment by encouraging or motivating clinicians or dentists to identify and document any early carious alterations or changes before cavitation occurs. In a dry, clean, in addition to sterile environment, ICDAS depends on both tactile and visual evidence or clues. Research studies and investigations, in addition to any epidemiological research, and standard or correct work and practice can all make applications for it. Compared to conventional techniques or ways that only classify teeth as having caries or not, validation tests demonstrate or show that it provides or allows superior diagnostic reliability and sensitivity with no mistakes (Marwaha et al., 2025).

Its complex grading system, however, necessitates more time and training, which can cause problems in hectic or busy clinics. The depth of lesions or spots is also graded or scored using X-ray scoring or grading systems, such as Ekstrand's radiographic or X-ray requirements, which range from initial enamel invasion to deep dentin extension. These tools facilitate or help in the development of standardized, consistent X-ray evaluations or assessments, enabling data from many research and organizations to be analyzed and interpreted. While interpretation still relies on the doctor’s calibration or perspective in addition to education, even with standardized signs or indicators. For instance, the ICDAS system requires or mandates adequate sufficient lighting and a dry, sterile area, which aren't usually possible in health care institutions and facilities (Marwaha et al., 2025)

Future diagnostic systems will probably take a hybrid approach, with objective data driven by artificially intelligent algorithms or programs supporting human capabilities rather than replacing them. **Figure 2** shows the descriptive scores or codes for the ICDAS AKA International Caries Detection and Assessment System (Jenson et al., 2007) (ICDAS,2016).

Figure 2. Descriptive scores for the International Caries Detection and Assessment System

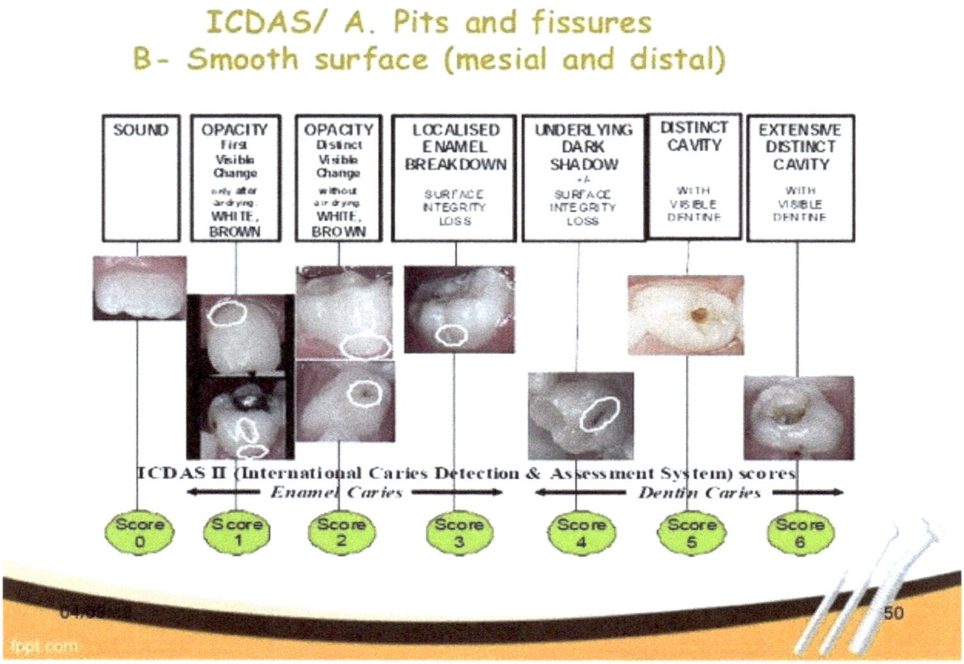

III. THEORETICAL FRAMEWORK

3. Introduction to Deep Learning in Dental Imaging

The field related to medical and dental X-ray radiographs, including oral cavity examination in addition to diagnosis with treatment, has already gone through many developments or advancements because of the AI programs, in particular the technique of AI deep learning. It makes it possible to develop models capable of highly accurate radiological X-ray data analysis. By training using massive collections of annotated or marked up radiography X-ray pictures, deep learning AI programs, particularly convolutional neural networks, have achieved impressive results for caries identification (Marwaha et al., 2025).

3.1 Basics of Deep Learning and CNNs for Image Analysis

The more than one or multiple-layered AI neural networks that are artificial are used in deep AI neural networks, an aspect of machine learning that aims to recognize complicated structures in data. The deep learning scenarios, particularly the CNNs, build structure features directly from raw or basic pixel info, in contrast to conventional approaches to image analysis involving manual choice of features. The CNNs' ability to analyze and interpret, in addition to figuring out the patterns of space, makes them particularly effective for image recognition and identification tasks or duties (Marwaha et al., 2025).

Convolutional layers use filters to detect and scan the image that is considered to be the input, layers for compromising and pooling any data, to a smaller in size, while fully linked and connected layers perform or carry out the classification in a traditional or usual CNN.

CNNs can identify or detect small or minute variations in gray scale in an X-ray radiograph of the oral cavity that point to or detect any structural changes and problems, demineralization, or decayed or carious spots. CNN programs or systems have been trained on marked dental imaging, identifying lesions using approaches to segmenting, in addition to categorizing or classifying surfaces as either sound or decayed. They are a useful tool for assisting or aiding dentists in making the right decision and lessening errors or mistakes in diagnosis because of their proficiency and capability with HD imaging information (Negi et al., 2024)

3.2 AI Model Training: Input Data, Labeling, and Ground Truth

A well-chosen data consisting of the input photos and their accompanying true markings is required to teach a model that uses deep learning. The input information for cavities identification usually consists of panoramic, bitewing, or PA X-rays. Each picture needs to be identified, either at the level of the object for recognition and detection tasks or at the level of the pixel for tasks like segmentation. The appropriate output that the system is meant to serve as is referred to as the ground truth. The ground truth in tooth decay detection is frequently established by treatment monitoring and follow-up, histology confirmation or acceptance among skilled dentists. Carious spots are carefully and manually labeled using tools for annotation like VGG Image or LabelMe Annotators. The accuracy of the model depends on this time consuming technique (Luke et al., 2025).

The performance of models is considerably affected by the quality of markings. Inadequate labels may result in less generality and predictions that are incorrect. In order to ensure accurate ground truth info, records must be carefully examined and cooperation between observers should be tested. Preprocessing techniques like scaling, normalizing, and comparison changes are also useful in unifying the provided or input data and enhancing model acceptance during training (Al-Khalifa et al., 2024).

3.3 Popular Datasets in Caries Detection

A major challenge faced by using deep learning methods in dental diagnosis and examination, in addition to treatment, is the limited number of significant freely or openly accessible data. Nevertheless, much data has been especially developed for the purpose or goal of screening decays or cavities screening. One of the most often cited openly or accessible and available data collections are the dental radiographs or X-ray Images data. It has several thousand bitewing and periapical gray scale images or radiographs identified for dental conditions and situations like root problems, cavities, and tooth loss. The collection of data it contains is mostly used by scientists or researchers for issues involving structure detection and grouping. Some dental imaging components can be found in the larger data like AI MED, in addition to ImageCLEFmed, which helps or aids in healthcare imaging classification. On the other hand, personal or individual clinical practice data gathered and found at private dentistry or at the dental college hospitals generally provide more radiography clarity and quality with a more reliable marking (Negi et al., 2024).

Nevertheless, since there are fears regarding patient privacy and confidentiality, these private and personal data tend not to become accessible and public. They are vital to teach and gain an efficient AI model training. Scientists use information enhancement methods, like rotation, image flipping, brightness changes and shifts, and zooming in and out, to intentionally expand the size of the data while boosting the efficiency of models in order to solve data lack and shortage. In order to improve dental radiography records, experts are also investigating artificially generated information produced using generative adversarial networks (GANs) (Al-Khalifa et al., 2024).

3.4 Model Architectures: ResNet, DenseNet, U-Net for Segmentation Tasks

In order to diagnose cavities in the mouth using excellent accuracy in diagnosing, the model structure or architectural design and selection is essential. A number of architectures indicate a potential (Negi et al., 2024):

- ResNet is a residual network, and it is a widely recognized Approach for, smooth and with no troubles, deep network training. The ResNet is successful in interpreting radiographs of teeth since it avoids layers through shortcut and rapid connections. Both multi class caries identification with its classification and binary caries make great use of it.

- The Densely Connected Convolutional Network or DenseNet is a system that uses a structure that suggests the reuse of features as well as efficient gradient transmission and flow by connecting the various layers to one another. It also functions excellently on small to medium size data and delivers good precision in dental evaluation with fewer criteria and parameters.
- A commonly standard used model or algorithm for tooth segmentation of images, The U-Net was originally created for the segmentation of bio medical pictures. Its decoder and encoder architecture with connections that skip making it possible to locate serious decays and carious spots exactly. Since the leveling of pixels markings is provided, The U-Net works especially well in enabling the system in precisely recognizing spots and lesions margins. To achieve particular healthcare objectives, which include identifying lesions and spots, assessing their risk, or their severity and extent grading, these structures can be adjusted or merged together. For improved consistency, numerous investigations gather and combine expectations or predictions from several algorithms or models via ensemble or group approaches (Budisak et al., 2023)

3.5 Transfer Learning for Small Dental Datasets

Having the ability for training and teaching the AI deep models from zero in imaging for dentistry is at times limited by an inadequate amount of info and data. By utilizing already trained algorithms or models formed on enormous data such as the ImageNet and correcting them on smaller in size information sets related to dentistry, in addition to, transferable learning tackles this issue. The approach begins by setting the algorithm or model with weight gathered from a broad picture recognition and detection job. The remaining layers are then modified for duties unique to the dental field. Even with just a little marked data, transferred learning assists the algorithm to interpret and generalize more successfully, speeds teaching or training, and boosts unity and convergence. For example, by switching out the last classification level or layer and re teaching on a dental health information set, an already trained DenseNet or ResNet can be further customized for the bitewing radiographic Xray classification (Marwaha et al., 2025).

In interacting with children with rare or minor lesions, where labeled information is hard for scientists to get by and get findings, this technique can be extremely helpful. Furthermore, scientists are investigating domain topic methods of adaptation that can close the spaces or gaps across information gathered through various facilities or radiological equipment. When used in practical situations, this improves the model's stability making it strong. Lastly, AI deep learning models are showing up as a significant factor in dental image processing, especially in the recognition and categorization of decayed spots. Experts and healthcare providers are capable of creating algorithms or models which might meet as well as beat individual's diagnosing skill with the help of convolutional neural networks or the CNNs along with powerful model designs like DenseNet, UNet, ResNet.

However, accurate data, proper marking, and ways like transferred learning for interacting with healthcare information concerns are all vital to these algorithms' or models' efficiency. AI Deep learning will be easier to include into routine dental work as more datasets that are marked be accessible and evolution in the computing methods. Gaining knowledge of those concepts is key to grasping and understanding the following chapters, which cover the dental AI acceptance, application in practice, and the ethical or moral pillars and the concerns of AI in dentistry (Talib et al., 2024).

IV. SOLUTIONS AND RECOMMENDATIONS

4. AI-Powered Caries Detection Systems

Dental caries is one of the most prominent and widespread oral diseases globally. Because they appear as a light color and faint on X rays in addition to human interpretation having its limits, the incipient and early cavitated lesions in the dentin and enamel often remain unnoticed. This happens even with improvements in diagnostic tools. One way to better detect and diagnose dental issues on X-rays is by using convolutional neural networks (CNNs), which are a type of artificial intelligence (Albano et al., 2024).

4.1 Application of CNNs on Radiographs for Caries Detection

Convolutional neural networks (CNNs) are a type of deep learning algorithm made for analyzing visual information. They can automatically learn and extract complicated information from images because of its organized layered structure, which has been designed after the human brain's cerebral cortex. When it comes to analyzing 2D radiographs, like bitewing and periapical images, to identify their existence, extent, and progress of tooth decay, the CNNs have delivered outstanding findings in the dentistry sector (Albano et al., 2024)

For training CNNs to tell the difference between carious and non-carious regions, experts are using huge sets of analyzed x-rays pictures. To improve the provided information, these CNNs generally do processing tasks such as raising contrast, lowering noise, and standardizing images (Oztekin et al., 2023)

The taught programs' ability to identify carious lesions is later assessed using a variety of validation data.

Importantly, CNNs have demonstrated competence in detecting early enamel caries, interproximal lesions, and occlusal caries that even highly qualified doctors can miss during eye inspections.

Complex model architectures such as ResNet, VGGNet, DenseNet, and U-Net have been used for tasks including segmentation and classification. For instance, U-Net, initially created for biological image segmentation, is now often used in dentistry to identify carious lesions pixel-by-pixel. In several studies, models based on U-Net achieved localization accuracy similar to expert annotations. It shows how AI can improve or even make the process of diagnosing way faster (Kamran et al., 2024). YOLOv7 Based Radiography Recognition Process and Workflow is shown in Figure 3 (Xu et al., 2023).

Figure 3. YOLOv7 based radiography recognition process and workflow

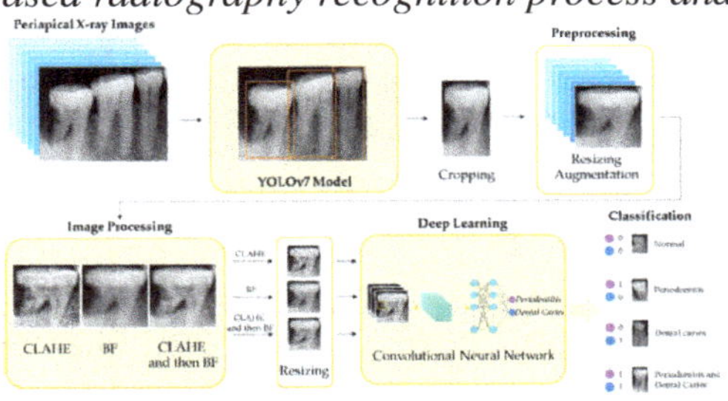

4.2 AI Model Performance Metrics: Accuracy, Sensitivity, Specificity

The value of AI power in the clinic is always there; furthermore, Caries detection algorithms must be assessed and evaluated by looking closely at some parameters, like specificity, in addition to sensitivity, and accuracy. In a lot of clinical diagnostic circumstances, these parameters help to demonstrate the reliability of the model.

- From many experts' points of view, Accuracy is the share and the number of correct results, which includes true negatives and true positives, within the entire population; it reflects and shows the model and its system's overall performance.
- Sensitivity, which is AKA the rate of all the true positives, and it measures the AI's capability to spot carious or decayed lesions, making it important for timely treatment (Albano et al., 2024).

- The actual negative rate, or AKA specificity, shows or demonstrates how well the model can exclude and remove the non-carious or the regions with no decay, allowing the dentists to minimize the need for any unnecessary treatment.

In recent studies, deep learning models have demonstrated good diagnostic performance. For instance, (Albano et al., 2024)[1] found that several AI models trained on panoramic pictures and bitewing radiographs showed sensitivity and specificity ranges of 0.85 to 0.98 and 0.44 to 0.86, respectively. In a different study (Kamran et al., 2024)[9] utilized or depended on the Grad CAM explainability in a model based on the ResNet. In this way, it was confirmed and ensured the high detection performance and how efficient it is, even for the early stage lesions and spots, achieving the accuracy of 96.6%, in addition to a sensitivity of 91.2%, nevertheless, a specificity of 94.8%.

Furthermore, it exceeded the usual interobserver agreement among general dental practitioners, which is usually calculated and estimated to be between 70 and 85 percent. These outstanding performances show and highlight the artificial intelligence's ability to lower diagnostic variability.

For the sake of clinical safety and generality, such models still require verification with other external data sets, a cross-valid techniques, and practical clinical trials.

4.3 AI vs. Dentists: Comparative Studies and Diagnostic Accuracy

Contrasting and comparing the AI's performance for diagnosis to that of practicing general dental practitioners is crucial or important to check if they are able to improve and maybe replace the standard methods of diagnosis. Some recent studies have examined whether AI can be a clinical tool to make diagnoses more error free and consistent while reducing errors, especially in challenging or difficult cases.

(Szabó et al., 2024) In a research study, researchers and experts contrasted and compared the abilities of diagnosis in the CNN models to those of a general dentist using intraoral X-ray radiographs. The AI showed and achieved a sensitivity between 0.51 and 0.76, in addition to a specificity that stands between 0.88 and 0.97. The performance was way better and higher than that of human dentists in the caries detection process. The outcomes and results show that AI, especially for the lesions that have just begun, can lower, and reduce false negatives while maintaining a good specificity.

Nevertheless, Carvalho et al., 2024, proved a cumulative sensitivity of 0.94 and specificity of 0.91 when comparing AI models with the human dentists for diagnosing caries on bitewing x-rays. This shows the AI's tool capability to spot difficult demineralization that might be missed in the daily practice.

More recently, (Szabó et al., 2024) conducted a multicenter trial to evaluate the Diagnocat AI platform using panoramic radiographs. The AI system showed similar performance to physicians, especially in detecting lesions in back teeth. It achieved faster diagnosis times and had lower differences in opinions among observers.

These benefits are important in busy clinics or tourist areas, where diagnostic efficiency matters.

Even with these positive results, human supervision is still essential. AI systems can make errors and misanalyze a structural overlap or artifacts that are anatomical, especially in cases of less uniform imaging or poorly taken X-rays. Humans' lack of contextual and dependent understanding, in addition to the skills of clinical reasoning, shows and implies why it's crucial to use AI as an additional tool, not as a replacement strategy. The AI can act as a reliable second opinion, helping dentists to reduce wrong diagnoses while maintaining and improving the accuracy with the right usage (Carvalho et al., 2024).

4.4 Case Examples: AI Detecting Early Lesions Missed by Clinicians

Artificial intelligence has shown its value in detecting dental cavities that might otherwise be missed. For example, the diagnosis software used a CNN model trained on more than 20,000 labeled bitewing radiographs during a pilot study at a private dental clinic in Stockholm, Sweden. The AI technology found early enamel problems that the treating dentists had missed in 37% of cases. Upon assessment, it was found that early cavities existed in more than 75% of these stated regions. (Oztekin et al., 2023)[2]

In another instance, an AI model was applied to do standard assessments on foreign patients receiving dental services at a clinic in Seoul, South Korea.

The model discovered 23 previously undetected cavities in 50 patients, allowing for conservative care and timely fluoride treatment. Patients reported higher satisfaction levels because they found the examination thorough and technically advanced, which is a key aspect of dental tourism experiences. (Kamran et al., 2024)[9]

These examples or instances show how AI can aid and help with diagnosis. They also highlight their effects on clinical workflow efficiency, patient confidence, and preventative care.

Figure 4 shows YOLOv7 Based the field of radiography Identification and recognition Mechanism and workflow (Oztekin et al., 2023).

Figure 4. YOLOv7 based the field of radiography identification and recognition mechanism and workflow

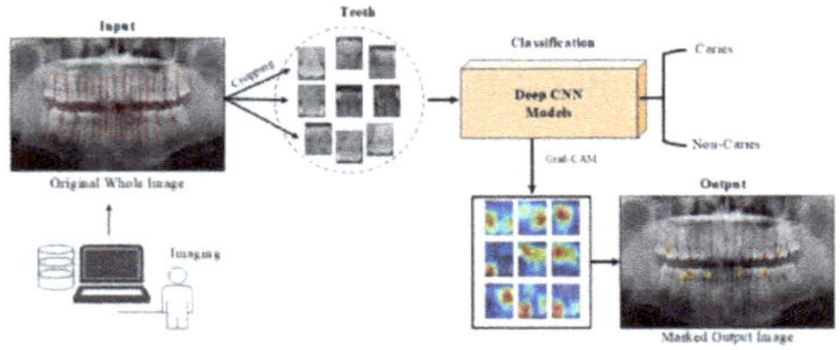

5. **Integration of AI into Clinical Dental Practice.**

The AI is being implemented significantly and a lot in the daily clinical dental work, quickly progressing and transforming from trial to research. The accuracy, productivity, and individualized treatments are all changing rapidly for general dentists as a result of implementing AI into the clinical diagnostic flow of work. As dental health tourism grows, these advancements are changing in chair diagnostics as they set the highest standards for patient care both locally and worldwide or internationally (Albano et al., 2024).

5.1 AI-Assisted Diagnostic Workflows: Real-Time Analysis During Patient Visits

To detect problems at the earliest possible moment or stage, like carious or decayed lesions, pulpal, or periapical illnesses. Analysis in real time is now accessible due to AI technology for diagnosis during routine dental visits. These techniques or methods often rely on convolutional neural networks that have been trained and taught on large or massive photo collections, such as bitewings, OPGs, and periapical films. (Albano et al., 2024)

Doctors and Clinicians can now upload images or take pictures with intraoral cameras or sensors to obtain real-time or on-the-spot diagnostic data, as artificial intelligence has been integrated into dental software programs as shown in Figure 5 (Thanh et al., 2023). For instance, Pearl's "Second Opinion®" and Overjet Dental, which are real-time radiograph analysis technologies including AI, can detect or identify potential bone loss and carious or decayed lesions within seconds of capturing or taking an image. The digital Practice management programs are easily integrated or incorporated with the programs or platforms. Thus, it makes it possible to share AI results with patients during clinical discussions, display them chairside, and overlay in addition to interpreting them on X-ray radiographs.

The decisions during the clinical process are made more quickly, delays in diagnosis are reduced, and appointment scheduling is made simpler and easier. By identifying or detecting early interproximal caries that may not be apparent or obvious to the eye or even to skilled doctors, a dentist using AI methods and technologies during a preventive appointment might improve early intervention techniques and outcomes (Wang et al., 2025).

Figure 5. Smartphone caries recognition and screening results

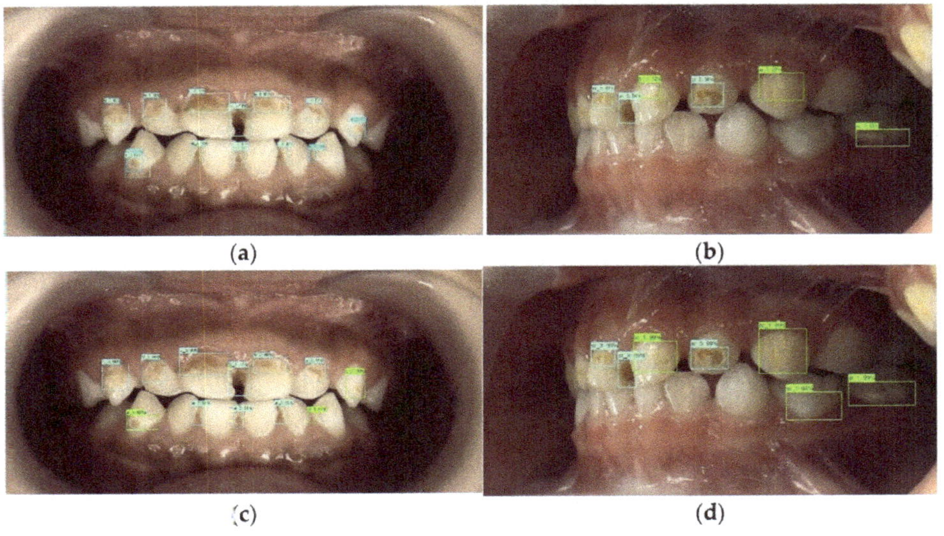

5.2 AI as a Second Opinion Tool for Dentists

One of the most significant clinical applications is the usage of AI in cases of making decisions during the dentist's diagnosis as a support system or a second point of view. AI systems or programs offer and show data-driven assessments, which are objective and repeatable, of radiography pictures, in contrast to conventional techniques that only rely on a clinician's experience and logic. This increases the confidence and dependability of diagnostics.

AI can lessen practitioner disagreements, according to many validity trials, which have demonstrated that.

According to Szabó et al., 2024, For example, the sensitivity of dentists in detecting and diagnosing early proximal decays ranged from approximately 51% to 76%. The AI programs, on the other hand, continuously produced and showed a greater sensitivity of 84% and specificity of 91%, thus reducing the number of early lesions that were missed or overlooked.

5.3 Reducing Diagnostic Errors and Improving Consistency

Diagnostic mistakes or errors can have major clinical impacts in dentistry, especially when caries are identified early. The wrong or False positive results have the potential to affect and harm healthy tooth structure, resulting in unnecessary interventions and treatment. However, when we find it false negative, it allows untreated lesions to progress and worsen, causing permanent or irreversible damage to the tooth layers.

According to researching and exploring, AI techniques that are trained on sizable, labeled datasets for both types of errors in diagnosis can be considerably and significantly decreased. CNNs are used or employed in these models to recognize and identify detailed visual characteristics associated with dentin involvement as well as initial enamel demineralization.

Some Researchers showed that their explainable approach of ResNet for early or initial stage lesion diagnosis had around accuracy of 96.1 percent and with a sensitivity of 90.9 percent, and a specificity of around 93.8 percent. Thus, it demonstrated its capability for clinical application and usage.

Even beyond statistical performance, a Provider's consistency is one of AI's biggest benefits in clinical practice. In group practices, rotating shifts, or health tourism clinics with diverse practitioner backgrounds, AI serves as a standardized interpretative layer.

By eliminating human factors like fatigue, experience gaps, or subjective bias, it encourages more uniform diagnostic results, a benefit particularly helpful in multinational dental organizations and the tourist facilities that are focused on oral health (Albano et al., 2024). **Figure 6.** Smartphone Based Dental Cavities Screening and recognition results or the Outputs (Overjet Inc., 2023).

Figure 6. Smartphone based dental cavities screening and recognition results or the outputs

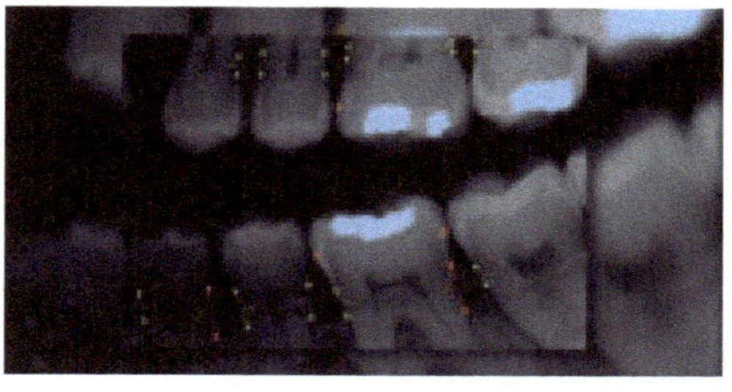

5.4 Benefits for Dental Health Tourism: Faster Diagnostics and Improved Care for International Patients

AI is meeting the demands with the required needs, which are, for example, nevertheless, improving and increasing treatment precision, fastening or speeding up the diagnosis and procedures, in addition to, enabling detailed discussions frequently on a single visit and there is an increasing and more demand for rapid or quick, accurate, and reasonably priced dental treatment or care.

AI programs are being used or employed by dental clinics in popular or prevalent destinations for dental tourism, like the UAE, Turkey, and Thailand, to assist or aid patients who are considered to be foreign in need of the same exact day diagnosis and treatment plans. Clinics may now offer complete treatment choices as soon as they receive radiographic images via AI, which reduces diagnostic waiting times from hours or days to minutes (Negi et al., 2024).

Lastly, the prestige and popularity of clinics are greatly increased. Clinics that use AI are considered to be modern and new dental offices that draw and attract more patients or clients seeking exceptional dental experiences. These clinics are thought to be more advanced and efficient (Wang et al., 2025).

6. Challenges and Limitations in AI-Based Caries Detection

AI has a lot of potential for dental diagnosis, especially for spotting and detecting early cavity lesions.

Several issues must be solved before AI is extensively adopted and applied in clinical dentistry. The performance of the models, physician acceptance, and patient trust are all impacted by these difficulties, which include clinical, legal, in addition to, moral, and technical concerns.

Data set restrictions remain a major obstacle from a technological perspective. Small, poorly labeled datasets that are skewed toward particular populations or radiography image types are used to train the majority of artificial intelligence programs. When models come with patient demographics, tooth forms, or radiography equipment that they have never seen before, weak generalizability occurs.

Adoption challenges like doubts regarding AI advice, a lack of clinician training, and problems integrating with existing imaging systems limit clinical application in the real world. According to (Szabó et al., 2024)[4] even successful AI systems like Diagnocat encountered difficulties when applied in real dentistry offices, especially in complex or uncommon situations where human judgment is still vital.

6.1 Data-Related Challenges: Annotation Quality, Dataset Bias, and Generalizability

The foundation and basis of any effective deep learning model is the quality of data, so we need an excellent info set. In order to detect dental caries, radiographic images are frequently categorized, and the lesions are labeled according to the standard diagnosis. However, the subjective and inconsistent nature of data markings is a major problem with contemporary AI research. Clinician differences introduce noise and uncertainty into training data sets when detecting early carious lesions, particularly teeth free of caries and any enamel alterations. Using the Reality clinical information has a direct impact on the system's learning process. Therefore, this results in decreased sensitivity and accuracy. (Albano et al., 2024)

Data set bias is yet another significant issue. Most caries detection models are trained on data collected from specific populations, imaging systems, or clinical practices.

Because of this, AI systems might perform well in their initial processing environment but not in other imaging modalities, age groups, ethnic communities, or clinical work. A CNN may not function well when applied to panoramic images from a public healthcare facility in Southeast Asia if it has only been trained on bitewing radiographs from a private clinic in Europe. The trustworthiness of AI systems in various healthcare scenarios is harmed by this lack of generalization, particularly in international applications such as dental health tourism.

This issue and confusion slow and might restrict dentists' innovations, making it more difficult for all humans to build models of AI (Holtkamp et al., 2021).

6.2 Ethical Considerations: Patient Privacy, Liability, and Professional Oversight

The application of AI in health centers raises questions and challenges, in addition to posing hard or difficult issues from its ethical aspects. For an AI model to learn and get better or improve, a lot of personal health data is required.

The Privacy of patients is, thus, crucial. If the info is collected or gathered with no appropriate encryption, anonymization, or a humanized way, in addition to consent, Confidentiality and privacy may be threatened or jeopardized. Since the process of transferring data across earth borders may include different and separate data privacy rules, for example, the HIPAA or the GDPR in the United States or in European nations, the hazards and risks are raised in the cases of tourism in the aspect of dental health tourism. Liability or accountability and its usage are still another crucial matter (Negi et al., 2024).

If an error related to Artificial intelligence happens or occurs during the diagnosis or the treatment phase, it is still unclear who is legally liable. The dentist, the workplace, and the clinic, the inventor and creator of the AI programs, all of them are involved in combination. Practitioners may be reluctant to completely depend on and use the AI in clinical scenarios and its decision making because of its vague or unclear legal rules and regulations as well as its issues or concerns about its misconduct.

Moreover, the continuous supervision under human eyes is mandatory for its ethical usage and implementation. Even though AI can help in making decisions, it shouldn't replace and take the place of dental experts' and scientists' environments, their critical thinking, and their empathy.

V. FUTURE RESEARCH DIRECTIONS

7. Future Directions

Fast and accurate detection and diagnosis are important factors in implementing appropriate prevention and treatment in patients with dental caries. When dental caries are not properly diagnosed, the lesion may progressively invade the enamel, dentin, and even pulp tissue, inducing severe pain, and ultimately leading to loss of tooth function. Using a deep CNN based on GoogLeNet Inception v3 architecture, which has superior performance in image detection, classification, and segmentation, compared to any other deep learning algorithm, has been extensively used in the medical field for classifying and diagnosing image and video sources including MRI, CT, microscopy, ultrasound, xray, mammography, and color fundus photos. By using this solution, we were able to achieve considerable accuracy and efficiency of detection and diagnosis of dental caries. This finding supports the concept that optimized deep learning architectures can be useful and effective in clinical dental practice (Mohammad-Rahimi et al., 2022).

7.1 Combining AI with other diagnostic tools: laser fluorescence, intraoral cameras

More precise information on the position and activity of lesions can be obtained with adjunct devices such as laser fluorescence (e.g., DIAGNOdent), transillumination, and quantitative light-induced fluorescence (QLF) (Al-Khalifa et al., 2024). However, they frequently have exorbitant costs and poor specificity. By combining these modalities with AI, their advantages could be maximized while their disadvantages are minimized. In order to classify caries on tooth surfaces, for instance, a

CNN applied to QLF images achieved ~86% sensitivity and precision (Park et al., 2023). In real life, an AI might be able to learn from both fluorescence patterns and X-ray features to enhance early caries diagnosis beyond what either technique could do on its own. A more comprehensive picture of incipient deterioration may be obtained by combining laser-based data with images from intraoral cameras or smartphones. According to one review, dentists should employ a variety of tests to ensure correctness (Al-Khalifa et al., 2024). AI might combine information from intraoral pictures, X-rays, and light-based technologies to more confidently detect problematic lesions.

a. AI and Laser Fluorescence Devices

Laser light is used by laser fluorescence (LF) equipment, like as DIAGNOdent, to identify fluorescence in dental structures. The degree of caries or demineralization is correlated with the fluorescence intensity. Historically, inter-operator variability and clinical skill were needed to interpret these fluorescence readings. To improve diagnosis reliability, AI models can be taught to examine these fluorescence readings in conjunction with information from other sources.

According to a study by Mertens et al. (2021), the diagnostic accuracy for identifying early carious lesions increased dramatically when fluorescence data and AI analysis were coupled. They reduced false positives frequently linked to LF alone by using machine learning methods to correlate LF values with histological validation.

b. AI and Intraoral Cameras

Intraoral cameras provide real-time, high-resolution images of the oral cavity, enabling clinicians to detect lesions, cracks, and restorations. Convolutional neural networks (CNNs), in particular, are AI models that have demonstrated potential in accurately diagnosing intraoral pictures.

A major research by Schwendicke et al. (2022) thoroughly examined deep learning applications in radiography and photography-based caries diagnosis. In comparison to or better than general dentists, the authors discovered that AI models trained on intraoral camera pictures were able to identify occlusal and proximal caries.

Thanh et al.'s 2022 work employed deep learning to identify dental cavities with smartphone images. They used 1,902 photos shot with an iPhone 7 to test four AI models: Faster R-CNN, YOLOv3, RetinaNet, and SSD. While all models discovered that early, non-cavitated lesions were more difficult to detect, the YOLOv3 and Faster R-CNN models performed best at identifying deeper (cavitated) cavities. After looking over the photos, a skilled dentist classified the teeth into four categories: healthy, early lesions (brown or white patches), moderate cavities (enamel degradation), and advanced cavities (open holes). This work demonstrates the potential of AI for early caries diagnosis using basic pictures, but it also emphasizes the need for additional advancements before it can be applied extensively in clinical settings. Figure 7 displays the method's flow chart.

Figure 7. Dental cavities detection using iPhone 7 images method's flow chart

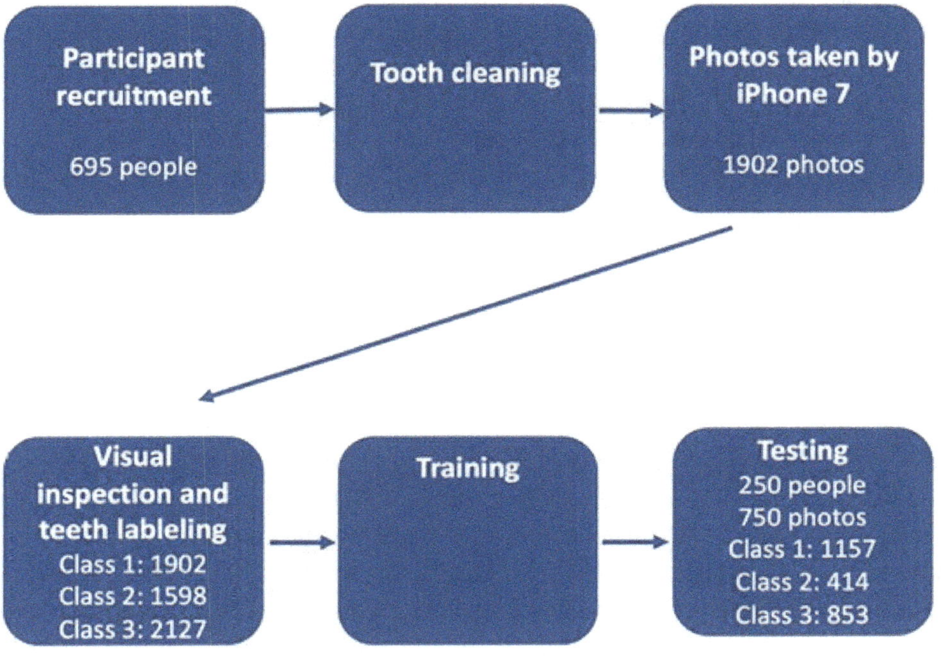

c. Integrated AI-Based Diagnostic Platforms

Combining LF and intraoral imagery with AI forms a multi-modal diagnostic approach. AI can integrate signals from both modalities, reducing false negatives and enhancing confidence in decision-making. Some commercial diagnostic software already implement such fusion, for example, platforms like **Overjet** and **Pearl** use AI to analyze radiographs and intraoral photos, and there is increasing interest in expanding this to fluorescence and optical coherence modalities.

A hybrid system trained on both fluorescence and imaging data can leverage the depth sensitivity of LF and the spatial resolution of imaging for a comprehensive caries profile, particularly beneficial for early-stage lesions where visual or tactile examination may fail.

7.2 Global Impact: AI for Dental Care Access in Underserved Regions

Access to dental care could be revolutionized by artificial intelligence (AI), especially in underdeveloped and resource-poor areas of the world. The infrastructure for dental treatment in many developing nations is beset by a lack of qualified personnel, diagnostic equipment, and educational opportunities. Scalable substitutes for in-person dental exams can be AI-driven diagnostic systems that are integrated into smartphones, portable intraoral cameras, or cloud-based apps. With the help of these technologies, non-specialist medical personnel may fairly accurately screen for and classify dental disorders such caries, periodontal disease, and oral diseases. A study by Esteva et al. (2021), for example, demonstrated that deep learning models trained on smartphone photos of oral cavities could classify common oral disorders with performance close to that of experts, making them appropriate for use in primary care settings without access to dentists.

In addition, AI-powered mobile health (mHealth) platforms have been tried in sub-Saharan Africa and South Asia to help community health professionals offer preventive oral health care and educational interventions (Alhayek & Hamed, 2020). These approaches not only make early detection and referral easier but also help collect epidemiological data for public health planning. The FDI World Dental Federation and the World Health Organization (WHO) are among the organizations that have emphasized digital dentistry as a key strategy for addressing global inequities in access to oral healthcare (World Health Organization, 2022). By integrating multilingual AI systems, speech-to-text interfaces, and natural language processing (NLP), such solutions can be customized for local languages and cultural contexts, making them more practical.

By enabling task-shifting strategies, decentralizing care, and providing remote communities with real-time, accurate diagnostic support, AI technology, as it becomes more affordable and accessible, offers a promising way to close the dental gap.

VI. CONCLUSION

AI serves as a promising tool in the diagnosis of dental cavities. The results of this study validate the high potential for developing accurate models for caries detection that facilitate the diagnosis and classification of dental caries. This, along with its rapid processing capabilities, positions AI as a highly effective diagnostic tool within this field.

In addition to convolutional neural networks (CNNs), various AI techniques, such as Artificial Neural Networks (ANNs) and Deep Convolutional Neural Networks (DCNNs), have shown significant potential in dental image analysis and cavity detection. These models offer diverse approaches to improving diagnostic accuracy and efficiency.

As this field progresses and becomes more established, with due regard for regulatory and ethical affairs, AI models can become a modern-day tool for dental image analysis and cavity detection. However, the following question remains: can AI models surpass the diagnostic abilities of dentists in identifying cavities in radiographic images and ultimately lead to improved clinical results for patients? Future research should continue to explore the integration of AI with other emerging technologies to enhance diagnostic capabilities and clinical outcomes (Al-Khalifa et al., 2024).

REFERENCES

Al-Khalifa, K. S., Ahmed, W. M., Azhari, A. A., Qaw, M., Alsheikh, R., Alqudaihi, F., & Alfaraj, A. (2024). The Use of Artificial Intelligence in Caries Detection: A Review. *Bioengineering (Basel, Switzerland)*, *11*(9), 936. DOI: 10.3390/bioengineering11090936 PMID: 39329679

Al-Khalifa, K. S., Ahmed, W. M., Azhari, A. A., Qaw, M., Alsheikh, R., Alqudaihi, F., & Alfaraj, A. (2024). The Use of Artificial Intelligence in Caries Detection: A Review. *Bioengineering (Basel, Switzerland)*, *11*(9), 936. DOI: 10.3390/bioengineering11090936 PMID: 39329679

Al-Khalifa, K. S., Ahmed, W. M., Azhari, A. A., Qaw, M., Alsheikh, R., Alqudaihi, F., & Alfaraj, A. (2024). The Use of Artificial Intelligence in Caries Detection: A Review. *Bioengineering (Basel, Switzerland)*, *11*(9), 936. DOI: 10.3390/bioengineering11090936 PMID: 39329679

Albano, D., Galiano, V., Basile, M., Di Luca, F., Gitto, S., Messina, C., Cagetti, M. G., Del Fabbro, M., Tartaglia, G. M., & Sconfienza, L. M. (2024). Artificial intelligence for radiographic imaging detection of caries lesions: A systematic review. *BMC Oral Health*, *24*(1), 274. DOI: 10.1186/s12903-024-04046-7 PMID: 38402191

Alhayek, S., & Hamed, R. (2020). Use of mobile technologies in low-resource dental care: A review. *Journal of Global Health Reports*, *4*, e2020034. DOI: 10.29392/001c.12294

Budisak, P., & Brizuela, M. (2023). Dental Caries Classification Systems. In *StatPearls*. StatPearls Publishing., DOI: 10.1016/j.adaj.2014.11.018

Carvalho, B. K. G., Nolden, E. L., Wenning, A. S., Kiss-Dala, S., Agócs, G., Róth, I., Kerémi, B., Géczi, Z., Hegyi, P., & Kivovics, M. (2024). Diagnostic accuracy of artificial intelligence for approximal caries on bitewing radiographs: A systematic review and meta-analysis. *Journal of Dentistry*, *151*, 105388. DOI: 10.1016/j.jdent.2024.105388 PMID: 39396775

Esteva, A., Robicquet, A., Ramsundar, B., Kuleshov, V., DePristo, M., Chou, K., Cui, C., Corrado, G., Thrun, S., & Dean, J. (2021). A guide to deep learning in healthcare. *Nature Medicine*, *25*(1), 24–29. DOI: 10.1038/s41591-018-0316-z PMID: 30617335

Holtkamp, A., Elhennawy, K., Cejudo Grano de Oro, J. E., Krois, J., Paris, S., & Schwendicke, F. (2021). Generalizability of Deep Learning Models for Caries Detection in Near-Infrared Light Transillumination Images. *Journal of Clinical Medicine*, *10*(5), 961. DOI: 10.3390/jcm10050961 PMID: 33804562

Jenson, L., Budenz, A. W., Featherstone, J. D., Ramos-Gomez, F., Spolsky, V. W., & Young, D. A. (2007). Clinical protocols for caries management by risk assessment. *Journal of the California Dental Association*, 35(10), 714–723. ICDAS Committee. (2016). *ICDAS: International Caries Detection and Assessment System™ — criteria manual.* Retrieved from https://iccms-web.com/uploads/asset/592846a55c8a2e4f18000008/ICDAS-Booklet.pdf

Kamran, M., Waseem, M., Shafi, N., & Zahid, A. (2024). Detection of Caries and Hypodontia using Deep Learning and Explainable AI. *2024 18th International Conference on Open Source Systems and Technologies (ICOSST)*, 1-6. DOI: 10.1109/ICOSST64562.2024.10871141

Kassebaum, N. J.GBD 2021 Oral Disorders Collaborators. (2025). Trends in the global, regional, and national burden of oral conditions from 1990 to 2021: A systematic analysis for the Global Burden of Disease Study 2021. *Lancet*, *405*(10482), 897–910. DOI: 10.1016/S0140-6736(24)02811-3 PMID: 40024264

Luke, A. M., & Rezallah, N. N. F. (2025). Accuracy of artificial intelligence in caries detection: A systematic review and meta-analysis. *Head & Face Medicine*, *21*(1), 24. DOI: 10.1186/s13005-025-00496-8 PMID: 40181403

Marwaha, J., Singla, M., Nath, A., & Arya, A. (2025). Revolutionizing the diagnosis of dental caries using artificial intelligence-based methods. *Journal of Conservative Dentistry and Endodontics*, *28*(5), 401–405. DOI: 10.4103/JCDE.JCDE_172_25 PMID: 40463673

Mertens, S.. (2021). Artificial intelligence for caries detection: Validation of a novel machine learning algorithm with laser fluorescence data. *Clinical Oral Investigations*, *25*, 1021–1030. DOI: 10.1007/s00784-020-03463-w

Mohammad-Rahimi, H., Motamedian, S. R., Rohban, M. H., Krois, J., Uribe, S. E., Mahmoudinia, E., Rokhshad, R., Nadimi, M., & Schwendicke, F. (2022). Deep learning for caries detection: A systematic review. *Journal of Dentistry*, *122*, 104115. DOI: 10.1016/j.jdent.2022.104115 PMID: 35367318

Negi, S., Mathur, A., Tripathy, S., Mehta, V., Snigdha, N. T., Adil, A. H., & Karobari, M. I. (2024). Artificial Intelligence in Dental Caries Diagnosis and Detection: An Umbrella Review. *Clinical and Experimental Dental Research*, *10*(4), e70004. DOI: 10.1002/cre2.70004 PMID: 39206581

Overjet Inc. (2023). Overjet AI for caries detection [Product demo]. Retrieved from https://www.overjet.com/ai-dental-caries-detection

Oztekin, F., Katar, O., Sadak, F., Yildirim, M., Cakar, H., Aydogan, M., Ozpolat, Z., Talo Yildirim, T., Yildirim, O., Faust, O., & Acharya, U. R. (2023). An Explainable Deep Learning Model to Prediction Dental Caries Using Panoramic Radiograph Images. *Diagnostics (Basel)*, *13*(2), 226. DOI: 10.3390/diagnostics13020226 PMID: 36673036

Park, E. Y., Jeong, S., Kang, S., Cho, J., Cho, J. Y., & Kim, E. K. (2023). Tooth caries classification with quantitative light-induced fluorescence (QLF) images using convolutional neural network for permanent teeth in vivo. *BMC Oral Health*, *23*(1), 981. DOI: 10.1186/s12903-023-03669-6 PMID: 38066624

Schwendicke, F.. (2022). Deep learning for caries detection: A systematic review. *Journal of Dentistry*, *122*, 104115. DOI: 10.1016/j.jdent.2022.104115 PMID: 35367318

Szabó, V., Szabó, B. T., Orhan, K., Veres, D. S., Manulis, D., Ezhov, M., & Sanders, A. (2024). Validation of artificial intelligence application for dental caries diagnosis on intraoral bitewing and periapical radiographs. *Journal of Dentistry*, *147*, 105105. DOI: 10.1016/j.jdent.2024.105105 PMID: 38821394

Talib, M. A., Moufti, M. A., Nasir, Q., Kabbani, Y., Aljaghber, D., & Afadar, Y. (2024). Transfer Learning-Based Classifier to Automate the Extraction of False X-Ray Images From Hospital's Database. *International Dental Journal*, *74*(6), 1471–1482. DOI: 10.1016/j.identj.2024.08.002 PMID: 39232939

Tartaglia, G., Del Fabbro, M., Gitto, S., Messina, C., Di Luca, F., Sconfienza, L., Galiano, V., Cagetti, M., Basile, M., & Albano, D. (2024). Artificial intelligence for radiographic imaging detection of caries lesions: A systematic review. *BMC Oral Health*, *24*(1), 274. Advance online publication. DOI: 10.1186/s12903-024-04046-7 PMID: 38402191

Thanh, M. T. G., Hoang, D., & Le, H.. (2022). Deep Learning Application in Dental Caries Detection Using Intraoral Photos Taken by Smartphones. *Applied Sciences (Basel, Switzerland)*, *12*(11), 5504. DOI: 10.3390/app12115504

Thanh, M. T. G., Toan, N. V., Ngoc, V. T. N., Tra, N. T., Giap, C. N., & Nguyen, D. M. (2023). Deep learning application in dental caries detection using intraoral photographs. *International Journal of Computer Applications in Technology*, *72*(4), 233–242. DOI: 10.1504/IJCAT.2023.10056912

Wang, Y., Chen, T., Vinayahalingam, S., Wu, T., Chang, C., Chang, H., Wei, H., Chen, M., Ko, C., Moin, D., Ginneken, B., Xi, T., Tsai, H., Chen, M., Hsu, T., & Chou, H. (2025). Artificial Intelligence to Assess Dental Findings from Panoramic Radiographs — A Multinational Study._.DOI: 10.485502502.10277

World Health Organization. (2022). *Global oral health status report: Towards universal health coverage for oral health by 2030.* https://www.who.int/publications/i/item/9789240061484

Xu, M., Wang, Y., Liu, H., & Zhang, Y. (2023). Deep learning-based recognition of periodontitis and dental caries in dental X-ray images. *Computerized Medical Imaging and Graphics*, *106*, 102173. DOI: 10.1016/j.compmedimag.2023.102173

KEY TERMS AND DEFINITIONS

Convolutional Neural Network (CNN): A deep learning architecture designed to process image data through convolutional layers that detect visual features (edges, textures, lesions). CNNs are widely used in dental caries detection models.

Deep Learning (DL): A subset of machine learning that uses multi-layered artificial neural networks to automatically learn complex patterns from large datasets, such as dental radiographs, without manual feature engineering.

Dental Caries: A biofilm-mediated, sugar-driven, multifactorial disease that leads to the demineralization and destruction of tooth structure. In AI systems, it refers to detectable lesions on dental images.

Radiographic Image Analysis: The computational interpretation of dental X-rays (bitewing, periapical, panoramic) using algorithms like CNNs to identify signs of caries, including early enamel lesions that may be difficult to detect visually.

Segmentation: A deep learning technique that partitions an image into regions (e.g., tooth surfaces, caries-affected areas). It enables pixel-level localization of lesions in dental radiographs.

Sensitivity and Specificity: Performance metrics used to evaluate AI diagnostic models. Sensitivity measures the model's ability to correctly detect carious lesions (true positives), while specificity measures its ability to avoid false positives.

Transfer Learning: A technique where a model pre-trained on large general datasets (e.g., ImageNet) is fine-tuned on dental radiographs, reducing training time and improving performance for caries detection tasks.

Compilation of References

Adams, K., Snyder, J., Crooks, V. A., & Berry, N. S. (2018). A critical examination of empowerment discourse in medical tourism: The case of the dental tourism industry in Los Algodones, Mexico. *Globalization and Health*, *14*(1), 70. DOI: 10.1186/s12992-018-0392-3 PMID: 30029610

Afshari, Z., Khademi, A., & Iranmanesh, P. (2024). Prospects of artificial intelligence in dentistry. *Dental Research Journal (Isfahan)*, *21*(1). Advance online publication. DOI: 10.4103/drj.drj_30_24 PMID: 39188386

Aggarwal, J., & Singh, P. (2024). Artificial intelligence in dental practice: An integrated approach. *Journal of Dental Specialities*, *12*(2), 72–76. DOI: 10.18231/j.jds.2024.015

Ahmadimanesh, F., Paydar, M. M., & Asadi-Gangraj, E. (2019). Designing a mathematical model for dental tourism supply chain. *Tourism Management*, *75*, 404–417. DOI: 10.1016/j.tourman.2019.06.001

Ahmadimanesh, F., Pourmehdi, M., & Paydar, M. M. (2021). Evaluation and prioritisation of potential locations for investment in dental tourism. *Soft Computing*, *25*(24), 15313–15333. DOI: 10.1007/s00500-021-06124-2

Ahmad, Z., Rahim, S., Zubair, M., & Abdul-Ghafar, J. (2021). Artificial intelligence (AI) in medicine, current applications and future role with special emphasis on its potential and promise in pathology: Present and future impact, obstacles including costs and acceptance among pathologists, practical and philosophical considerations. A comprehensive review. *Diagnostic Pathology*, *16*(1), 1–16. DOI: 10.1186/s13000-021-01085-4 PMID: 33731170

Ajam, M., Sadeghifar, J., Anjomshoa, M., Mahmoudi, S., Honarvar, H., & Mousavi, S. M. (2014). Assessing the quality of healthcare service by the SERVQUAL model: A case study of a field hospital. *Journal of Military Medicine*, *15*(4), 273–279.

Akbar, F. H., Rivai, F., Abdullah, A. Z., & Awang, A. H. (2021). Relationship between information access, service quality, costs saving, cultural similarity and supporting service towards medical (dental) tourism patients' satisfaction. *Journal of Dentomaxillofacial Science*, *6*(1), 31. DOI: 10.15562/jdmfs.v6i1.1106

Akbar, F., Krishnan, V., Yusoh, M., Senin, M. S., Ismail, A., & Abbas, M. (2022). Dental Tourism in Bali Province, Indonesia. *NeuroQuantology : An Interdisciplinary Journal of Neuroscience and Quantum Physics*, *20*(1), 340–347. DOI: 10.14704/nq.2022.20.1.NQ22301

Albano, D., Galiano, V., Basile, M., Di Luca, F., Gitto, S., Messina, C., Cagetti, M. G., Del Fabbro, M., Tartaglia, G. M., & Sconfienza, L. M. (2024). Artificial intelligence for radiographic imaging detection of caries lesions: A systematic review. *BMC Oral Health*, *24*(1), 274. DOI: 10.1186/s12903-024-04046-7 PMID: 38402191

Alhayek, S., & Hamed, R. (2020). Use of mobile technologies in low-resource dental care: A review. *Journal of Global Health Reports*, *4*, e2020034. DOI: 10.29392/001c.12294

Al-Khalifa, K. S., Ahmed, W. M., Azhari, A. A., Qaw, M., Alsheikh, R., Alqudaihi, F., & Alfaraj, A. (2024). The Use of Artificial Intelligence in Caries Detection: A Review. *Bioengineering (Basel, Switzerland)*, *11*(9), 936. DOI: 10.3390/bioengineering11090936 PMID: 39329679

Alkier Tomić, R., Okicic, J., & Milojica, V. (2024). *Measuring Satisfaction of Tourists with Dental Services in Kvarner Region*. https://doi.org/DOI: 10.15308/Sitcon-2024-95-104

Allied Market Research. (2023). *Dental tourism market by treatment type: Global opportunity analysis and industry forecast, 2021–2031*.

Al-Neyadi, H. S., Abdallah, S., & Malik, M. (2018). Measuring patient's satisfaction of healthcare services in the UAE hospitals: Using SERVQUAL. *International Journal of Healthcare Management*, *11*(2), 96–105. DOI: 10.1080/20479700.2016.1266804

AlOmari, F. (2020). Measuring gaps in healthcare quality using SERVQUAL model: Challenges and opportunities in developing countries. *Measuring Business Excellence*. Advance online publication. DOI: 10.1108/MBE-11-2019-0104

Alotaibi, S., & Deligianni, E. (2024). AI in oral medicine: Is the future already here? A literature review. *British Dental Journal*, *237*(10), 765–770. DOI: 10.1038/s41415-024-8029-9 PMID: 39572810

Al-Romeedy, B. S., Emam, M. E., Hussein, H., Singh, A., & Tyagi, P. K. (2025). Digital passports to wellness: How technology is shaping medical tourism. In Ezzat, R. E. R., & Ali, M. F. (Eds.), *Revolutionizing healthcare experience with digital medical tourism*. IGI Global., DOI: 10.4018/979-8-3693-7888-5.ch004

Aminoshariae, A., Kulild, J., & Nagendrababu, V. (2021). Artificial intelligence in endodontics: Current applications and future directions. *Journal of Endodontics*, *47*(9), 1352–1357. DOI: 10.1016/j.joen.2021.06.003 PMID: 34119562

Ancy, R. J., Shenoy, R. P., Jodalli, P. S., & Pasha, I. M. (2020). Benefits of medical and dental tourism–a review. *IOSR Journal of Dental and Medical Sciences*, *19*(3), 26–31.

Anjalin, U., Sohel-Uz-Zaman, A. S. M., Mazumdar, A., & Khan, M. I. (2025). The Prospects and Intricacies of Dental Tourism in South Asia. In Hamdan, R. K. (Ed.), *Sustainable Data Management: Navigating Big Data, Communication Technology, and Business Digital Leadership* (Vol. 2, pp. 461–469). Springer Nature Switzerland., DOI: 10.1007/978-3-031-83915-3_37

Arends, B. (2011). Inward dental tourism. *British Dental Journal*, *211*(12), 584. DOI: 10.1038/sj.bdj.2011.1062 PMID: 22193468

Ashiti, S., & Moshkun, C. (2021). Dental tourists: Treat, re-treat or do not treat? *British Dental Journal*, *230*(2), 73–76. DOI: 10.1038/s41415-020-2591-6 PMID: 33483660

Aydin, G., & Karamehmet, B. (2017). Factors affecting health tourism and international health-care facility choice. *International Journal of Pharmaceutical and Healthcare Marketing*, *11*(1), 16–36. DOI: 10.1108/IJPHM-05-2015-0018

Badawy, M. (2023). Integrating Artificial Intelligence and Big Data into Smart Healthcare Systems: A Comprehensive Review of Current Practices and Future Directions. *Artificial Intelligence Evolution*, 133-153.

Badri, S. A., & Yarmohamadi, N. (2022). A game theory–based model for dental centers in a competitive market of dental tourism under government intervention. *Journal of Applied Research on Industrial Engineering*, *9*(1), 78–94. DOI: 10.22105/jarie.2021.300196.1370

Badruddoza, T. Mohammad, Sanjeev, K., & Kumar, T., Pankaj. (2024a). *Impact of AI and Tech-Driven Solutions in Hospitality and Tourism*. IGI Global.

Badruddoza, T. Mohammad, Sanjeev, K., & Kumar, T., Pankaj. (2024b). *Impact of AI and Tech-Driven Solutions in Hospitality and Tourism*. IGI Global.

Bagga, T., Vishnoi, S. K., Jain, S., & Sharma, R. (2020). Medical tourism: Treatment, therapy and tourism. *International Journal of Scientific and Technology Research*, *9*(3), 4447–4453.

Baglivo, F., De Angelis, L., Cruschelli, G., & Rizzo, C. (2024). A decalogue for personalized travel health assistance with AI-driven chatbots. *Journal of Travel Medicine*, *31*(4), taae026. Advance online publication. DOI: 10.1093/jtm/taae026 PMID: 38345410

Bamashmous, M. (2025). The Role of Artificial Intelligence in Transforming Dental Public Health: Current Applications, Ethical Considerations, and Future Directions. *The Open Dentistry Journal*, *19*(1), e18742106363413. Advance online publication. DOI: 10.2174/0118742106363413250211053942

Barrowman, R. A., Grubor, D., & Chandu, A. (2010). Dental implant tourism. *Australian Dental Journal*, *55*(4), 441–445. DOI: 10.1111/j.1834-7819.2010.01267.x PMID: 21133945

Basu, S., Andrews, J., Kishore, S., Panjabi, R., & Stuckler, D. (2012). Comparative performance of private and public healthcare systems in low- and middle-income countries: A systematic review. *PLoS Medicine*, *9*(6), e1001244. DOI: 10.1371/journal.pmed.1001244 PMID: 22723748

Battista, M., Kernitsky, J., & Dibart, S. (2023). Artificial Intelligence Chatbots in Patient Communication: Current Possibilities. *The International Journal of Periodontics & Restorative Dentistry*. Advance online publication. DOI: 10.11607/prd.6925 PMID: 37819844

Behrmann, J., & Smith, E. (2010). Top 7 issues in medical tourism: Challenges, knowledge gaps, and future directions for research and policy development. *Global Journal of Health Science*, *2*(2), 80. DOI: 10.5539/gjhs.v2n2p80

Beladi, H., Chao, C. C., Ee, M. S., & Hollas, D. (2019). Does medical tourism promote economic growth? A cross-country analysis. *Journal of Travel Research*, *58*(1), 121–135. DOI: 10.1177/0047287517735909

Béland, D., & Zarzeczny, A. (2018). Medical tourism and national health care systems: An institutionalist research agenda. *Globalization and Health*, *14*(1), 68. DOI: 10.1186/s12992-018-0387-0 PMID: 30012218

Bertl, M., Lamo, Y., Leucker, M., Margaria, T., Mohammadi, E., Mukhiya, S. K., Pechmann, L., Piho, G., & Rabbi, F. (2024). Challenges for AI in healthcare systems. In *Lecture notes in computer science* (pp. 165–186). DOI: 10.1007/978-3-031-73741-1_11

Bharti, P., Agarwal, P., & Gupta, N. (2021). Medical and dental tourism in India: Opportunities and challenges. *Journal of Health Management*, *23*(2), 107–120.

Białk-Wolf, A. (2025). Developments in the medical tourism market in Poland from the perspective of international factors. *Worldwide Hospitality and Tourism Themes*, *17*(2), 261–272. DOI: 10.1108/WHATT-01-2025-0020

Budisak, P., & Brizuela, M. (2023). Dental Caries Classification Systems. In *StatPearls*. StatPearls Publishing., DOI: 10.1016/j.adaj.2014.11.018

Carrera, P. M., & Bridges, J. F. P. (2006). Globalization and healthcare: Understanding health and medical tourism. *Expert Review of Pharmacoeconomics & Outcomes Research*, *6*(4), 447–454. DOI: 10.1586/14737167.6.4.447 PMID: 20528514

Carvalho, B. K. G., Nolden, E. L., Wenning, A. S., Kiss-Dala, S., Agócs, G., Róth, I., Kerémi, B., Géczi, Z., Hegyi, P., & Kivovics, M. (2024). Diagnostic accuracy of artificial intelligence for approximal caries on bitewing radiographs: A systematic review and meta-analysis. *Journal of Dentistry*, *151*, 105388. DOI: 10.1016/j.jdent.2024.105388 PMID: 39396775

Cham, T. H., Lim, Y. M., Sia, B. C., Cheah, J. H., & Ting, H. (2021). Medical tourism destination image and its relationship with the intention to revisit: A study of Chinese medical tourists in Malaysia. *Journal of China Tourism Research*, *17*(2), 163–191. DOI: 10.1080/19388160.2020.1734514

Charati, M. K., Gholian-Jouybari, F., Hajiaghaei-Keshteli, M., Paydar, M. M., & Sadeghi, F. (2024). Designing a sustainable dental tourism supply chain considering waste treatment. *Annals of Operations Research*, *342*(1), 173–214. DOI: 10.1007/s10479-023-05779-4

Chongthanavanit, P., & Kheokao, J. (2018). Factors Influencing the Use of Dental Services by Foreign Tourists in Thailand. *Asian Journal for Public Opinion Research*, *5*(2), 63–83. DOI: 10.15206/AJPOR.2018.5.2.63

Chou, C., Chang, H., & Yang, Y. (2020). The impact of online reviews on patient decision-making in dental tourism. *Journal of Tourism Research*, *29*(3), 201–212.

Chou, Y., Wang, M., & Li, C. (2021). Virtual reality in medical tourism: Enhancing patient experience through immersive technology. *Journal of Healthcare Innovation*, *11*(2), 108–118.

Chuang, T. C., Liu, J. S., Lu, L. Y., & Lee, Y. (2014). The main paths of medical tourism: From transplantation to beautification. *Tourism Management*, *45*, 49–58. DOI: 10.1016/j.tourman.2014.03.016

Chung, W., Lee, M., & Kim, H. (2020). Blockchain-based medical record management in dental tourism: Enhancing data security and patient trust. *Journal of Medical Tourism*, *19*(3), 112–120.

Ciki, K. D., & Tanriverdi, H. (2023). Self-determination theory in the field of tourism: A bibliometric analysis. Tourism. *Tourism (Zagreb)*, *71*(4), 769–781. DOI: 10.37741/t.71.4.8

Collins, L. (2022). The burden of dental tourism. *British Dental Journal*, *233*(7), 516–516. DOI: 10.1038/s41415-022-5109-6 PMID: 36241780

Connell, J. (2006). Medical tourism: Sea, sun, sand and … surgery. *Tourism Management*, *27*(6), 1093–1100. DOI: 10.1016/j.tourman.2005.11.005

Convolutional Neural Networks (CNN) and Deep Learning. (n.d.). Intel. https://www.intel.com/content/www/us/en/internet-of-things/computer-vision/convolutional-neural-networks.html

Crooks, V. A., Kingsbury, P., Snyder, J., & Johnston, R. (2010). What is known about the patient's experience of medical tourism? *BMC Health Services Research*, *10*(1), 266. DOI: 10.1186/1472-6963-10-266 PMID: 20825667

Da'Costa, A., Teke, J., Origbo, J. E., Osonuga, A., Egbon, E., & Olawade, D. B. (2025). Ai-driven triage in emergency departments: A review of benefits, challenges, and future directions. *International Journal of Medical Informatics*, *197*, 105838. DOI: 10.1016/j.ijmedinf.2025.105838 PMID: 39965433

Dang, H.-S., Nguyen, T.-M.-T., Wang, C.-N., Day, J.-D., & Dang, T. M. H. (2020). Grey System Theory in the Study of Medical Tourism Industry and Its Economic Impact. *International Journal of Environmental Research and Public Health*, *17*(3), 961. DOI: 10.3390/ijerph17030961 PMID: 32033177

Das, I. R., Talukder, M. B., & Kumar, S. (2024). Implication of Artificial Intelligence in Hospitality Marketing. In Kumar, S., Talukder, M. B., & Pego, A. (Eds.), *Advances in Hospitality, Tourism, and the Services Industry* (pp. 291–310). IGI Global., DOI: 10.4018/979-8-3693-1978-9.ch014

De Arellano, A. B. R. (2007). Patients without borders: The emergence of medical tourism. *International Journal of Health Services*, *37*(1), 193–198. DOI: 10.2190/4857-468G-2325-47UU PMID: 17436992

De la Hoz-Correa, A., Muñoz-Leiva, F., & Bakucz, M. (2018). Past themes and future trends in medical tourism research: A co-word analysis. *Tourism Management*, *65*, 200–211. DOI: 10.1016/j.tourman.2017.10.001

Demonja, D., & Uglješić, N. (2020). Dental Tourism and Business Risks: The Example of the Republic of Croatia. *Interdisciplinary Description of Complex Systems : INDECS, 18*(4), 425–445. DOI: 10.7906/indecs.18.4.3

DentalMonitoring. (2023). *Remote orthodontic monitoring platform*. https://dental-monitoring.com

Dhama, K., Patthi, B., Singla, A., Gupta, R., Niraj, L. K., Ali, I., Kumar, J. K., & Prasad, M. (2016). Global tourist guide to oral care - A systematic review. *Journal of Clinical and Diagnostic Research : JCDR, 10*(9). Advance online publication. DOI: 10.7860/JCDR/2016/19438.8408 PMID: 27790595

Diagnocat. (2023). *AI for dental radiology and diagnostics*. https://diagnocat.com

Ding, H., Wu, J., Zhao, W., Matinlinna, J. P., Burrow, M. F., & Tsoi, J. K. (2023). Artificial intelligence in dentistry—A review. *Frontiers in Dental Medicine, 4*, 1085251. DOI: 10.3389/fdmed.2023.1085251 PMID: 39935549

Ebrahim, A. H., & Ganguli, S. (2019). A comparative analysis of medical tourism competitiveness of India, Thailand, and Singapore. *Tourism an International Interdisciplinary Journal, 67*(2), 102–115.

Ekert, T., Krois, J., Meinhold, L., Elhennawy, K., Emara, R., Golla, T., & Schwendicke, F. (2019). Deep learning for the radiographic detection of apical lesions. *Journal of Endodontics, 45*(7), 917–922. DOI: 10.1016/j.joen.2019.03.016 PMID: 31160078

El Khoury, N., Hadid, D., & El-Outa, A. (2025). Exploring the Ethical Landscape of Artificial Intelligence in Dentistry: Insights From a Cross-Sectional Study. *Cureus, 17*(4), e82667. DOI: 10.7759/cureus.82667 PMID: 40400857

Enache, E. N., Gabor, M.-R., & Morozan, C. (2013). Considerations about dental tourism development and its specific marketing in Romania. *Management Strategies Journal, 22*(Special), 420–426.

Esteva, A., Robicquet, A., Ramsundar, B., Kuleshov, V., DePristo, M., Chou, K., Cui, C., Corrado, G., Thrun, S., & Dean, J. (2021). A guide to deep learning in healthcare. *Nature Medicine, 25*(1), 24–29. DOI: 10.1038/s41591-018-0316-z PMID: 30617335

Fahim, A., Saleem, Z., Malik, K. A., Atta, K., Mahmood, R., Alam, M. K., & Sethi, A. (2022). Exploring challenges and mitigation strategies towards practicing teledentistry. *BMC Oral Health, 22*(1), 658. DOI: 10.1186/s12903-022-02685-2 PMID: 36585644

Farhadi Nia, M., Ahmadi, M., & Irankhah, E. (2024). Transforming dental diagnostics with artificial intelligence: Advanced integration of ChatGPT and large language models for patient care. *Frontiers in Dental Medicine*, *5*, 1456208. Advance online publication. DOI: 10.3389/fdmed.2024.1456208 PMID: 39917691

Farsi, D. (2021). Social media and health care, Part I: Literature review of social media use by health care providers. *Journal of Medical Internet Research*, *23*(4), e23205. DOI: 10.2196/23205 PMID: 33664014

Felkai, P. P., Flaherty, G., & Felkai, T. (2021). International dental tourism in a post-COVID era: Pre-travel advice. *Journal of Travel Medicine*, *28*(7), taab108. Advance online publication. DOI: 10.1093/jtm/taab108 PMID: 34272850

Felkai, P. P., Nakdimon, I., Felkai, T., Levin, L., & Zadik, Y. (2023). Dental tourism and the risk of barotrauma and barodontalgia. *British Dental Journal*, *234*(2), 115–117. DOI: 10.1038/s41415-023-5449-x PMID: 36707585

Fetscherin, M., & Stephano, R. M. (2016). The medical tourism index: Scale development and validation. *Tourism Management*, *52*, 539–556. DOI: 10.1016/j.tourman.2015.08.010

Figueiredo, N., Abrantes, J. L., & Costa, S. (2024). Mapping the sustainable development in health tourism: A systematic literature review. *Sustainability (Basel)*, *16*(5), 1901. DOI: 10.3390/su16051901

Ganguli, S., & Ebrahim, A. H. (2017). A qualitative analysis of Singapore's medical tourism competitiveness. *Tourism Management Perspectives*, *21*, 74–84. DOI: 10.1016/j.tmp.2016.12.002

Gan, L. L., & Frederick, J. R. (2011). Medical tourism facilitators: Patterns of service differentiation. *Journal of Vacation Marketing*, *17*(3), 165–183. DOI: 10.1177/1356766711409181

Gao, S., Wang, X., Xia, Z., Zhang, H., Yu, J., & Yang, F. (2025). Artificial Intelligence in Dentistry: A Narrative Review of Diagnostic and Therapeutic Applications. *Medical Science Monitor*, *31*, e946676. DOI: 10.12659/MSM.946676 PMID: 40195079

Garner, R. (2019). Implications of dental tourism Examining US patients travelling to Mexico for dental care. *BDJ In Practice*, *32*(10), 20–23. DOI: 10.1038/s41404-019-0182-5

GeeksforGeeks. (2025, May 29). *Convolutional Neural Network (CNN) in machine learning*. GeeksforGeeks. https://www.geeksforgeeks.org/deep-learning/convolutional-neural-network-cnn-in-machine-learning/

Ghaffari, M., Zhu, Y., & Shrestha, A. (2024). A review of advancements of artificial intelligence in dentistry. *Dentistry Review*, *4*(2), 100081. DOI: 10.1016/j.dentre.2024.100081

Ghosh, T., & Mandal, S. (2019). Medical tourism experience: Conceptualization, scale development, and validation. *Journal of Travel Research*, *58*(8), 1288–1301. DOI: 10.1177/0047287518813469

Goh, C., Lee, W., & Tan, R. (2021). The impact of digital marketing on the dental tourism industry: A study of SEO and content marketing strategies. *International Journal of Digital Marketing*, *15*(3), 113–128.

Goodacre, B. J. (2022). Digital workflow for 3D printed implant surgical guides. *The Journal of Prosthetic Dentistry*, *127*(2), 205. DOI: 10.1016/j.prosdent.2022.01.002 PMID: 35241263

Gupta, M., Mishra, P., Srivastava, R., & Jyoti, B. (2015). Holistic oral health care in India: A corporate perspective. *Journal of Indian Academy of Oral Medicine and Radiology*, *27*(2), 237–240. DOI: 10.4103/0972-1363.170144

Hackley, D. M., & Luca, J. (2024). Sustainability in Dentistry: An Overview for Oral Healthcare Team Members. *Journal of the California Dental Association*, *52*(1), 2422150. DOI: 10.1080/19424396.2024.2422150

Hall, C. M. (2011). Health and medical tourism: A kill or cure for global public health? *Tourism Review*, *66*(1-2), 4–15. DOI: 10.1108/16605371111127198

Hanefeld, J., Smith, R., Horsfall, D., & Lunt, N. (2014). What do we know about medical tourism? A review of the literature with discussion of its implications for the UK National Health Service as an example of a public health care system. *Journal of Travel Medicine*, *21*(6), 410–417. DOI: 10.1111/jtm.12147 PMID: 25156070

Haque, S., Nurunnabi, M., Akhter, F., & Bianoony, A. A. M. (2024). Attitude Towards Sustainability in Dentistry: The Evidence From Riyadh City, Saudi Arabia. *International Dental Journal*, *74*(4), 884–891. DOI: 10.1016/j.identj.2024.01.007 PMID: 38368236

Hernandez, M. (2022). Leveraging patient reviews for dental tourism success: The case of Dental Departures. *International Journal of Dental Tourism*, *14*(4), 245–258.

Holtkamp, A., Elhennawy, K., Cejudo Grano de Oro, J. E., Krois, J., Paris, S., & Schwendicke, F. (2021). Generalizability of Deep Learning Models for Caries Detection in Near-Infrared Light Transillumination Images. *Journal of Clinical Medicine*, *10*(5), 961. DOI: 10.3390/jcm10050961 PMID: 33804562

Huda, Md. N., Talukder, M. B., & Kumar, S. (2024). Securing Healthcare AI: Applied Federal Learning. In P. Bhattacharya, H. Liu, P. K. Dutta, J. J. P. C. Rodrigues, & G. Sethi (Eds.), *Revolutionizing Healthcare 5.0: The Power of Generative AI: Advancements in Patient Care Through Generative AI Algorithms* (pp. 255–272). Springer Nature Switzerland. DOI: 10.1007/978-3-031-75771-6_17

Hu, F., Wen, J., Zheng, D., & Wang, W. (2023). Travel medicine in hospitality: An interdisciplinary perspective. *International Journal of Contemporary Hospitality Management*, *35*(9), 3134–3153. DOI: 10.1108/IJCHM-05-2022-0574

Hung, K. F., Ai, Q. Y. H., Wong, L. M., Yeung, A. W. K., Li, D. T. S., & Leung, Y. Y. (2022). Current applications of deep learning and radiomics on CT and CBCT for maxillofacial diseases. *Diagnostics (Basel)*, *13*(1), 110. DOI: 10.3390/diagnostics13010110 PMID: 36611402

Hussain, Z., Khan, N. A., Haider, N. H. A., Naz, N. F., Iqbal, N. R., Burki, N. S., Almagharbeh, N. W. T., & Khan, N. H. (2025). COMPARING THE EFFICACY OF AI-ASSISTED VS. TRADITIONAL DIAGNOSTIC IMAGING IN RADIOLOGY – A META-ANALYSIS. *Journal of Health and Rehabilitation*, *3*(2 (Health&Rehab)), 163–171. DOI: 10.71000/vd11kz38

Hyder, A. S., Rydback, M., Borg, E., & Osarenkhoe, A. (2019). Medical tourism in emerging markets: The role of trust, networks, and word-of-mouth. *Health Marketing Quarterly*, *36*(3), 203–219. DOI: 10.1080/07359683.2019.1618008 PMID: 31210584

Iqbal, M. A. (2023). Dental Tourism in Bangladesh: A Growing Opportunity. *Update Dental College Journal*, *13*(2), 1–2. DOI: 10.3329/updcj.v13i2.69143

Iruvuri, A. G., Miryala, G., Khan, Y., Ramalingam, N. T., Sevugaperumal, B., Soman, M., & Padmanabhan, A. (2023). Revolutionizing Dental Imaging: A comprehensive study on the integration of artificial intelligence in dental and maxillofacial radiology. *Cureus*. Advance online publication. DOI: 10.7759/cureus.50292 PMID: 38205468

Jaapar, M., Musa, G., Moghavvemi, S., & Saub, R. (2017). Dental tourism: Examining tourist profiles, motivation and satisfaction. *Tourism Management*, *61*, 538–552. DOI: 10.1016/j.tourman.2017.02.023

Jensen, C. B. (2008). Sociology, systems and (patient) safety: Knowledge translations in healthcare policy. *Sociology of Health & Illness*, *30*(1), 100–114. DOI: 10.1111/j.1467-9566.2007.01035.x PMID: 18290938

Jenson, L., Budenz, A. W., Featherstone, J. D., Ramos-Gomez, F., Spolsky, V. W., & Young, D. A. (2007). Clinical protocols for caries management by risk assessment. *Journal of the California Dental Association*, 35(10), 714–723. ICDAS Committee. (2016). *ICDAS: International Caries Detection and Assessment System™ — criteria manual*. Retrieved from https://iccms-web.com/uploads/asset/592846a55c8a2e4f18000008/ICDAS-Booklet.pdf

Kamran, M., Waseem, M., Shafi, N., & Zahid, A. (2024). Detection of Caries and Hypodontia using Deep Learning and Explainable AI. *2024 18th International Conference on Open Source Systems and Technologies (ICOSST)*, 1-6. DOI: 10.1109/ICOSST64562.2024.10871141

Kassebaum, N. J.GBD 2021 Oral Disorders Collaborators. (2025). Trends in the global, regional, and national burden of oral conditions from 1990 to 2021: A systematic analysis for the Global Burden of Disease Study 2021. *Lancet*, *405*(10482), 897–910. DOI: 10.1016/S0140-6736(24)02811-3 PMID: 40024264

Kato, T., Suzuki, H., & Tanaka, K. (2023). Augmented reality in dental tourism: Improving patient decision-making and satisfaction. *International Journal of Dental Tourism*, *12*(3), 150–160.

Kaur, R., & Hira, J. K. (2021). Enquiring the dental practitioners' perceptions about dental tourism: A phenomenological viewpoint. *World Review of Entrepreneurship, Management and Sustainable Development*, *17*(2/3), 323. DOI: 10.1504/WREMSD.2021.114438

Kesar, O., & Mikulić, J. (2017). Medical tourist satisfaction and dissatisfaction with dental care services: An exploratory case study. In Tourism in Southern and Eastern Europe 2017: Tourism and Creative Industries: Trends and Challenges (pp. 243-258). University of Rijeka, Faculty of Tourism and Hospitality Management. DOI: 10.20867/tosee.04.41

Khanbhai, M., Flott, K., Darzi, A., & Mayer, E. (2019). Evaluating digital maturity and patient acceptability of real-time patient experience feedback systems: Systematic review. *Journal of Medical Internet Research*, *21*(1), e9076. DOI: 10.2196/jmir.9076 PMID: 31344680

Kim, J., & Lee, H. (2021). The role of online reviews in medical and dental tourism: Building trust through patient feedback. *Journal of Health Marketing*, *23*(2), 79–89.

Koh, T., Tan, E., & Ng, Y. (2020). Leveraging SEO for success: A digital marketing strategy for dental tourism. *JMR, Journal of Marketing Research*, *32*(2), 56–65.

Kokshagina, O. (2021). Managing shifts to value-based healthcare and value digitalization as a multi-level dynamic capability development process. *Technological Forecasting and Social Change*, *172*, 121072. DOI: 10.1016/j.techfore.2021.121072

Kopmaz, B., Kitapci, N. S., Kitapci, O. C., Bulu, S. B., Aksu, P. K., Koksal, L., & Mumcu, G. (2019). Dental Websites as New Media Tools for Patients in Dental Health Tourism. *Acta Informatica Medica*, *27*(2), 128–132. DOI: 10.5455/aim.2019.27.128-132 PMID: 31452572

Kovacs, E., & Szocska, G. (2013). Vacation for your teeth' - Dental tourists in Hungary from the perspective of Hungarian dentists. *British Dental Journal*, *215*(8), 415–418. DOI: 10.1038/sj.bdj.2013.995 PMID: 24157766

Kowalska, N., & Ostręga, A. (2020). Using SERVQUAL method to assess tourist service quality by the example of the Silesian Museum Established on the post-mining area. *Land (Basel)*, *9*(9), 333. DOI: 10.3390/land9090333

Kusumawardhani, Y., Hilmiana, H., Widianto, S., & Azis, Y. (2024). Smart tourism practice in the scope of sustainable tourism in emerging markets: A systematic literature review. *Cogent Social Sciences*, *10*(1), 2384193. DOI: 10.1080/23311886.2024.2384193

Lal, A., Nooruddin, A., & Umer, F. (2025). Concerns regarding deployment of AI-based applications in dentistry - a review. *BDJ Open*, *11*(1), 27. DOI: 10.1038/s41405-025-00319-7 PMID: 40133287

Lam, S., Lee, V., Ooi, K., & Phusavat, K. (2012). A structural equation model of TQM, market orientation and service quality: Evidence from a developing nation. *Managing Service Quality*, *22*(3), 281–309. DOI: 10.1108/09604521211230996

Lee, S., Kim, J., & Choi, J. (2022). AI-powered chatbots in dental tourism marketing: Enhancing customer service and engagement. *Journal of Digital Healthcare*, *18*(4), 205–215.

Lee, S., Oh, S., Jo, J., Kang, S., Shin, Y., & Park, J. (2021). Deep learning for early dental caries detection in bitewing radiographs. *Scientific Reports*, *11*(1), 16807. Advance online publication. DOI: 10.1038/s41598-021-96368-7 PMID: 34413414

Leggat, P., & Kedjarune, U. (2009). Dental health, "dental tourism" and travellers. *Travel Medicine and Infectious Disease*, *7*(3), 123–124. DOI: 10.1016/j.tmaid.2009.02.001 PMID: 19411039

Li, C., Lin, S., Chou, H., Chen, T., Chen, Y., Liu, S., Liu, Y., Chen, C., Huang, Y., Chen, S., Mao, Y., Abu, P. R., Chiang, W., & Lo, W. (2021). Detection of dental apical lesions using CNNs on periapical radiograph. *Sensors (Basel)*, *21*(21), 7049. DOI: 10.3390/s21217049 PMID: 34770356

Lina, F. Y., & Talukder, M. B. (2025). AI in Tourism: Business and Economic Perspectives. In *Innovation Management for a Resilient Digital Economy* (pp. 81–104). IGI Global Scientific Publishing. DOI: 10.4018/979-8-3693-8357-5.ch004

Lin, H., Chang, M., & Li, J. (2020). Emotional engagement in dental tourism marketing: The power of patient testimonials. *Journal of Health Care Marketing*, *25*(3), 87–99.

Lin, P., Chen, T., Lin, C., Huang, C., Tsai, Y., Tsai, Y., & Wang, C. (2024). The use of augmented reality (AR) and virtual reality (VR) in dental surgery education and practice: A narrative review. *Journal of Dental Sciences*, *19*, S91–S101. DOI: 10.1016/j.jds.2024.10.011 PMID: 39807259

Lovelock, B., Lovelock, K., & Lyons, K. (2018). The impact of outbound medical (dental) tourism on the generating region: New Zealand dental professionals' perspectives. *Tourism Management*, *67*, 399–410. DOI: 10.1016/j.tourman.2018.02.001

Lubowiecki-Vikuk, A. (2018). Consumption of dental services: Medical tourism in CEE. *European Journal of Service Management, 27*(3/1), 135–142.

Lubowiecki-Vikuk, A. (2018). Consumption of dental services: Medical tourism in CEE. *European Journal of Service Management*, *27*, 135–142. DOI: 10.18276/ejsm.2018.27/1-16

Lubowiecki-Vikuk, A., & Dryglas, D. (2019). Medical tourism services and medical tourism destinations in Central and Eastern Europe—The opinion of Britons and Germans. *Economic Research -. Ekonomska Istrazivanja*, *32*(1), 1256–1274. DOI: 10.1080/1331677X.2019.1627892

Luke, A. M., & Rezallah, N. N. F. (2025). Accuracy of artificial intelligence in caries detection: A systematic review and meta-analysis. *Head & Face Medicine*, *21*(1), 24. DOI: 10.1186/s13005-025-00496-8 PMID: 40181403

Lunt, N., Horsfall, D., & Hanefeld, J. (2016). Medical tourism: A snapshot of evidence on treatment abroad. *Maturitas*, *88*, 37–44. DOI: 10.1016/j.maturitas.2016.03.001 PMID: 27105695

Lunt, N., Jin, K. N., Horsfall, D., & Hanefeld, J. (2014). Insights on medical tourism: Markets as networks and the role of strong ties. *Korean Social Science Journal*, *41*(1), 19–37. DOI: 10.1007/s40483-014-0012-7

Lwin, H. N. N., Punnakitikashem, P., & Thananusak, T. (2021). The level and determinants of international patient satisfaction with dental tourism in Bangkok, Thailand. *Cogent Business & Management*, *8*(1), 1898316. Advance online publication. DOI: 10.1080/23311975.2021.1898316

Mahadev Madgule, N. (2023). Vinayaka, Yeshwant M. Sonkhaskar, Dhiren Ramanbhai Patel, R. Karthikeyan, P. Selvakumar,(2023). Mechanical properties and microstructure of activated TIG welded similar joints of Inconel alloys by desirability approaches. *Materials Today: Proceedings*, *77*, 528–533. DOI: 10.1016/j.matpr.2022.12.250

Mallineni, S. K., Sethi, M., Punugoti, D., Kotha, S. B., Alkhayal, Z., Mubaraki, S., Almotawah, F. N., Kotha, S. L., Sajja, R., Nettam, V., Thakare, A. A., & Sakhamuri, S. (2024). Artificial Intelligence in Dentistry: A Descriptive Review. *Bioengineering (Basel, Switzerland)*, *11*(12), 1267. DOI: 10.3390/bioengineering11121267 PMID: 39768085

Mandagi, D. W., & Tappy, Y. P. (2024). Determinants of Health Tourism Destination Attractiveness: A Comprehensive Systematic Review. *Jurnal Studi Perhotelan Dan Pariwisata*, *2*(2), 57–69. DOI: 10.35912/jspp.v2i2.3261

Marcus, K., Balasubramanian, M., Short, S. D., & Sohn, W. (2022). Dental diaspora: Oral health care attitudes and experiences in culturally and linguistically diverse mothers in Australia. *BMC Health Services Research*, *22*(1), 1314. DOI: 10.1186/s12913-022-08708-6 PMID: 36329526

Marr, B. (2019). *Artificial intelligence in practice: how 50 successful companies used AI and machine learning to solve problems*. John Wiley & Sons.

Martinez, D., & Hernandez, F. (2022). Exploring the impact of dental tourism on Mexico's economy: A study on cost-efficiency and patient satisfaction. *Journal of Tourism and Health*, *45*(3), 210–220.

Marwaha, J., Singla, M., Nath, A., & Arya, A. (2025). Revolutionizing the diagnosis of dental caries using artificial intelligence-based methods. *Journal of Conservative Dentistry and Endodontics*, *28*(5), 401–405. DOI: 10.4103/JCDE.JCDE_172_25 PMID: 40463673

McMahan, J., Pritchard, T., & Zhang, Y. (2021). Emerging technologies in healthcare: Blockchain and edge computing in dental tourism marketing. *Journal of Health Care Marketing*, *32*(4), 215–230.

Mei, L., Deng, K., Cui, Z., Fang, Y., Li, Y., Lai, H., Tonetti, M. S., & Shen, D. (2024). Clinical knowledge-guided hybrid classification network for automatic periodontal disease diagnosis in X-ray image. *Medical Image Analysis*, *99*, 103376. DOI: 10.1016/j.media.2024.103376 PMID: 39536402

Mertens, S.. (2021). Artificial intelligence for caries detection: Validation of a novel machine learning algorithm with laser fluorescence data. *Clinical Oral Investigations*, *25*, 1021–1030. DOI: 10.1007/s00784-020-03463-w

Milosevic, A. (2009). DENTAL TOURISM—A GLOBAL ISSUE? *Journal of Esthetic and Restorative Dentistry*, *21*(5), 289–291. DOI: 10.1111/j.1708-8240.2009.00277.x PMID: 19796293

Mishra, V., Samuel, C., & Sharma, S. K. (2019). Patient's utility for various attributes of diabetes care services. *IIM Kozhikode Society and Management Review*, *8*(1), 1–9. DOI: 10.1177/2277975218798134

Moghavvemi, S., Ormond, M., Musa, G., Isa, C. R. M., Thirumoorthi, T., Mustapha, M. Z. B., & Chandy, J. J. C. (2017). Connecting with prospective medical tourists online: A cross-sectional analysis of private hospital websites promoting medical tourism in India, Malaysia, and Thailand. *Tourism Management*, *58*, 154–163. DOI: 10.1016/j.tourman.2016.10.010

Mohammad, B. T., & Iva, R. D. (2024). The technology impacts and AI solutions in hospitality. *I-Manager's Journal on Artificial Intelligence &. Machine Learning*, *2*(1), 56. DOI: 10.26634/jaim.2.1.20291

Mohammad-Rahimi, H., Motamedian, S. R., Rohban, M. H., Krois, J., Uribe, S. E., Mahmoudinia, E., Rokhshad, R., Nadimi, M., & Schwendicke, F. (2022). Deep learning for caries detection: A systematic review. *Journal of Dentistry*, *122*, 104115. DOI: 10.1016/j.jdent.2022.104115 PMID: 35367318

Musleh, D., Almossaeed, H., Balhareth, F., Alqahtani, G., Alobaidan, N., Altalag, J., & Aldossary, M. I. (2024). Advancing Dental Diagnostics: A Review of Artificial Intelligence Applications and Challenges in Dentistry. *Big Data and Cognitive Computing*, *8*(6), 66. DOI: 10.3390/bdcc8060066

Nadee, W., Kaewkitipong, L., Ractham, P., & Sayruamyat, S. (2024). An Investigation of the Intention to Visit Smart Tourism Destinations: Domestic Travelers vs. International Travelers. *Sustainability (Basel)*, *16*(23), 23. Advance online publication. DOI: 10.3390/su162310484

Naik, N., Hameed, B. M. Z., Shetty, D. K., Swain, D., Shah, M., Paul, R., Aggarwal, K., Ibrahim, S., Patil, V., Smriti, K., Shetty, S., Rai, B. P., Chlosta, P., & Somani, B. K. (2022). Legal and ethical consideration in artificial intelligence in healthcare: Who takes responsibility? *Frontiers in Surgery*, *9*, 862322. Advance online publication. DOI: 10.3389/fsurg.2022.862322 PMID: 35360424

Negi, S., Mathur, A., Tripathy, S., Mehta, V., Snigdha, N. T., Adil, A. H., & Karobari, M. I. (2024). Artificial Intelligence in Dental Caries Diagnosis and Detection: An Umbrella Review. *Clinical and Experimental Dental Research*, *10*(4), e70004. DOI: 10.1002/cre2.70004 PMID: 39206581

Nexhipi, O. (2018). Medical Tourism Management Challenges—The Case of Dental Tourism in Albania. *European Journal of Interdisciplinary Studies*, *10*(1), 80. DOI: 10.26417/ejis.v10i1.p80-86

Ní Ríordáin, R., & McCreary, C. (2009). Dental patients' use of the Internet. *British Dental Journal*, *207*(12), 583–586. DOI: 10.1038/sj.bdj.2009.1137 PMID: 20019727

Nitecki, D. A., & Hernon, P. (2000). Measuring service quality at Yale university's libraries. *Journal of Academic Librarianship*, *26*(4), 259–273. DOI: 10.1016/S0099-1333(00)00117-8

Nyumba, T. O., Wilson, K., Derrick, C. J., & Mukherjee, N. (2018). The use of focus group discussion methodology: Insights from two decades of application in conservation. *Methods in Ecology and Evolution*, *9*(1), 20–32. DOI: 10.1111/2041-210X.12860

Okazaki, S., Mine, Y., Yoshimi, Y., Iwamoto, Y., Ito, S., Peng, T., Nishimura, T., Suehiro, T., Koizumi, Y., Nomura, R., Tanimoto, K., Kakimoto, N., & Murayama, T. (2024). *RadImageNet and ImageNet as datasets for transfer learning in the assessment of dental radiographs: A Comparative study*. Deleted Journal., DOI: 10.1007/s10278-024-01204-9

Oltean, F. D., Gabor, M. R., Stăncioiu, A.-F., Kardos, M., Kiss, M., & Marinescu, R. C. (2020). Aspects of Marketing in Dental Tourism—Factor of Sustainable Development in Romania. *Sustainability (Basel)*, *12*(10), 4320. DOI: 10.3390/su12104320

Orlic, E., Spalj, S., Ivancic Jokic, N., Bakarcic, D., Cicvaric, O., & Grzic, R. (2023). Pandemic Financial Stress in Dental Medicine in Croatia. *Dentistry Journal*, *11*(1), 9. Advance online publication. DOI: 10.3390/dj11010009 PMID: 36661546

Ossowska, A., Kusiak, A., & Świetlik, D. (2022). Artificial Intelligence in Dentistry—Narrative Review. *International Journal of Environmental Research and Public Health*, *19*(6), 3449. DOI: 10.3390/ijerph19063449 PMID: 35329136

Ostojic, B., Bajramovic, D., & Cvjetkovic, M. (2025). The impact of digital marketing on customer satisfaction in dental tourism in Serbia. Menadžment u hotelijerstvu i turizmu, 13(1), 131–144. DOI: 10.5937/menhottur2500008O

Overjet Inc. (2023). Overjet AI for caries detection [Product demo]. Retrieved from https://www.overjet.com/ai-dental-caries-detection

Overjet. (2023). *AI for dental providers.* https://www.overjet.com

Ozbek, O., & Hassan, A. (2022). Medical Tourism and the Application of Technology. In *Handbook of Technology Application in Tourism in Asia* (pp. 607–627). Springer., DOI: 10.1007/978-981-16-2210-6_28

Oztekin, F., Katar, O., Sadak, F., Yildirim, M., Cakar, H., Aydogan, M., Ozpolat, Z., Talo Yildirim, T., Yildirim, O., Faust, O., & Acharya, U. R. (2023). An Explainable Deep Learning Model to Prediction Dental Caries Using Panoramic Radiograph Images. *Diagnostics (Basel)*, *13*(2), 226. DOI: 10.3390/diagnostics13020226 PMID: 36673036

Page, S. J. (2009). Current issue in tourism: The evolution of travel medicine research: A new research agenda for tourism? *Tourism Management*, *30*(2), 149–157. DOI: 10.1016/j.tourman.2008.04.011 PMID: 32287728

Paisi, M., Baines, R., Burns, L., Plessas, A., Radford, P., Shawe, J., & Witton, R. (2020). Barriers and facilitators to dental care access among asylum seekers and refugees in highly developed countries: A systematic review. *BMC Oral Health*, *20*(1), 337. DOI: 10.1186/s12903-020-01321-1 PMID: 33238954

Panahi, O., & Ezzati, A. (2025). AI in Dental-Medicine: Current Applications & Future Directions. *Journal of Digital Imaging*, *2*(1), 1–5. DOI: 10.61440/OAJ-CI.2025.v2.09

Papakoca, K., & Petrovski, M. (2021). Dental tourism -our perspectives. *Knowledge –. International Journal (Toronto, Ont.)*, *48*(3), 479–482.

Parasuraman, A., Berry, L., & Zeithaml, V. (2002). Refinement and reassessment of the SERVQUAL scale. *Journal of Retailing*, *67*(4), 114–139.

Park, E. Y., Jeong, S., Kang, S., Cho, J., Cho, J. Y., & Kim, E. K. (2023). Tooth caries classification with quantitative light-induced fluorescence (QLF) images using convolutional neural network for permanent teeth in vivo. *BMC Oral Health*, *23*(1), 981. DOI: 10.1186/s12903-023-03669-6 PMID: 38066624

Patil, A. V., Somasundaram, K. V., & Goyal, R. C. (2002). Current health scenario in rural India. *The Australian Journal of Rural Health, 10*(2), 129–135. DOI: 10.1111/j.1440-1584.2002.tb00022.x PMID: 12047509

Patton, M. Q. (2002). *Qualitative research and evaluation methods* (3rd ed.). Sage Publications.

Pearl. (2023). *Second Opinion®: AI-powered dental radiologic detection platform.*

Pérez-Campdesuñer, R., Sánchez-Rodríguez, A., García-Vidal, G., Martínez-Vivar, R., Valdés-Alarcón, M. E., & De Miguel-Guzmán, M. (2025). Demographic capital and the conditional validity of SERVPERF: Rethinking tourist satisfaction models in an emerging market destination. *Administrative Sciences, 15*(7), 272. DOI: 10.3390/admsci15070272

Peručić, D. (2019). Limitations and development opportunities of dental tourism: The case of Croatia. Ekonomski vjesnik/Econviews - Review of Contemporary Business. *Entrepreneurship and Economic Issues, 32*(1), 93–104.

Piya, S., Triki, C., Al Maimani, A., & Mokhtarzadeh, M. (2023). Optimization model for designing personalized tourism packages. *Computers & Industrial Engineering, 175*, 108839. DOI: 10.1016/j.cie.2022.108839

Prasert, N., Chia, L., & Tith, L. (2020). The role of digital marketing in dental tourism: A case study of Thailand. *International Journal of Healthcare Marketing, 35*(4), 324–330.

Puyt, R. W., Lie, F. B., & Wilderom, C. P. M. (2023). The origins of SWOT analysis. *Long Range Planning, 56*(3), 102304. DOI: 10.1016/j.lrp.2023.102304

Qolipour, M., Torabipour, A., Khiavi, F. F., & Malehi, A. S. (2018). Assessing medical tourism services quality using SERVQUAL model: A patient's perspective. *Iranian Journal of Public Health, 47*(1), 103–110. PMID: 29318124

Ramakrishnan, T., Mohan Gift, M. D., Chitradevi, S., Jegan, R., & Subha Hency Jose, P. Nagaraja, Rajneesh Sharma H.N., Selvakumar P., Sintayehu Mekuria Hailegiorgis, (2022). "Study of Numerous Resins Used in Polymer Matrix Composite Materials", Advances in Materials Science and Engineering, vol. 2022, Article ID 1088926, 8 pages, 2022. DOI: 10.1155/2022/1088926

Ramos, K., & Cuamea, O. (2023). Dental tourism: Factors influencing travelers' revisit intention to the Mexican border. *International Journal of Tourism Cities, 9*(3), 806–831. DOI: 10.1108/IJTC-03-2023-0046

Samancioglu, E., Kumlu, S., & Ozkul, E. (2024). Smart tourism destinations and sustainability: Evidence from the tourism industry. *Worldwide Hospitality and Tourism Themes*, *16*(6), 680–693. Advance online publication. DOI: 10.1108/WHATT-07-2024-0167

Sandberg, D. S. (2017). Medical tourism: An emerging global healthcare industry. *International Journal of Healthcare Management*, *10*(4), 281–288. DOI: 10.1080/20479700.2017.1296213

Sandhu, R. (2018). Dental Tourism: A Review. *International Healthcare Research Journal*, *2*(3), 55–58. DOI: 10.26440/IHRJ/02_03/172

Sanjeev, K., & Badruddoza, T. Mohammad, & Ana, P. (2024). *Utilizing Smart Technology and AI in Hybrid Tourism and Hospitality*. IGI Global.

Saxena, V., Deheriya, M., & Datla, A. (2023, June 1). *Bibliometric Analysis of Dental Tourism: A Global Perspective. | EBSCOhost*. DOI: 10.30491/IJT-MGH.2023.387742.1349

Schwendicke, F. A., Samek, W., & Krois, J. (2020). Artificial intelligence in dentistry: Chances and challenges. *Journal of Dental Research*, *99*(7), 769–774. DOI: 10.1177/0022034520915714 PMID: 32315260

Schwendicke, F., Golla, T., Dreher, M., & Krois, J. (2019). Convolutional neural networks for dental image diagnostics: A scoping review. *Journal of Dentistry*, *91*, 103226. DOI: 10.1016/j.jdent.2019.103226 PMID: 31704386

Simon, B. D., Ozyoruk, K. B., Gelikman, D. G., Harmon, S. A., & Türkbey, B. (2024). *The future of multimodal artificial intelligence models for integrating imaging and clinical metadata: a narrative review*. Diagnostic and Interventional Radiology., DOI: 10.4274/dir.2024.242631

Snyder, J., Dharamsi, S., & Crooks, V. A. (2011). Fly-by medical care: Conceptualizing the global and local social responsibilities of medical tourists and physician voluntourists. *Globalization and Health*, *7*(1), 6. Advance online publication. DOI: 10.1186/1744-8603-7-6 PMID: 21470415

Sreenivasulu, A., & Manimozhi, T. Satheesh kumar P., Selvakumar P. and Singh P.,(2022). "The Model of Smart Sensing Device For Sensitive Nanoclusters Modification in Sensing Properties," 2022 2nd International Conference on Advance Computing and Innovative Technologies in Engineering (ICACITE), Greater Noida, India, 2022, pp. 1043-1047, DOI: 10.1109/ICACITE53722.2022.9823846

Stackpole, I., Ziemba, E., & Johnson, T. (2021). Looking around the corner: COVID-19 shocks and market dynamics in US medical tourism. *The International Journal of Health Planning and Management*, *36*(5), 1407–1416. DOI: 10.1002/hpm.3259 PMID: 34096092

Stefanac, S. J., & Nesbit, S. P. (2006). *Treatment planning in dentistry* (2nd ed.). Elsevier.

Sterle, A., Balázs, P., & Delgado, J. (2009). Travelling for teeth: Characteristics and perspectives of dental care tourism in Hungary. *British Dental Journal*, *206*(8), 425–428. DOI: 10.1038/sj.bdj.2009.308 PMID: 19396208

Sugumaran, K. M. D., Pandiyarajan V., Y. B S, Selvakumar P. and M. S, (2024). "Analysis of Electromyography Signals for Control of Mechanical Prosthesis using Machine Learning Techniques," 2024 2nd International Conference on Intelligent Data Communication Technologies and Internet of Things (IDCIoT), Bengaluru, India, 2024, pp. 1059-1067, DOI: 10.1109/IDCIoT59759.2024.10467707

Surdu, A., Budala, D. G., Luchian, I., Foia, L. G., Botnariu, G. E., & Scutariu, M. M. (2024). Using AI in Optimizing Oral and Dental Diagnoses - A Narrative Review. *Diagnostics (Basel)*, *14*(24), 2804. DOI: 10.3390/diagnostics14242804 PMID: 39767164

Swenson, M. S., & Bansal, A. (2024). *Medical, Dental, and Wellness Tourism: A Post-Pandemic Perspective*. Apple Academic Press., DOI: 10.1201/9781003433569

Szabó, V., Szabó, B. T., Orhan, K., Veres, D. S., Manulis, D., Ezhov, M., & Sanders, A. (2024). Validation of artificial intelligence application for dental caries diagnosis on intraoral bitewing and periapical radiographs. *Journal of Dentistry*, *147*, 105105. DOI: 10.1016/j.jdent.2024.105105 PMID: 38821394

Talib, M. A., Moufti, M. A., Nasir, Q., Kabbani, Y., Aljaghber, D., & Afadar, Y. (2024). Transfer Learning-Based Classifier to Automate the Extraction of False X-Ray Images From Hospital's Database. *International Dental Journal*, *74*(6), 1471–1482. DOI: 10.1016/j.identj.2024.08.002 PMID: 39232939

Talukder, M. B., & Afchar, M. N. (2025). Vision Hotels: Shaping the Future of Hospitality Through Innovation, Sustainability, and Technology. In *Global Practices and Innovations in Sustainable Homestay Tourism* (pp. 269–294). IGI Global Scientific Publishing. DOI: 10.4018/979-8-3373-0427-4.ch012

Talukder, M. B., & Hoque, M. (2025). Navigating the Digital Horizon: Transforming Travel Agencies in the Digital Era. In *Perspectives on Digital Transformation in Contemporary Business* (pp. 383–410). IGI Global Scientific Publishing. DOI: 10.4018/979-8-3693-5966-2.ch014

Talukder, M. B., Hossain, S. E., Ferdous, F. A., & Khan, M. R. (2025). Exploring the Rise of Wellness Tourism: Trends, Benefits, and Market Potential. In *AI Technologies and Advancements for Psychological Well-Being and Healthcare* (pp. 351–378). IGI Global Scientific Publishing. DOI: 10.4018/979-8-3693-9158-7.ch013

Talukder, M. B., Khan, M. R., & Haghi, A. K. (2025). Redefining Hospital Waste Management: Circular Economy Strategies for Reducing Toxicity. In *Sustainable Business Ecosystems and Social Perspectives* (pp. 335–358). IGI Global Scientific Publishing. DOI: 10.4018/979-8-3693-8437-4.ch015

Talukder, M. B., Khan, M. R., Kumar, S., & Singh, K. (2025). Blockchain and Tourism: Enhancing Community Participation and Sustainability. In *Open Innovation and Technology in Tourism and Hospitality* (pp. 279–302). IGI Global Scientific Publishing. DOI: 10.4018/979-8-3693-8633-0.ch015

Talukder, M. B. (2024). Implementing Artificial Intelligence and Virtual Experiences in Hospitality. In *Innovative Technologies for Increasing Service Productivity* (pp. 145–160). IGI Global Scientific Publishing., DOI: 10.4018/979-8-3693-2019-8.ch009

Talukder, M. B. (2025). Current Trends and Future Research Directions of Eco-Friendly Steps of Hotel Industry. *RPER*, *71*(71), 7–18. DOI: 10.59072/rper.vi71.695

Talukder, M. B., Huda, M. N., Kumar, S., & Hasan, M. M. (2025). Metaverse Future of Digital Medical Tourism. In *Revolutionizing Healthcare Experience With Digital Medical Tourism* (pp. 173–198). IGI Global Scientific Publishing., DOI: 10.4018/979-8-3693-7888-5.ch007

Talukder, M. B., Kabir, F., & Jibon, F. A. (2025). AI-Driven Personalized Room Management in the Modern Hotel Industry. In *AI Technologies for Personalized and Sustainable Tourism* (pp. 59–82). IGI Global Scientific Publishing., DOI: 10.4018/979-8-3693-5678-4.ch003

Talukder, M. B., Khan, M. R., Kumar, S., Singh, K., & Lina, F. Y. (2025). AI Strategies for Tourism Development in Emerging Markets. In *Practical Strategies and Case Studies for Online Marketing 6.0* (pp. 117–138). IGI Global Scientific Publishing., DOI: 10.4018/979-8-3373-2058-8.ch007

Talukder, M. B., Rahman, M. Z., & Khan, M. R. (2025). Enhancing Guest Experience Through Smart Hotel Technologies. In *Adapting to Evolving Consumer Experiences in Hospitality and Tourism* (pp. 301–324). IGI Global Scientific Publishing., DOI: 10.4018/979-8-3693-7021-6.ch011

Tanriverdi, H., Çiki, K. D., Uygun, N., & Çiki, S. (2025). Narratives of medical tourists travelling for hair transplant: A case of Turkiye. *Tourism Recreation Research*, 1–13. Advance online publication. DOI: 10.1080/02508281.2025.2471484

Thanh, M. T. G., Hoang, D., & Le, H.. (2022). Deep Learning Application in Dental Caries Detection Using Intraoral Photos Taken by Smartphones. *Applied Sciences (Basel, Switzerland)*, *12*(11), 5504. DOI: 10.3390/app12115504

Thanh, M. T. G., Toan, N. V., Ngoc, V. T. N., Tra, N. T., Giap, C. N., & Nguyen, D. M. (2023). Deep learning application in dental caries detection using intraoral photographs. *International Journal of Computer Applications in Technology*, *72*(4), 233–242. DOI: 10.1504/IJCAT.2023.10056912

The Future of Healthcare: Multimodal AI for precision medicine. (n.d.). https://www.akira.ai/blog/multi-modal-in-healthcare

Thorat, V., Rao, P., Joshi, N., Talreja, P., & Shetty, A. R. (2024). Role of Artificial Intelligence (AI) in Patient Education and Communication in Dentistry. *Cureus*, *16*(5). Advance online publication. DOI: 10.7759/cureus.59799 PMID: 38846249

Topol, E. (2019). *Deep medicine: how artificial intelligence can make healthcare human again*.

Tripathi, S. N., & Siddiqui, M. H. (2018). Assessing the quality of healthcare services: A SERVQUAL approach. *International Journal of Healthcare Management*. Advance online publication. DOI: 10.1080/20479700.2018.1469212

Tsekouropoulos, G., Vasileiou, A., Hoxha, G., Dimitriadis, A., & Zervas, I. (2024). Sustainable Approaches to Medical Tourism: Strategies for Central Macedonia/Greece. *Sustainability (Basel)*, *16*(1), 121. DOI: 10.3390/su16010121

Turner, L. (2008). Cross-border dental care: 'Dental tourism' and patient mobility. *British Dental Journal*, *204*(10), 553–554. DOI: 10.1038/sj.bdj.2008.403 PMID: 18500297

Turner, L. G. (2011). Quality in health care and globalization of health services: Accreditation and regulatory oversight of medical tourism companies. *International Journal for Quality in Health Care : Journal of the International Society for Quality in Health Care*, *23*(1), 1–7. DOI: 10.1093/intqhc/mzq078 PMID: 21148210

Uribe, S., Issa, J., Sohrabniya, F., Denny, A., Kim, N., Dayo, A., Chaurasia, A., Sofi-Mahmudi, A., Büttner, M., & Schwendicke, F. (2024). Publicly available dental image datasets for artificial intelligence. *Journal of Dental Research*, *103*(13), 1365–1374. DOI: 10.1177/00220345241272052 PMID: 39422586

Vahdati, A., Khadivi, G., Ghorbani, Z., Vahdati Helan, E., Ranjbar, A., & Azimi, S. (2024). Accessibility of special care dentistry across countries: A scoping review. *Health Care*, *12*(23), 2376. DOI: 10.3390/healthcare12232376 PMID: 39684998

Van Eck, N. J., & Waltman, L. (2010). Software survey: VOSviewer, a computer program for bibliometric mapping. *Scientometrics*, *84*(2), 523–538. DOI: 10.1007/s11192-009-0146-3 PMID: 20585380

Vanatta, L. (2025). AI and elevating the dental patient experience. *DrBicuspid.com*. https://www.drbicuspid.com/dental-practice/patient-communication/article/15748243/ai-and-elevating-the-dental-patient-experience

Vijayakumar, G., Rajkumar, M., Rajiv Chandar, N., Selvakumar, P., & Duraisamy, R. (2024). Muniyandi Rajkumar, Rajiv Chandar N, Selvakumar P and Ramesh Duraisamy, (2024). Environmentally friendly TDS removal from waste water by electrochemical ion exchange batch-type recirculation (EIR) technique. *Environmental Science. Water Research & Technology*, *10*(4), 826–835. DOI: 10.1039/D3EW00793F

Vijaya, R. M. (2010). Medical tourism: Revenue generation or international transfer of healthcare problems? *Journal of Economic Issues*, *44*(1), 53–70. DOI: 10.2753/JEI0021-3624440103

Virani, A., Wellstead, A. M., & Howlett, M. (2020). Where is the policy? A bibliometric analysis of the state of policy research on medical tourism. *Global Health Research and Policy*, *5*(1), 19. DOI: 10.1186/s41256-020-00147-2 PMID: 32391438

Wang, H., Ghasemi, M., Ghadiri Nejad, M., & Khandan, A. S. (2023). Assessing the potential growth of Iran's hospitals with regard to the sustainable management of medical tourism. *Health & Social Care in the Community*, *2023*, 1–12. Advance online publication. DOI: 10.1155/2023/8734482

Wang, Y., Chen, T., Vinayahalingam, S., Wu, T., Chang, C., Chang, H., Wei, H., Chen, M., Ko, C., Moin, D., Ginneken, B., Xi, T., Tsai, H., Chen, M., Hsu, T., & Chou, H. (2025). Artificial Intelligence to Assess Dental Findings from Panoramic Radiographs — A Multinational Study._.DOI: 10.485502502.10277

Wei, W., Önder, I., & Uysal, M. (2024). Smart tourism destination (STD): Developing and validating an impact scale using residents' overall life satisfaction. *Current Issues in Tourism*, *27*(17), 2849–2872. DOI: 10.1080/13683500.2023.2296587

Wernz, C., Thakur Wernz, P., & Phusavat, K. (2014). Service convergence and service integration in medical tourism. *Industrial Management & Data Systems*, *114*(7), 1094–1106. DOI: 10.1108/IMDS-04-2014-0115

Wong, K. M., & Musa, G. (2012). Medical tourism in Asia: Thailand, Singapore, Malaysia, and India. Medical tourism: The ethics, regulation, and marketing of health mobility. Routledge.

Wong, B. K. M., & Hazley, S. A. S. (2021). The future of health tourism in the industrial revolution 4.0 era. *Journal of Tourism Futures*, *7*(2), 267–272. DOI: 10.1108/JTF-01-2020-0006

World Health Organization. (2022). *Global oral health status report: Towards universal health coverage for oral health by 2030.* https://www.who.int/publications/i/item/9789240061484

Xu, M., Wang, Y., Liu, H., & Zhang, Y. (2023). Deep learning-based recognition of periodontitis and dental caries in dental X-ray images. *Computerized Medical Imaging and Graphics*, *106*, 102173. DOI: 10.1016/j.compmedimag.2023.102173

Xu, T., Wang, W., & Du, J. (2020). An integrative review of patients' experience in the medical tourism. INQUIRY. *Inquiry : a Journal of Medical Care Organization, Provision and Financing*, *57*, 1–13. DOI: 10.1177/0046958020926762 PMID: 32513038

Yeganeh, H. (2019). An analysis of emerging trends and transformations in global healthcare. *International Journal of Health Governance*, *24*(2), 169–180. DOI: 10.1108/IJHG-02-2019-0012

Yomi. (2023). *Robot-assisted dental surgery system.* https://www.neocis.com/yomi

Zeng, X., Wang, Y., & Li, H. (2022). Influencer marketing in healthcare: An emerging strategy for dental tourism success. *International Journal of Digital Marketing*, *14*(2), 73–86.

Zhang, L., Lin, Z., & Wang, J. (2021). The role of online reviews in shaping trust in dental tourism: Evidence from China. *JMR, Journal of Marketing Research*, *58*(1), 55–72.

Zhao, H., Zheng, Y., Chen, S., & Han, T. (2024). Enhancing user experience in the digital service environment: A comprehensive study on the design and evaluation of internet-based healthcare products. *Journal of Evaluation in Clinical Practice*, *30*(8), 1471–1790. DOI: 10.1111/jep.14088 PMID: 38973104

Zhao, X., Bai, C., & Hui, Y. V. (2002). An empirical assessment and application of SERVQUAL in a mainland Chinese department store. *Total Quality Management*, *13*(2), 241–254. DOI: 10.1080/09544120120102478

Zolfagharian, M., Rajamma, R. K., Naderi, I., & Torkzadeh, S. (2018). Determinants of medical tourism destination selection process. *Journal of Hospitality Marketing & Management*, *27*(7), 775–794. DOI: 10.1080/19368623.2018.1444527

About the Contributors

Ömer Faruk Şarkbay was born on January 3, 1970 in Ankara. He graduated from the Faculty of Dentistry Istanbul University in 1991. He specialized in Oral Implantology at Bezmialem University Faculty of Dentistry. He served in the field of Maxillofacial Surgery for 4 years. He completed his master's degree in Business Administration at Marmara University Social Sciences Institute and his doctorate education at Istanbul Gelisim University. He started working as a faculty member at Istanbul Gelişim University Department of Faculty of Health Sciences. He works in the fields of health management, artificial intelligent sustainability and efficiency. He has participated in many congresses at home and abroad. His article was published nationally and internationally. He served as a manager in many projects related to his field. He opened his own clinic in 1992. He currently works as both managing partner and Oral surgeon at a dental hospital where 58 people work. He worked on corporate social responsibility projects. He worked as an administrator and volunteer in business and charity associations. As a volunteer doctor, he provided treatment services to child and adult patients in Afghanistan, Somalia, Ethiopia,Iraq and in refugee camps Syria.

Aslı Kaya graduated from the Faculty of Economics and Administrative Sciences, Dumlupınar University (1999-2003), specializing in Management and Organization. She completed her Master's degree in the Department of Business Administration, Management, and Organization at Dumlupınar University between 2003-2006, having the title of "Business Administration and Organization Science Specialist." On September 6, 2021, she graduated from the Department of Health Management, Faculty of Health Sciences, Suleyman Demirel University, in the field of Health Institutions Management, receiving the title of "Doctor." Simultaneously, she completed the PhD. program in Accounting and Finance at the Department of Business Administration, Inönü University, and had the title of "Doctor" on February 22, 2024. Her research focuses on academic subjects in which health management, organizational behavior, behavioral accounting and finance, management and strategic management, health tourism and health economy. She has served as the editor of several scholarly and professional books, including Clinical Management in Disasters and Epidemics: Resilience and Sustainability (2026), Intersecting AI, Neurofinance, and Behavioral Finance for Decision Making (2026), Next-Generation Treatment Methods and Destinations in Dental Health Tourism (2026), Academic Organizational Behaviour (2025), Green Leadership Strategies for Increased Employee Engagement and Performance (2025), Integrating Organizational Theories With Sustainable Development (2024), Green Management Approaches to Organizational Behavior (2025), Health Economics from Different Perspectives (2025), Journey to Health: Health Tourism (2024), Academician Poets Shaping Poetry (2020), and My World (2013).

***

Kartal Doğukan Çıkı received his bachelor's degree from Gazi University, Department of Travel Management and Tourism Guidance (2014-2017). Kartal Doğukan Çıkı completed his master's degree in Travel Management and Tourism Guidance at Hacı Bayram Veli University in 2020. He received his PhD degree in Tourism Management from Istanbul University in 2024. He works as a full-time Research Assistant (PhD) at Istanbul Gelisim University Faculty of Economics, Administrative and Social Sciences (2019-Present). Research Areas: Tourist guiding, tourism management, tourism and accommodation, recreation and recreational activities, tourist experience and other tourism related fields (gastronomy tourism, tourist motivation etc.). Istanbul Gelisim University; Faculty of Economics, Administrative and Social Sciences; Department of Tourism Guidance; kdciki@gelisim.edu.tr; ORCID: 0000-0002-8307-8561; Web of Science Researcher ID: ABL-7919-2022

Narendra Kumar is currently working as Assistant Professor at Amity Institute of Travel & Tourism, Amity University, Noida. With 23 years of experience in travel & tourism industry and academia, he has made significant contributions to the area of tourism education. Dr. Kumar has a strong interest in Business travel, tourist behaviour and visitor experiences has published extensively on related topics. In addition to his academic pursuits, Dr. Kumar is actively involved in helping young graduates of tourism and hospitality domain to help them in establishing their own start-ups. He has been invited to speak at numerous conferences and seminars on tourism and related fields and his current research focuses on student mentoring. Dr. Kumar's previous works include one edited book on "Tourist Behaviour" published by Apple Academic Press, USA; one book on "Digital Marketing" and one on

"Ethical Aspects of Business in Tourism". Recent works from Dr. Kumar includes two books from IGI Global Publishing themed at Bleisure Tourism.

Sanjeev Kumar Is a Professor in Lovely Professional University Punjab India. He received Undergraduate in Hotel Management from Osmania University, Postgraduate in Tourism Management from Madurai Kamaraj University. He completed Doctor of Philosophy in Hospitality Management in 2019 from Amity University Jaipur India. His research areas lies in food Service Industry, his research focuses on Alcoholic beverages, Event management and Sustainable Management Practices, Metaverse, AI Machine Learning and Artificial Intelligence. He published more than 80 research papers, articles and chapters in Scopus Indexed, UGC Approved and peer reviewed Journals and books. Dr. Sanjeev Kumar participated and acted as resource person in various National and International conferences, seminars, session chair, research workshops and industry talks and his work has been widely cited. Dr. Sanjeev also edited more than 20 books with various International Publishers such as IGI Global, Cambridge Scholars, Emerald, CABI, Bentham Science, Taylor & Francis. Dr Sanjeev is an active researcher and has published numerous research articles in prestigious National and International journals and books.

R. Bhuvaneswari working as an Assistant Professor of English at Dr.Mahalingam College of Engineering and Technology, Pollachi. To her credit she completed 10 NPTEL / SWAYAM and published few articles in Scopus indexed journals.

R. Velmurugan presently working as Professor, Department of Commerce, Karpagam Academy of Higher Education, Coimbatore. He started his career as a Project Fellow under UGC Sponsored Major Research Project at NGM College, Pollachi. He has 19 years of teaching experience has 15 years of research experience. To his credit he produced 22 Ph.D. Scholars and 5 M.Phil. Scholars. At present 1 scholar submitter his thesis, 6 Ph.D. Scholars are under his guidance. Moreover, to his credit he published 168 articles in various International Journals, of which 94 articles are published in Scopus Indexed Journals and 15 articles in Web of Science and 76 articles in edited volumes. He also participates and presented 27 papers in various International Seminar / Conference and 54 National Seminar / Conference. He acted as an external examiner for various M.Phil. and Ph.D. Viva voce examinations. He acted as a Vice Chancellor nominee for Doctoral Committee Expert at Bharathiar University, Coimbatore and Periyar University, Salem. He acted as a Chairperson at various National Level Conferences. He also acted as an Expert for Syllabus Scrutiny Committee, Question Paper Scrutiny Committee and Expert members for Board of Studies at various reputed Colleges. Considering his meritorious contribution, he received awards like Best Paper Presenter, Best Research Supervisor and Best Faculty Awards from various research foundations and councils. He too acted as a resource person for 27 Guest Lectures, 30 Workshops and 10 faculty development programmes.

Affaan Shaikh is the Founder & CEO of IntelliDent AI. As an AI engineer, researcher and neuroscientist, he develops cutting-edge solutions at the intersection of artificial intelligence, neuroscience, and medical technology. His research spans neurodegenerative disease diagnosis, brain-computer interfaces (BCIs), and AI in aerospace. With over 10 peer-reviewed papers in journals like IEEE and Springer, Affaan is an active contributor to the tech community. He has mentored 20+ aspiring researchers and writers and is passionate about innovation, leadership, and public engagement.

Mohammad Badruddoza Talukder is an Associate Professor at the College of Tourism and Hospitality Management at the International University of Business Agriculture and Technology (IUBAT) in Dhaka, Bangladesh. Holding a PhD from Lovely Professional University, India, he is renowned for his innovative integration of cutting-edge technologies such as Artificial Intelligence (AI), the Internet of Things (IoT), and Blockchain into tourism and hospitality management. His research explores the transformative impact of these technologies on smart tourism, cloud kitchens, and the broader industry landscape. As a prolific author, Dr. Talukder has published numerous scholarly articles and books, with forthcoming titles that address AI innovations in hospitality, the evolution of cloud kitchens, and the enhancement of digital literacy within hospitality education. His work shapes contemporary tourism and hospitality practices, skillfully marrying technological advancements with practical industry applications. Since 2008, Dr. Talukder has imparted his knowledge through a diverse array of courses in tourism and hospitality across various universities in Bangladesh.

Ravi Thirumalaisamy working as an Assistant Professor, Department of Business and Economics, Modern College of Business and Science. To his credit, he published more than 16 articles in Scopus indexed journals.

Suraj Yadav is an accomplished professional with a background in Hospitality, holding a bachelor's degree from Pune University and a Master in Hotel Management & Tourism from Madurai Kamaraj University, Madurai. Currently serving as an Assistant Professor and Training & Placement Officer at D Y Patil School of Hospitality in Kolhapur, Maharashtra, India, he brings extensive expertise to the field. Suraj is also dedicated to furthering his academic pursuits and is actively pursuing a Ph.D. at D Y Patil Agricultural & Technical University in Kolhapur. His commitment to education and training has made a significant impact in the realm of hospitality.

Index

www.ingramcontent.com/pod-product-compliance
Lightning Source LLC
LaVergne TN
LVHW081521300926
849161LV00006B/1251